'This book really manages to capture the multi-layered and multi-faceted nature of life story work. It sets life stories within the bigger frameworks of health, psychology, policy, culture change, identity, equality and diversity. We hear about life stories from many people living with dementia, families and professionals covering care at home, care homes, housing, hospitals, end of life, memory assessment services and arts venues. It ranges from the practical to the existential and fizzes with case studies, top tips, and research evidence.'

— *Professor Dawn Brooker, Association for Dementia Studies,*
University of Worcester

'Life stories, a strand in psychological therapy with older people and people with dementia, has been unfolding over the past 25 years. This timely book brings the many facets of this work together.

Here is a sparkling treasure trove of a book containing all you might want to know about life story work and dementia. Written with clarity and in an accessible style suitable for lay persons, it also contains all professionals might want to inform their practice and develop services that place the person with their unique life story at the centre.'

— *Reinhard Guss, Chair, Dementia Workstream Lead, Faculty of the Psychology*
of Older People, BPS, Consultant Clinical Psychologist, KMPT

'This is a really good and useful contribution. It is full of well-curated information and practical advice, but above all it is full of the humanity of people with dementia and the value of their stories. I thoroughly recommend this book.'

— *Sube Banerjee, Professor of Dementia, Centre for Dementia*
Studies, Brighton and Sussex Medical School

of related interest

A Creative Toolkit for Communication in Dementia Care
Karrie Marshall
ISBN 978 1 84905 694 6
eISBN 978 1 78450 206 5

Facilitating Spiritual Reminiscence for People with Dementia
A Learning Guide
Elizabeth MacKinlay and Corinne Trevitt
ISBN 978 1 84905 573 4
eISBN 978 1 78450 018 4

Reminiscence and Life Story Work
A Practice Guide
Faith Gibson
ISBN 978 1 84905 151 4
eISBN 978 0 85700 338 6

Life Story Work with People with Dementia

ORDINARY LIVES, EXTRAORDINARY PEOPLE

EDITED BY

Polly Kaiser and Ruth Eley

Foreword by Tommy and Joyce Dunne

Jessica Kingsley *Publishers*
London and Philadelphia

First published in 2017
by Jessica Kingsley Publishers
73 Collier Street
London N1 9BE, UK
and
400 Market Street, Suite 400
Philadelphia, PA 19106, USA

www.jkp.com

Library of Congress Cataloging in Publication Data
Names: Kaiser, Polly. | Eley, Ruth, editor.
Title: Life story work with people with dementia : ordinary lives, extraordinary people / edited by Polly Kaiser and Ruth Eley ; foreword by Dawn Brooker.
Description: London ; Philadelphia : Jessica Kingsley Publishers, 2017. | Includes bibliographical references and index.
Identifiers: LCCN 2016013089 | ISBN 9781849055055 (alk. paper)
Subjects: LCSH: Dementia--Patients--Care. | Narrative therapy. | Autobiography--Therapeutic care.
Classification: LCC RC521 .L54 2017 | DDC 616.8/3--dc23 LC record available at https://urldefense.proofpoint.com/v2/url?u=https-3A__lccn.loc.gov_2016013089&d=BQIFAg&c=euGZstcaTDllvimEN8b7jXrwqOf-v5A_CdpgnVfiiMM&r=4EemtO9R1x-uacXap7EaQ1RHPq9-MnYBwnfuC-ulpHU&m=PA_lYmrSaEfTEjlHXYIz-fwyz0MfVKPwcw803twS2v8&s=_rWZ6ahO4Ks7FkxGfz163PBE4PpbFBfsgG4QtYDEElo&e=

British Library Cataloguing in Publication Data
A CIP catalogue record for this book is available from the British Library

ISBN 978 1 84905 505 5
eISBN 978 0 85700 914 2

Printed and bound in Great Britain

MIX
Paper from
responsible sources
FSC® C013056

Contents

Foreword

As a person living with dementia, I can't stress enough the importance of life stories and involving the person with dementia in creating their own life story. After all, the best perspective for understanding behaviour is from the internal reference of the individual themselves.

Every day we lose another piece of our life that will be gone forever unless our family, friends and carers are able to reinforce those memories by going through our life story –whether it is a book, photo album or memory box – with us over and over again. Without this, people will never know the person behind the dementia. In a care home or hospital we would just be a resident or patient with *Dementia* instead of a *Person* with dementia.

They say that knowledge is power, so what better way to have the knowledge to be able to communicate with a person with dementia than to find out what was important to them in terms of their memories, experiences, life events, values and beliefs.

It's vital that people know about what type of food I like, whether I'm a vegan/vegetarian, what my religious beliefs are, did I like pets, did I play sports, what school I went to and my employment history. The life story should contain such details as the name I liked to be called by, whether I was married, names of children and grandchildren, parents and friends, as well as my employment experiences and hobbies.

We can take away a lot of stress for people who will be caring for us by detailing our wishes regarding health and financial matters, so why not detail our life story to enable people to have empathy with us.

Care homes would benefit from life stories as they allow staff to enter into the world of the person with dementia. They can go through the book each day with the person and learn about their life, their likes and dislikes. They can help add to the book because it is an ongoing work in process.

It's a great experience for a person with dementia to sit with someone over time to make a personal record of important experiences, people, places and events in their life and provide a way of communicating with them (and their family carers) about their life.

I personally hope that my own life story will give people an insight into the person I was and the person that I now am. But I urge my peers and everyone else to start their own life story today because you never know what the future will bring.

Tommy Dunne

As Tommy's wife – and now his carer – I do worry that I may not always be there to look after him, but through having his life story book I know that people will be able to get to know him and see all that he has achieved.

A life story book epitomises a person's life and can help achieve person-centred and relationship-centred care tailored to meet individual needs. It assists care-planning and helps ensure that the person receives the best possible type of care for their wellbeing. As life stories draw on residual long-term memory, they can provide a medium for communication that promotes self-esteem and wellbeing – vital to help prevent isolation.

Having a life story book is a great way of communicating, because if you 'know' about the person you will be more relaxed and that is something that the person will pick up on. Having the book helps to make the person feel proud, valued and appreciated.

Sometimes a person with dementia does not recognise their spouse, children or friends, because in their memory that person is living at an earlier time and should look much younger. Using photos of an earlier time will often help their recognition of family and friends.

A life story book can be a great distraction, and distraction is what all good carers must master to help the person maintain their happiness. It also safeguards personal identity and can increase carers' understanding of confused or agitated behaviour.

The book can help care home staff to appreciate the person with dementia in the context of their whole life. It should help them understand the person better and change negative views and assumptions about the person.

The tools in this book will help you make a great life story.

Joyce Dunne

Acknowledgements

In a book of this nature there are so many people to say thank you to.

Thanks go first to Ken Holt, who not only founded the Oldham Life Story Group, but who was the inspiration for the national Life Story Network. Thanks to Lesley Jones for those first workshops in Oldham (the best three bottles of wine Polly has ever bought!) and to members of the Oldham Life Story Group past and present, especially Frank Kenyon, John Starkey, Linda Green, Nicola Shore, Chris Newton and Joyce Brown.

To Bob Woods who encouraged this book to be written in the first place, helping us to believe in it, providing timely nudging and suggestions in our darker days of the process – and responding to our own nudges in return…

To Jean Tottie and Tony Jameson Allen – for pioneering leadership in establishing the original network.

To Anna Gaughan, Steve Amos, Sally Rogers and Veronica Brown for the earlier years and the 2008 conference; Suzanne Whitman and all her colleagues and all the above for the 2010 conference, along with Dawn Brooker, Graham Stokes and Toby Williamson.

Our fellow members of the Life Story Network (CIC): Jean Tottie, Anna Gaughan, Pat Broster, John Shaw and Julie McManus for their passion about life story work.

To Tommy and Joyce Dunn, to Ken and Janice Clasper and all the other people with dementia and family carers we have had the privilege of working with who are passionate about life story work and its benefits.

To Life Story Network associates past and present with special thanks to Rachel Niblock, Ann Kiney, Gail Scouthern, Penny Redwood and Damien Murphy.

To all our contributors who have been so patient with us and responded to our (not so gentle) prods, and to Jessica Kingsley Publishers for their patience and support.

To all the people who have participated in our workshops and projects over the years and from whom we have learnt so much.

Friends and supporters of this endeavour – Barbara Mackay, John Osborne, Lucy Houghton-Burnett, Rhona Brown and Pat Gray – whose feedback has been so valuable.

Last but not least, our friends and families, whose patience, belief, support and cups of tea have been so much appreciated.

Polly Kaiser and Ruth Eley

Introduction
Ruth Eley and Polly Kaiser

Ken Holt's story[1]

Ken Holt was a great connector, communicator and organiser. His vast experience in local politics and community groups meant he had good relationships with people, while not being afraid to speak his mind. He met his wife Alice during the war and they married in 1946. They shared many interests including a great love of motorcycling and were involved in setting up and running the North West and then the national moto cross association.

Ken had always been an activist, so when his wife Alice received her diagnosis of dementia he threw himself into being active in that world. He became chair of the local Alzheimer's Society, the Oldham carers' forum and various strategy groups, including Oldham Council's health overview and scrutiny committee.

When Alice eventually had to go to into a care home, Ken, who knew her so well, was able to write Alice's life story for the staff. He knew what was important for staff to know. He knew of her war time fears when she would often stay dressed at night in case she had to make a quick dash to the air raid shelter; some nights she would stay dressed come what may. Ken was able to let the staff know this as part of her life story.

Of course, the staff realised, 'this is why Alice needs to stay dressed at night.' Not knowing the history, the staff might have prescribed unnecessary tranquilisers to calm her down. Instead they could see the world from her point of view – no more bedtime agitation when staff brought out her nightdress.

This experience gave Ken Holt an insight: stories can have a therapeutic value for us when they help us understand ourselves, our hopes, our fears and our dreams and, importantly, when we can communicate these to others. He was so convinced of the benefits of this approach that he went on to found the Oldham Life Story Group in 2003. He shared his vison for a national network at a psychology conference in York in 2008. Both the editors of this book worked at the Department of Health around that time and, working with many others, were able to launch the national Life Story Network at a conference in Leeds in February 2010. Thankfully Ken lived to see that vison come to fruition before he died later that year. Many of the contributors in this book were also at the conference and have been part of this work and influenced it. They have been using, advocating and researching life story work for many years and we are delighted and honoured that so many have contributed to gathering this knowledge into one place for the first time. The members of the national Life Story Network have changed over time but the work continues in many ways, particularly with the work they are doing supporting the national network of carers – TIDE (Together in Dementia Every Day) – something we hope Ken would be proud of.

Why is this book needed now?

Since Charlie Murphy's work *It Started with a Seashell: Life Story Work and People with Dementia* (1994) there has been a growth in the use of life story work that has outpaced its definition, research and evaluation as an intervention (Subramaniam and Woods 2012). As a consequence, there is no consistent definition of life story work; if you ask six people, you are likely to receive six different answers, depending on the purpose and context of the work. The term life story work is used to describe a wide range of activities. At one end of the continuum this can be putting one's life into perspective through therapeutic life review, as described by Butler (1963), or as part of a very structured (Haight 1992) or unstructured (Heliker 1997) life review process. This is done on a one-to-one basis with the person. The other end of the spectrum might be the development of a one-page profile like those developed by Helen Sanderson (Sanderson 2016); this might be put together by a family carer or staff working with the family and not necessarily by the person themselves.

The purpose of life story work may also differ, as discussed in Chapter 1. For some people, the purpose might be to focus on a person's sense of identity, improving their self-esteem and wellbeing. For others it might be to inform a person-centred care plan in order to decrease so called 'challenging behaviour' (McKeown 2006; Moos and Bjorn 2006).

The authors of this book come from various perspectives and describe the work from their context. Some authors, such as Bob Woods, have been researching this area for many years – from the perspective of individual reminiscence and life review. Practitioners and researchers like Lesley Jones, Jane McKeown and Rachel Thompson are pioneers in their areas and the challenges of embedding life story work in practice. Researchers like Kate Gridley are newer to the field and have pioneered having the voice of people with dementia at the heart of the research.

The one perspective that is fundamental and we all share is about the power and potential of stories to improve the quality of life for people with a diagnosis of dementia.

The aim of this book is to share what is currently known about life story work. Our aim is to give you an overview from different perspectives – from people with dementia themselves, carers, staff – and across different settings – in-patient wards, acute hospitals, memory services and care homes. It will help you to access policy and legislation in arguing for service development. We want it to be practical – to encourage you to get started whilst understanding some of the tools, techniques, complexities and pitfalls to be aware of. However, whilst we are strong advocates of life story work, it is not always right for everyone. Jane McKeown, Kate Gridley and Nada Savitch in Chapter 16 highlight some of the cautions and concerns that need to be taken into account, as does Steve Milton's Chapter 7 from listening to people with dementia themselves. So policies or targets that say 'everyone must have a life story' might be counterproductive. As life story work has grown and developed, so too have some myths and potentially rigid ideas about what it is and isn't and who you can and should do it with. Our intention is that this book will give you an overview of the many ways it can be used, along with some ideas and advice about when it might not be helpful.

Definitions – what are we talking about?

What is dementia?

This book is about using life story work with people with dementia, so it is important to be explicit about the condition and its impact on individuals. The Diagnostic and Statistical Manual (DSM), version 5, used by the medical profession, categorises dementia as a neurocognitive disorder. It has been defined as 'an acquired global impairment of intellect, memory and personality but without impairment of consciousness' (Lishman 1978, p.9).

The number of people with a dementia is growing. There are an estimated 835,000 people with dementia in the United Kingdom (Alzheimer's Society 2014a). There is a misconception that it is a disease of old age; however, there are an estimated 42,325 people with young onset dementia (aged under 65) (Alzheimer's Society 2014a). Dementia affects roughly 5 per cent of people over 65 and 20 per cent of people over 80 (Jorm, Kortn and Hendersen 1987). Dementia is not one disease but a syndrome of many diseases. The symptoms of dementia include change and impairment in a range of mental functioning, not just memory. The most common type is Alzheimer's disease and this affects about 62 per cent of people living with dementia. Vascular dementia and those with a mixed dementia of both Alzheimer's disease and vascular dementia account for about 30 per cent. The remaining 8 per cent comprise Lewy Body dementia, fronto-temporal lobe dementia, dementia associated with Parkinson's disease and other rarer conditions (National Audit Office 2007). People living with dementia may have problems with visual perception, word-finding, fine finger movements, auditory hallucinations, concentration, and planning and carrying out day-to-day activities such as making a cup of tea or getting dressed in the morning. If the frontal lobes are affected, people may become disinhibited and act out of character.

As the illness progresses, people may cease to recognise individuals, such as family members, their home or even themselves, as their memories may revert to their younger years. All of these manifestations can be distressing and frustrating for them and for people aiming to support them:

> My abilities to be able to cook are steadily diminishing… I am losing my ability to sequence, plan, prepare and cook. I hate packing – I

pick up one thing, put it down, look for another thing, look for the first thing you put down and it's not there. You end up not knowing where anything is. You try to be logical but you cannot be logical when you've got Alzheimer's. (Agnes Houston – from the Scottish Dementia Working Group via Dementia Information)

Besides neurological impairments, numerous factors can affect the experience of a person with a dementia, such as their physical health, their own biography and personality and the social environment they are in (Brooker 2007; Kitwood 1997); Kitwood's concept of 'Malignant Social Psychology' is discussed in more detail in Chapter 1. It is here that the power of narrative approaches and life story has potential to reduce disability.

Life story work

As described above, there are numerous definitions of life story work. One linked at the identity end of the spectrum is: 'Life stories are psychosocial constructions, co-authored by the person himself or herself and the cultural context within which that person's life is embedded' (McAdams 2001, p.101). Another definition, linked more to care, is:

> Life story work is a term given to biographical approaches in health and social care that give people the opportunity to talk about their life experiences. It involves recording relevant aspects of a person's past and present lives in some way, and then using this life story to benefit them in their present situation. (McKeown 2006, p.238, cited in Murphy 2000)

This definition still holds good, although there is also a drive to move life story work away from just health and social care settings to communities, as described in Chapter 10. Much of our approach seeks to speak to you as busy practitioners who tend to glean people's stories each day in the course of your work. This book aims to extend your idea of what life story work can be in valuing and using the 'snippets' you hear and capturing these in such a way as to be of practical use in your setting.

Our definition of life story work

Life story work is, above all, a process that involves having helpful conversations to elicit, capture and use stories about a person, in order to promote their personhood and their wellbeing and keep them connected with family, friends and communities.

The difference between reminiscence and life story work

Imagine a big family event in your life, maybe a Christmas gathering or a wedding or a funeral. When you gather as a family you may reminisce together about that event – what stories are told? Not only are your memories likely to be different, but each person's relationship to that event will be different. In the case of a wedding, the event may be a core part of the life story of the bride but not mean as much to her little brother; for him it might have been the first time he was allowed alcohol or for Aunty May that she got up and danced. The life story and meaning for each individual at that event will be different.

Life story work is usually personal, individual and more than reminiscence; it is about capturing memories, reminiscences and future hopes. These may be modest – the opportunity to go outside in the fresh air – or more substantial, such as meeting a friend again or visiting a special place. In the example above, hopes may range from enjoying a long marriage, to having another beer or to starting dancing again. Whatever the aspirations gathered in a life story, we must not set these in stone or assume that they will remain the same for that person for ever.

What the book is about

Conversations to elicit stories may be between family members, a family carer and the person with a diagnosis. It may be between a person with a diagnosis and a therapist (occupational therapist, speech and language therapist or psychologist) or, as illustrated in Chapters 9, 11, 12 and 13, with nurses or care staff. Or it may be between a person with dementia and a volunteer (see the case study in Chapter 11). The conversations might result in a book, photo album, DVD, one-page profile or CD of music, or they might not result in anything so tangible. Any product that is an outcome of the work depends on the purpose, and the purpose will depend on your setting – be that a mental health assessment ward (Chapter 9), a general hospital (Chapter 12) or a care home (Chapter 13). The main issue is that these stories are used rather than gather dust on a shelf. Someone could have the most beautifully bound photo life story – but it is of limited value if it is not used. Whilst this book does give examples of available products (they are evolving all the time), its focus is on how to initiate these vital conversations that honour a person, who they are and who they want to be, not just who they have been. These skills will endure despite the products and the technologies. The whole area of art and dementia is a growing and flourishing one who can give ideas about ways of engaging with people who do not rely on the written word. Maria Parsons describes some of these in more detail in Chapter 17 and this should give you more ideas. We want to inspire you to 'have a go'.

Life story work is not like genealogy, researching family history or drawing up a family tree; it is about helping people to tell their stories in whatever way is best for them, which may not result in a tidy chronological account that is factually accurate. It is important to know how to ask questions and to encourage people to respond. At the same time, it is helpful to know some of the known benefits not just to people with a diagnosis, carers and staff (Chapters 7, 8 and 9) but also in terms of the evidence and outcomes that can be achieved, so that the work is undertaken in the knowledge that it has validity (Chapters 5 and 6). We therefore want the book to provide practical examples, ideas and suggestions that readers can adapt to their own circumstances.

Part 1 describes where these ideas have come from and the policy context.

In Part 2, Bob Woods, Ponnusamy Subramanian and Kate Gridley look at the current evidence base for life story work so far.

Part 3 looks at why life story work is important. For the first time, the views and perspectives of people with dementia are included in the debate. The benefits for carers are discussed from the perspective of a former carer and some of the work we have done together at the Life Story Network. Then we hear about ways in which it is important to staff and how it can help them.

Part 4 is the most practical section and describes the variety of settings in which life story work is taking place, its core applications – from community, memory services, hospital wards, care homes and end of life – and the use of person-centred approaches further afield in Europe. Jane McKeown, Nada Savitch and Kate Gridley explore the challenges of life story work, whilst Mara Parsons illustrates some of the creative approaches that can be taken.

In Part 5 we are grateful to Marie-Jo Guisset Martinez for a broader European perspective that opens up new opportunities.

Finally, we pull together an overview of the work and current practice and explore what the future might hold.

What do we want to achieve?

From our discussions with practitioners, family carers and people with dementia themselves, it is clear that there is enthusiasm and commitment for embarking on life story work, but it can be difficult to know where to start or the best approach to take.

The chapters include many examples of how life story work has helped people living with dementia to reconnect with their families, friends and communities and enabled staff to support them better by understanding who they have been, who they are and who they want to be. We therefore want the book to inspire people to have a go and to discover the rich, extraordinary lives of people who are often overlooked and only seen in terms of their diagnosis and the problems that this appears to present to others around them. It is hoped that the book will appeal to people with dementia themselves and their family carers, as well as paid staff and volunteers in various settings.

Note

1.   A version of Ken's story appeared in *The Tablet* (Kaiser *et al.* 2008).

Part 1

Where Has Life Story Work Come From?

The Context of Life Story Work

1

Narrative Approaches to Life Story Work

Polly Kaiser

A man is always a teller of stories, he lives surrounded by his own stories and those of other people, he sees everything that happens to him in terms of these stories and he tries to live his life as if he were recounting it.

J. P. Sartre, *Nausea* (1936, p.61)

I have had such an interesting life…if only I could remember it.

'Elsie', interviewed in 1985

Introduction

These quotations reveal some of the paradoxes of life story work. Elsie may well have valued a life story book that could help her to remember some of the facts and chronology of her life. Even without that she would be living her life through the stories she told herself. The challenge is knowing what these stories are and how they might be helpful. What was important to Elsie was that she had an 'interesting life'. It has been acknowledged for a long time now that reminiscence and putting one's life in perspective are normal and valuable activities of old age (Butler 1963; Erikson 1997).

My experience of meeting Janine

Before I knew what was happening I was ushered into 'Janine's' apartment, an elderly woman with dementia – I was told to sit and wait for her daughter whilst the carers got her ready. I was a researcher – 24 years old in Lyon, France. I am not sure who was more startled, me or Janine! She was being lifted from her bed by a hoist. The carers did not look at her, speak with her or reassure her...she could have been a sack of potatoes... She had a look of utter terror in her eyes that seemed to say 'Help me!' 'What is going on?'... I knew I should not have been there to see her in such an undignified state. When they were done I wasn't sure what to do. Janine could not speak. I sat with her. We held hands...and waited for her daughter to arrive.

The carers did not know her and they did not seem to want to know her. What did she need? She needed to feel safe, to have them speak with her in a kindly way, to be valued and noticed, her hand held ...she needed comfort, connection and kindness.

My motivation for life story work comes from stories like these and others in my career: the importance of treating people well, for '*seldom heard voices*' (Robson *et al.* 2008) to be heard so that a person can be supported in the choices they wish to make to keep them well: to support what Tom Kitwood would call 'personhood'. He defined this as '*a standing or status that is bestowed upon one human being by others in the context of relationship and social being. It implies recognition, respect and trust*' (Kitwood 1997, p.8). The key phrase here is '*in the context of relationship and social beings*'. How can we do this?

We need to know the people we work with, and life story work is a central part of this endeavour. 'You never really understand a person until you consider things from his point of view.' (Lee, H. p.30)

? Reflection points

- Can you think of a time when you did not feel listened to? How did that make you feel?

- Can you bring to mind a person you have worked with who you wished you had known better?

- What difference would knowing more about their life have made?

Principles

The principles and philosophy that have shaped the development of life story work for me have a number of roots. First, are my undergraduate lectures in social psychology by John Shotter and reading Ken Gergen (1973), who talked about social constructionism and the evolving nature of psychological ideas in history. Second, came the ideas of person-centred care as espoused by Tom Kitwood. These were such a breath of fresh air when he gave me a copy of his manuscript of *Person to Person* (Kitwood and Bredin1992) to read when I first qualified as a psychologist. Finally, there was my training in narrative therapy with Hugh Fox and workshops with Michael White and others. These form part of my story and my relationship to life story work and provide the background to its principles. First, I will define some terms and then illustrate the principles.

Social constructionism

Social constructionism is a sociological theory (Berger and Luckman 1966) that places great emphasis on everyday interactions between people and the way we use language to understand our reality (Anderson 2012). One person's understanding shapes another's; we do not develop in isolation. We develop shared meaning and understandings in relationship with each other. Think about how a mother looks at her infant and how a child begins to understand their environment through verbal and non-verbal communication. These meanings and practices become 'taken for granted' realities we learn about the rules of our particular culture and the 'way things are done'. As we shall see, these realities are socially constructed and change over time.

Kitwood and person-centred care

Tom Kitwood has been a huge influence for many. He said that the aim of good dementia care is to 'maintain personhood in the face of failing mental powers' (1997, p.20). Besides the neurological impairment that accompanies dementia there are numerous factors that affect the experience of a person with a diagnosis, such as their physical health, their own biography and personality, and the social environment they are in (Brooker 2007; Kitwood 1997). The environment around a person can be disabling, as Kitwood described in his observations of what he termed 'Malignant Social Psychology', such as when people with dementia are intimidated, outpaced, not responded to, infantilised, labelled, disparaged, blamed, overpowered, stigmatised or ignored (Kitwood 1997). Shotter (2009) talks about the importance of how we listen to one another and of listening well.

Narrative practices

Narrative practices and therapy have developed as ways of putting ideas from social constructionism into practice (Morgan 2000; White and Epstein 1990). Narrative approaches seek to be respectful and non-blaming. They centre people as the experts in their own lives. A narrative approach is one that 'views problems as separate from people and assumes people have many skills, competencies, beliefs, values, commitments and abilities that will assist them to reduce the influence of problems in their lives' (Morgan 2000, p2). Narrative approaches include practices such as 'outsider witness' and re-membering practices. Outsider witness is a particular form of speaking, listening and being heard, used as part of narrative practices (Fox, Tench and Tench 2002). It derived from Barbara Myerhoff's (1982) innovative work, which influenced Michael White (2000) and others in considering how a supportive group 'sustains a sense of identity in a potentially alienating environment' (Claire 2009, p.3). It offers a structure of telling, listening and retelling and has been used not just in training for professionals but also in the *Family Carers Matter* training described by Jean Tottie in Chapter 8. Re-membering practices (Hedtke 2003; White 1988) are described in more detail in Chapter 15.

I will now explore the general principles behind the narrative approach (Fox 2003).

The stories of people's lives are socially constructed

Stories are of a time and place (Gergen 1973). The story of dementia is socially constructed and this is changing dramatically over time. We may take for granted the idea that person-centred care that honours the personhood of someone with a dementia has always been with us, but it is easy to forget that the term 'person-centred care' was coined by Tom Kitwood only in the late 1980s; it was not until 1997 that he published his seminal book *Dementia Reconsidered* (Kitwood 1997). Other practitioners, such as Bob Woods and many others, were promoting psychosocial interventions (e.g. Brooker 2007; Downs 1997; Keady and Nolan 1994; Stokes and Goudie 1990) as part of what Keady has since referred to as 'the person centred care movement' (Keady, Williams and Hughes-Roberts 2007). The idea that people with a dementia could lead fulfilling lives was radical at that time, so much so that in the early 1990s I remember being warned off Tom and his then 'new-fangled' ideas!

The dominance of the biological discourse around dementia was, and still is, very persistent. There was a huge struggle to introduce psychosocial ideas into the realm of dementia care. Even as Kitwood's work was emerging, there was strong scepticism that therapy was possible with someone with a dementia; thankfully this 'taken for granted' idea is being laid to rest (e.g. Cheston 1998; Guss *et al.* 2014; Woods 1996).

Despite the changing language and approaches to dementia care there is still a challenge about how to 'do' person-centred care in practice. This is being addressed by people like Dawn Brooker at the Worcester Association of Dementia Studies[1] and Murna Downs at the Bradford Dementia Centre.[2] Knowing the person is central to the concept of person-centred care and life story work is just one tool to help to put the principles into practice.

Life story itself is a socially constructed idea and it will be interesting to see new evidence and ideas in this area emerge to challenge further what we understand life story work to be and how it is put into practice. This book is bringing together our current knowledge in the field in one place for the first time, including the voice of people with dementia themselves.

The stories of people themselves are helping to shape how dementia is viewed. 'Living well with dementia' was a term coined by Peter Ashley, who had dementia and was a member of the external reference group for the English National Dementia Strategy (DH 2009a). He wanted to give the message that people could still live well with a diagnosis. *My Name is Not Dementia* (Alzheimer's Society 2010) gives another strong statement that people are more than the label of their illness. Stigma is continuing to be challenged. The Dementia Engagement and Empowerment Project (DEEP), funded by the Joseph Rowntree Foundation, is a collaboration between the Mental Health Foundation[3] and Innovations in Dementia.[4] It is a network of groups and projects led by or actively involving people with dementia and is growing from strength to strength.

'On Our Radar – Dementia Diaries' is a UK-wide project that brings together people's diverse experiences of living with dementia as a series of audio diaries. They are recorded on special handsets that are linked to a dedicated voicemail and are automatically sent to the editorial team at On Our Radar. The team listen, transcribe and curate it for publication.[5] Paul Myles, editorial manager, explains that 'a lot of reporters [people with a dementia] thought, "Oh I've been written off…once I had dementia I never thought I'd get the chance to be a new technology user and to be developing my storytelling skills and to be featured on national media and other places".'[6]

I include these as illustrations of the continually evolving context in which life stories are being created.

Stories have real effects in shaping our futures

As the above example shows, stories about dementia are now being told by people living with dementia and are beginning to shape not only the way people with dementia see themselves but also the way they view their possible futures. How people view themselves after a diagnosis can change how they behave and how others behave towards them. A label comes with a diagnosis and a person's identity can become the label. Researcher Gloria Sterin described her dementia label as transformative and said that 'one is never looked at in the same way again' (Keady *et al.* 2007, p.8). As one individual told me recently, 'I thought because I had a diagnosis of dementia I had to act "demented."' Once this person came to a post-diagnostic group and understood more, shared and heard stories, they realised that they were still themselves. Stories and reputation can shape what happens to people. If a person feels 'written off' by others, that may indeed affect how they view themselves and their future. That is one of the powerful benefits of life story work, particularly if it results in a written document; the person does not feel 'written off' but, potentially, writes their own stories.

Our lives are multi-storied

We are surrounded by stories and we make sense of ourselves and each other by stories (Bruner 1991). How important might this be for people with a diagnosis of dementia? Stories and approaches that do not pathologise or blame people are vital for people who have been diagnosed with dementia. Any story we tell can only be a partial description of our lives, but how we choose which story can be a challenge.

In the newly discovered, unasked for role of 'carer,' sometimes the good things can be forgotten: 'I forgot that my mother loves to shop… we went shopping the other day and she bought six new outfits! She didn't need them but we had such fun' (carer, Family Carers Matter programme). People are more than their diagnosis; reconnecting them with their values and hopes can be transforming. We are all multi-storied. One woman I worked with said she wanted at least three life stories: one for her family, one for her friends and one for her work colleagues. One of the most important aspects of life story work is the focus on eliciting and recording stories of competency, skill and knowledge. These are enabling to the person and can help others see the person, not just their diagnosis. As explored in Chapters 14 and 16, this does not mean sad or difficult stories cannot be told; they may show how a person survived other difficult periods in their life. Or there may be 'no go areas': Ken Holt would never talk about his time in the war. Identities come alive through telling and retelling our stories, and for people living with dementia this can be vital. Their stories can be silenced too readily.

The process

Many people, family and staff alike, can feel overwhelmed as to where to start with life story work and sometimes where to finish. One Age UK advocate told us that 'when he began to tell me the name of the pet goldfish he had when he was eight I knew it was time to stop!'

This may explain why templates are popular. They give us a structure and often follow a culturally familiar narrative path of family, school, work, marriage and children. Traditionally, people use structured interview techniques to sit down and elicit stories that then result in a book (Haight 1992; Subramaniam, Woods and Whitaker 2014). As can be seen in later chapters, there is good evidence for this approach in the context of skilled life review.

However, such a prescriptive approach does not always fit with people's experiences. Cognitive psychologists have studied how autobiographical memory works (Rubin 1989) and this can illuminate the process of eliciting life stories. Autobiographical stories are built from many different ingredients – snippets of what actually happened (Schachter 1996). These are what people remember as 'self-defining memories' (Singer 1995; Singer and Salovey 1993), which tend to be those charged with more emotion. As Bower (1981) noted emotions are important in how memories are made and how they can be recalled. A personal example is from George. George (aged 92) always recounts the story of his home being hit by a bomb in the war. Fortunately, he survived along with his parents *and* the grandfather clock, which is still in pride of place in his home.

Involuntary autobiographical memories (IAMs)

Involuntary autobiographical memories are a normal part of our lives. They occur spontaneously, perhaps three to five times a day (Bernstein 1996). They have been described as seeming to 'pop into consciousness more easily and more frequently than voluntary memory, occurring without any deliberate attempt at retrieval and often during undemanding activities. IAMs appear to be more resistant to ageing and dementia' (Bradley, Moulin and Kvavilashvili 2013, p.190). These automatic routes to memory seem to remain intact and can provide a fast route to perhaps previously untapped autobiographical memories. This may help to explain how sensory reminiscence activities and music are so powerful and effective for people with dementia, as discussed in Chapter 17. These memories have been described by Mace (2007) as three types: 'precious fragments' (from Linton 1982), 'bi-products of other memories' (involuntary memories produced by other memories) and 'not so precious fragments', which result from traumatic experiences (Mace 2007, p.3). Such memories are not chronological and, as Victoria Metcalfe illustrates in Chapter 13, the process of life story work does not have to be either. So how do we choose which story to tell or help someone else tell their story?

Conclusion

Narrative approaches encourage listening for stories of ability, skills and competence. Using approaches like a 'tree of life', as described by Eleanor Martin and colleagues (Clayton *et al.* 2012), might produce a more fluid, less linear narrative. No research has been done yet in this area. Such narrative approaches try to reconnect a person to these stories in order to reignite hope (Milton and Hansen 2010) and allow people to tell their preferred story.

This chapter has discussed some of the psychological theories that underpin life story work, some of the guiding principles and some of the processes that need to be considered when starting out.

Notes

1. Established in 2009 at the University of Worcester, the aim of the Association of Dementia Studies is to make a substantial contribution to building evidence-based practical ways of working with people living with dementia and their families that enable them to live well. They do this primarily through research, education and scholarship. Further information is available at www.worcester.ac.uk/discover/association-for-dementia-studies.html
2. Bradford Dementia Group, based at Bradford University, is a multidisciplinary, multi-professional group committed to making a difference to policy and practice in dementia care, through excellence in research, education and training. Further information is available at http://dementiapartnerships.com/project/bradford-dementia-group
3. The Mental Health Foundation is a charity that provides support and research for good mental health. Find further information at www.mentalhealth.org.uk
4. Innovations in Dementia is a community interest company that works nationally with people with dementia, partner organisations and professionals, with the aim of developing and testing projects that will enhance the lives of people with dementia.
5. See www.dementiadiaries.org
6. Further information can be found at www.journalism.co.uk/news/-life-after-diagnosis-dementia-diaries-stigma-and-the-media/s2/a565025

2

The Policy Context

Life Story Work and People with Dementia

Ruth Eley

Introduction

This chapter will consider the importance of understanding the policy context within which life story work takes place. Policy sets out what is expected – and sometimes what is required – and can therefore be instrumental in shaping what is commissioned and how it is provided. There is no doubt that the publication of dementia strategies and plans in the four countries of the UK, with associated incentives, has raised dementia up the priority list, not only for health and social care but also for other sectors such as housing, leisure, arts and culture, resulting in part in the development of Dementia Action Alliances. The implications of other policy exhortations such as person-centred care, choice and control, and what happens when things go wrong are also considered. Staff in particular should pay attention to policy objectives when drafting business cases for service changes to make sure they present the right evidence in support. They should also look out for opportunities to influence policy and how it is implemented locally.

My inspiration – why life story work matters

As the national programme lead for older people and dementia in the Department of Health (DH) I also had the lead for the Dignity Campaign. We were always looking for ways to make the campaign real – more than an exhortation to do good works – and to turn the care minister's mission to create Dementia Champions into something that made sense to busy practitioners. In 2008, I attended the annual conference of the Psychology Special Interest Group in the Elderly to speak about the draft national dementia strategy, which had just gone out for consultation, and took the opportunity to attend a workshop run by Polly Kaiser about life story work. During the workshop Polly showed a video interview with Ken Holt, whose wife had dementia and had recently moved to a care home. As described in the Introduction, he had produced her life story to help the staff understand a bit about her life and how this might affect her behaviour, so that they could support her better. When Polly asked Ken what his vision for life story work was, he replied, 'We need a national network so that we can spread the word about life story work and get everyone involved.' I immediately saw the opportunity that this idea presented to make what 'dignity' meant more tangible and was able to allocate a small amount of money to bring interested people together to work out how such a network could be set up and maintained. Two years later, the inaugural Life Story Network conference in Leeds was attended by 250 people (500 more had to be turned away). It was clear that there were many people who saw life story work as a valuable tool that could help them provide dignified, respectful care based on knowing individual needs, preferences and aspirations – giving them a tangible hook on which to hang their local Dignity Campaign.

The magic of life story work is that not only does it bring huge benefits to individuals – as discussed elsewhere in this book – but it also helps practitioners and clinicians 'do' policy, which can often seem dry and impenetrable and the responsibility of only senior executives. This chapter will therefore give some pointers to how policy can be used in our everyday work and readers will be able to say 'so that's what it means!'

Early days

When I started my social work career in the 1970s, it was hard to get anyone to take responsibility for confused older people – we didn't talk about dementia in those days, but chronic brain failure. Geriatricians were the most likely to take an interest, as old age psychiatrists were rare at that time. In the late 1960s there were only eight psycho-geriatricians in the UK and the specialty was not recognised in the National Health Service (NHS) until 1989.

This was in the context of older people generally being a low priority; in the newly formed social services departments, the old welfare service trailed behind child care and mental health in terms of status, priority and resources. In the NHS, older people were still living in long stay geriatric dormitory wards. In the 1980s, changes in the social security regulations meant that people requiring residential or nursing home care could claim benefits towards their fees in the private sector if the local authority was not prepared to pay, leading, in part, to a reduction in NHS provision. The community care reforms of the 1990s led to an expansion of independent sector provision and a shift in thresholds of care, resulting in frail older people being looked after by social care rather than the NHS. At the same time, the discipline of old age psychiatry was gaining ground; by 1999 there were 450 consultant posts along with elements of service such as day hospitals, community mental health teams and liaison psychiatry (Bewley, undated).

However, the debate about where dementia fitted in the policy landscape continued. The National Service Framework (NSF) for Mental Health (DH 1999) specifically excluded older people and people with dementia from its considerations and therefore from the additional resources that accompanied its implementation. Two years later, the NSF for Older People (DH 2001) included a standard on mental health, with a detailed service model. It stated that, inter alia, treatment for dementia should involve 'at all stages emphasising the unique qualities of the individual with dementia and recognising their personal and social needs' (p.98). This NSF was implemented without additional resources, however, and in the years that followed, people with dementia were still falling between the disciplines of mental health and older people.

Recent initiatives

The National Dementia Strategy for England (NDSE) (DH 2009a) was published with cross-party consensus and was a major driver in shifting the attention of the health and social care system to this group of people who use the whole spectrum of services – primary, community and acute NHS services and generic adult social care services as well as specialist mental health provision – yet report poor experiences of care and support. Importantly, the strategy was developed with the involvement of people with dementia and their carers; the title

Living Well with Dementia was at their insistence, reflecting the need to promote the possibilities of healthy and fulfilling lives after diagnosis and the reality that an individual is the same person the day after receiving the news. The NDSE included in its section on 'Improving care for people with dementia in care homes' a reference to life story work as an important ingredient in excellent residential care for people with dementia, describing it as 'an effective vehicle for care home staff to communicate and develop relationships with residents, based on their unique life experiences' (p.58).

Now, dementia has never been higher up the policy agenda. Wales, Scotland and Northern Ireland have each developed their own approaches, while internationally there have been various summits at European and global levels. Dementia is no respecter of international boundaries and increasingly nations are exploring ways of collaborating in research. In March 2015, the World Health Organization hosted their first Ministerial Dementia Conference, building on the work of the G7 under the UK's leadership. In England, the Prime Minister launched his Challenge on dementia in 2012 (DH 2012b), which set out his priorities as better health and social care, creating dementia-friendly communities and better research. The Challenge included a Dementia Care and Support Compact, which was signed by 11 leaders in the care sector and pledged six commitments, including: 'We will focus on quality of life for people with dementia as well as quality of care. By knowing their life history and their personal culture, our staff will deliver a personalised package of care and support.' Since then, we have had *Compassion in Practice: Nursing, Midwifery and Care Staff – Our Vision and Strategy* (DH 2012a), *Making a Difference in Dementia: Nursing Vision and Strategy* (DH 2013a) and *Dementia: A State of the Nation Report on Dementia Care and Support in England* (DH 2013b). In 2014, Public Health England identified dementia as one of its seven priority areas, with the aim of reducing incidence and prevalence amongst 65–74-year-olds. The following year the National Institute for Health and Clinical Excellence (NICE) published guidance aimed at changing lifestyle habits in mid-life to delay or prevent the onset of dementia (NICE 2015). The new Care Act, implemented in April 2015, created a single, consistent route to establishing an entitlement to public care and support and, for the first time, entitlement to support for carers on a similar basis. In 2015 the Prime Minister announced a further Challenge (DH 2015b), in which he said he 'wanted England to be the best country in the world for dementia care and support and for people with dementia, their carers and families to live'. It contains 50 commitments. The *Dementia Implementation Plan* (DH 2016) split these across four themes: risk reduction, health and care, awareness and social action, and research. It proposes action across two phases: up to 2018, with funding already set; and indicative actions, with no allocated funding, from 2018 to 2020. The government's stated vision is 'to create a society by 2020 where every person with dementia, their families and carers – whatever their background, geographical location, age, gender, sexual orientation, ability or ethnicity – receive high quality, compassionate and culturally competent care' (DH 2016, p.29). The test is whether this aspiration is translated into real change in the lived experiences of people with dementia and their carers, without yet another raft of police and guidance exhorting us to do better.

Policy and person-centred care

What do personalisation and person-centred care actually mean? Brooker and Latham (2015) define the latter by means of their VIPS framework: **V**alues, **I**ndividualised approaches, understanding the world from the **P**erspective of the person with dementia and a supportive **S**ocial environment. It values people irrespective of their age or cognitive ability and recognises that each individual is unique. Yet the lived experience of many people with dementia falls short of these expectations.

? Reflection points

- What does person-centred care mean for you?

- Could you explain it in simple terms to your next door neighbour or the person sitting next to you on the train?

Alongside policy exhortations there has been a series of reports that catalogue the mediocre, neglectful and abusive care of vulnerable adults. These include: the Parliamentary and Health Service Ombudsman's review of cases concerning older people (2011); the Francis report into hospital care in Mid-Staffordshire (Francis 2013); the Equalities and

Human Rights Commission inquiry into home care (2011); the report of the Older People's Commissioner for Wales into hospital care for older people (2011); *Winterbourne View Hospital: A Serious Case Review* (Flynn and Citarella 2012); and *In Search of Accountability: A Review of the Neglect of Older People Living in Care Homes Investigated as Operation Jasmine* (Flynn 2015). All highlight the failure of organisations, managers and staff to recognise and respond to the unique needs of individuals respectfully and with compassion. Specific reports relating to people living with dementia include: *Home from Home* (Alzheimers Society 2011); *A Road less Rocky* (Newbronner *et al.* 2013); *Building on the National Dementia Strategy in England* (All Party Parliamentary Group on Dementia 2011, 2014); and *Cracks in the Pathway* (Care Quality Commission 2014). These reports highlight the fact that despite policy initiatives across the UK, the experiences of older people generally and people living with dementia specifically are often of services that fail to treat them with respect and to recognise their unique value as individuals. Fifteen-minute calls for people needing home care are still commissioned by many local authorities; the numbers of people whose discharges from hospital are delayed are increasing significantly; and in many parts of the country admission to residential care remains the default response to people needing intensive support. Anna Gaughan considers the implications of these service failures and how we can better respect people's human rights in more detail in Chapter 3.

So why has the rhetoric around personalisation, choice and control not delivered real change for how people with dementia experience care and support? There is no doubt that the policy of austerity and the severe reductions in public finances, particularly for local government, have had a significant impact. Commissioning services based on quality outcomes rather than on cost and volume and maintaining the quality of provision with reducing resources have put many services under pressure; at the time of writing, some local authorities have not raised fee levels in care homes for four years and some tenders for home care services are awarded by reverse auction – the cheapest bidder gets the goods. In such circumstances, psychosocial interventions, such as life story work, to support person-centred care can often be seen as the icing on the cake. Perhaps the most straightforward explanation, however, is that ageism is alive and well. Older people are not seen as vibrant, valuable members of society who have knowledge and skills to contribute; rather, they are portrayed as unproductive, a burden to the state, boring and to be pitied. We rarely celebrate the fact that life expectancy has increased significantly over the last century, with most older people leading fulfilling lives, but focus on the 'burden' on the NHS and social care that larger numbers have created and we have failed to plan for.

? Reflection points

- Why do you think things go badly wrong in services?

- Can you think of ways of making this less likely to happen?

Yet there are examples of organisations that have found different ways of providing good quality services. By investing in staff training and development, enabling staff to make the most of time spent with people and encouraging innovation and creativity, some providers are able to ensure care is tailored to individuals and goes far beyond the minimalist 'one size fits all' approach that can so often characterise communal care settings. The Joseph Rowntree Foundation's *Better Life Programme* (Katz *et al.* 2011) confirmed that older people with high support needs want *a quality of life that includes relationships*, as well as living in a pleasant environment, being involved in making decisions and the opportunity to mix with other people. *John Kennedy's Care Home Inquiry* (Kennedy 2014) explored what relationship-centred care means. One contributor via Facebook stated that he took for granted the necessary physical care and housekeeping in a care home; he wanted to know that staff 'are interested in me, that you know I like to get on my soap-box and rant…that I am a football pundit and love to bet on the footie (so I'll need Wi-Fi and a laptop) and that I married the girl of my dreams' (p.23). Kennedy concluded that 'If care staff are to be able to prioritise relationships they need the time, space, confidence and encouragement to invest in them. The system needs to provide this environment for the right culture to prevail' (p.24).

These comments from a care home resident illustrate what the policy aspirations such as 'person-centred care' and 'choice and control' really mean. A life story work approach goes beyond meeting physical care needs (essential though they are); it enables staff to get to know the person and understand what makes them tick, why they might behave in particular ways and what will help them lead more fulfilling lives.

In recognition of the fact that policy can be interpreted in different ways – or indeed may be difficult to interpret at all – guidance is often developed to ensure consistency and to support policy. Examples include the NICE/SCIE guideline (2006), and Dementia Quality Standard (NICE/SCIE 2010), which provide clear evidence-based guidance on what care and treatments are effective in supporting people living with dementia and their carers throughout the course of the illness. The DH guidance on Intermediate Care was updated in 2009 and included specific reference to the needs of people with dementia and various models of service delivery to meet their needs (DH 2009b). The NDSE commissioning pack (DH 2011) included service specifications, financial models and evidence bases for early intervention and diagnosis, community-based care (in people's own homes, care homes and other residential settings), care in acute and community hospitals and the use of anti-psychotic medication in line with NICE/SCIE guidelines. It emphasised the fact that most people with dementia live at home and commissioners need to ensure that generic services such as home care, community nursing and intermediate care are able to meet the needs of people living with dementia. The promotion of life story work features in several guidance documents, including *Common Core Principles for Supporting People with Dementia* (Skills for Care 2011). These make specific reference to making use 'of the person's past experiences and life story to support communicating with them' (p.8) and 'understanding the personal history of the person and their life story in order to address the causes of challenging behaviour' (p.11).

Policies generated from different government departments may not always be aligned. For example, the Department of Health's stated action to 'work with the Dementia and Housing working group to raise the profile of housing, highlight and promote good practice, and further the integration of housing in health and social care policy on the issue of dementia' (DH 2016, p.40) seems at odds with the welfare reforms related to housing, which would catastrophically threaten the viability of social housing provision such as extra care and sheltered housing, announced by the Department of Work and Pensions.

People with dementia are often assumed to be 'at risk' because of their memory loss or other cognitive impairments, yet professionals may not consider how people with dementia themselves define risks and the strategies they may have developed to mitigate them. *Nothing Ventured, Nothing Gained: Risk Guidance for People with Dementia* (DH 2010) explores these issues in detail and promotes the concept of risk enablement rather than risk management. Taking risks is part of everyone's everyday experience, and how we deal with risks is an essential part of our identity. Using narrative approaches as part of assessing risks for people with dementia should enable more realistic risk enablement strategies to be negotiated that recognise the benefits as well as the potential dangers of undertaking certain activities or being in particular situations.

One of the most promising recent initiatives is the development and growth of Dementia Action Alliances (DAAs),[1] beginning initially as a national Alliance in 2010 and given impetus by the two Prime Minister's Challenges to encourage communities to become dementia friendly. Following a 'think tank' hosted by the Department of Health in 2011, early work on dementia-friendly communities in the UK was led by the Local Government Association (2012) and the Joseph Rowntree Foundation, the latter funding the 'Dementia Without Walls' project to explore how York could become a more dementia-friendly city (Crampton, Dean and Eley 2012). People living with dementia want to live at home and be part of their communities, continuing to participate in the activities that they enjoy and contributing as local citizens alongside everyone else. They are often prevented from doing so by stigma and ignorance about dementia among the wider population, hence efforts to raise awareness and increase understanding so that people with dementia and their carers can be assured that they will be welcomed, supported and included as they go shopping, use local transport, visit the theatre and eat in restaurants, for example. At the time of writing, the Liverpool DAA[2] had nearly 40 member organisations, ranging across health and social care and including arts and cultural organisations, housing and the business sector. Crucial to its success is the Service Users Reference Forum (SURF), comprising people with dementia and family carers. The group sets the priorities for the DAA and holds the organisation to account through its involvement in the various projects and representation in the core co-ordinating group. The challenge is to move the debate on from 'dementia-friendly' (suggesting tolerance and the granting of permission) to 'dementia-inclusive' communities that enable and empower people with dementia to play a full role as equal citizens.

Why does policy matter?

Policy is there for a purpose. It sets the parameters within which decisions are made, actions are taken and funding is allocated, whether at a national or local level. Whilst it does not in itself ensure compliance, it sets out what is expected and is a benchmark by which performance is measured. However, there is so much policy and guidance out there that it is easy to be overwhelmed. The challenge for practitioners is to make sense of all this and translate what the policy says – for example, to 'provide person-centred and meaningful post-diagnosis support, which meets the needs of people affected by dementia' (DH 2016, p.32) – into practical action to support individuals in particular circumstances. In times of sustained austerity and financial cut-backs, staff will need to gear their proposals for developments and improvements to what commissioners and managers will be looking for to enable them to meet the local and national policy objectives. Family carers and people with dementia who are involved in local working groups will also benefit from understanding national policy and what their clinical commissioning group (CCG) and local council see as priorities, so that they contribute to discussions about future developments from an informed perspective and challenge these priorities when they believe it is necessary. Narrative approaches such as life story work can be powerful tools in helping to understand what matters to individuals and how to help them realise their aspirations. These matters are considered in more detail in the following chapters.

:Q: TOP TIPS

- Don't be overwhelmed by the amount of policy and guidance that is available. Decide what is most important to you – it might be workforce development and training, personal care or mental capacity and decision making, for example – and familiarise yourself with what is expected (policy) and how to do it (guidance).

- Find out if your local NHS and council have a joint dementia strategy. If so, make sure you know what their priorities are.

- Many of these policies promote person-centred care so you can use them to support your practice.

- Conversely, use your knowledge of what policies say should happen in order to challenge local decisions that seem to be contrary to these

Notes

1. Further information is available at www.dementiaaction.org.uk
2. Information on the Liverpool DAA is available at www.dementiaaction.org.uk/local_alliances/3012_liverpool_dementia_action_alliance

3

Values, Rights and a Compassionate Culture

The Bedrock of High Quality Care and Support

Anna Gaughan

Introduction

Tom's story

This chapter is underpinned by my personal experience of supporting my mother-in-law, Beryl, in caring for my father-in-law, Tom, who had been diagnosed with vascular dementia some years earlier. What transpired on the afternoon that Tom was admitted as an emergency to an acute ward changed my perspective. It would make me even more resolute in facilitating and influencing the much needed change in the culture of care from one of finance, activity and performance targets to one focusing on people and relationships.

When it came to the section on the admission sheet that asked for information about occupation and past history, the nurse who was admitting Tom used her pen to put a line through that section, without a single glance at Beryl or me. In that one moment, with that simple yet powerful gesture and without any spoken words, this nurse began the process of devaluing Tom as a human being – one hopes unintentionally. What she saw in that moment was an elderly man with a diagnosis of dementia. What she did not see was Tom as a gentleman and a retired police sergeant, someone who had a big part to play in a loving, close-knit family, with a wonderful wife, Beryl, two grown-up sons and a daughter-in-law, as well as two beautiful granddaughters who adored their 'Taid' (Welsh for grandad). Beryl and I have reflected on the insensitivity of that moment many times since then. In the words of Maya Angelou:

> People will forget what you said; people will forget what you did; but people will never forget how you made them feel (cited in Kelly 2003).

This chapter will demonstrate the importance of retaining a clear focus on the whole person with dementia and not just on what we see, which at times is coloured by our own prejudices and attitudes. Often, we do not allow ourselves the time to stop and think of what it might be like for the person 'to be on the receiving end of me' (Lake 2015). It explores the need for leaders and staff to take the time to examine and become more aware of their own values, their own sense of who they really are and what is important to them and recognise that 'patients' and 'service users' are just like them.

From my experience, the importance of 'being present moment by moment' is the only way in which we will restore 'humanity' into words like *respect, equality, dignity, compassion and kindness* and enable us to connect as human beings.

I will draw on our experience in the Life Story Network of delivering training programmes to achieve cultural change. The chapter is designed to offer the reader a greater level of knowledge, understanding and confidence in the following areas:

- What are values and rights and why are they important?

- The interdependencies between values, rights and creating a culture of compassion – what does compassion really mean?

- Creating a culture of compassionate care – embedding values and the use of people's stories.

- Approaches to and theories underpinning cultural change and leading change in practice.

Understanding the key concepts will enable the reader to reflect on their own practice and explore how we as individuals can be the instruments of change we want to see in our care system.

When things go badly wrong

Scandals of poor care and treatment of older people and vulnerable adults are not a recent phenomenon (Walshe and Higgins 2002), but the Serious Case Review on Winterbourne View Hospital (Flynn and Citarella 2012) and the Francis Report (2013) are heralded as critical milestones in the history of our care services. They bring into sharp focus the devastating consequences of losing touch with some of our most fundamental values, resulting in the abuse, degrading treatment and assault of many people with learning disabilities in Winterbourne View Hospital and the neglect, humiliating treatment and even deaths of hundreds of people at Mid Staffordshire NHS Foundation Trust.

Poor care and neglect do not just occur in our care organisations, but also in people's own homes. The Equality and Human Rights Commission's *Care Close to Home* (EHRC 2011) highlighted the appalling ways in which many people's human rights were breached when receiving care at home. In some of the worst cases, many people were left without access to food and water or left in soiled clothes and linen. In others, people were ignored, humiliated, talked over and put to bed in the early afternoon.

In the aftermath of these inquiries there have been increasing calls for a sustainable transformative change in culture across the whole care system, from one focused on throughputs, targets and the bottom line to one that places the person and what matters to them at the centre of everything that we do. In particular, there is an emphasis on embedding core values in the care system, namely equality, dignity, respect, autonomy and compassion. However, we should not assume that there is consistency in defining and understanding these. Consequently, I will explore some of these concepts in more detail, aiming to understand the interdependencies between them and their relationship with organisational cultures, and examine the importance of collective, distributed leadership if we are to achieve excellent care across the whole system.

The common enabling factor in achieving a better understanding of values, rights and changing cultures is why and how we use the art of storytelling as a basis for creating the emotional connection with people at individual, team and organisational levels. Story telling is one of the most powerful means of communication and learning and has existed for centuries. Stories well told capture our hearts, our minds and our imagination. They allow us to build up a picture and set of values and beliefs around the person and what is happening in their lives, what really matters to them and how they are connecting to others in the world around them. Culture, either from a wider societal perspective or within organisations, is often defined as 'how things are done around here' (The Kings Fund 2013) – in other words, what stories are being told, what is influencing our beliefs, norms, practices and behaviours. Finally, in order to inspire people to change behaviours and cultures, we need to 'capture their hearts and minds', to offer professionals the opportunity to create the space for reflecting on their own moral compass and to begin to develop shared understandings to make progress (Drumm 2013).

Values and rights: what are they and why are they important?

> *Your beliefs become your thoughts. Your thoughts become your words. Your words become your actions. Your actions become your habits. Your habits become your values. Your values become your destiny.*
>
> Mahatma Gandhi

Values are intrinsic to what we stand for and what really matters to us; they influence how we live our lives and how we behave to meet our needs (Ciulla 1999; Posner and Munson 1979). These in turn can be influenced by the context in which we live. When we can achieve and meet our needs (values), our sense of wellbeing and happiness is increased. Conversely, when we feel that there has been an infringement of our values and our needs are not being met, this can lead to anxiety, fear and depression (Barrett and Clothier 2013). Whilst most of us would readily recognise the importance of our own personal values, care staff may forget the integral nature of a person's values to their sense of wellbeing, identity and happiness when viewing individuals with labels such as 'patient', 'service user' or 'client'. The *Your Story Matters* programme (Life Story Network 2012b) highlighted the difficulties that staff encounter when trying to work according to their values within pressured environments. As one participant said:

> Life story work reminded me [of] the ultimate purpose of health care work, to reconnect with our patients in a meaningful and valued way. On a depressing note, it reminded me how far we

have strayed from this fundamental principle in our therapeutic relationships.

Providing *compassionate* care, which recognises and respects the individuality, identity, dignity and privacy of the person, is central to the quality of care and support that individuals and families receive (Dewar and Christley 2013; Dewar and Nolan 2013; Kings Fund 2013; Porter and Lee 2013; Posner and Munson 1979). Further, 'improving health outcomes' is a core contributory factor in the job satisfaction experienced by staff (West *et al.* 2011).

Human rights are not a privilege conferred by government. They are every human being's entitlement by virtue of his humanity.

Mother Theresa

Human rights are there to protect everyone in every aspect of our lives. They are about our rights to be treated with dignity, respect and fairness. The Human Rights Act (HRA) (1998) came into force in 2000 and provides a legislative framework to implement the European Convention on Human Rights (ECHR). Under the HRA, all public authorities (including courts, police, NHS Trusts, local authorities and care homes) have a legal obligation to be compliant and ensure that people's human rights are respected in all that they do, as well as to positively promote the HRA.

The following six articles are of special relevance to the care sector and people living with dementia:

- **Article 2**: the right to life (with virtually no exceptions)

- **Article 3:** the right not to be tortured or treated in an inhuman or degrading way

- **Article 5**: the right to liberty and security of person (subject to lawful arrest or detention, which can include people with mental health disorders)

- **Article 8**: the right to respect for private and family life, home and correspondence

- **Article 12**: the right to marry and found a family (successfully used in some cases for people with learning disabilities and mental health needs)

- **Article 14**: the right not to be discriminated against in relation to any of the rights contained in the ECHR.

A simple and easy way to understand human rights is to see them as a vehicle for making Fairness, Respect, Equality, Dignity and Autonomy (FREDA) central to our lived experience. Human rights also form an integral part of the NHS Constitution (DH 2015), which states in the first principle that it 'has a duty to each and every individual that it serves and must respect their human rights' (p.3). Despite this, a review of the application of human rights in the UK undertaken in 2012 found that, although we should expect to be treated with dignity and respect when receiving care, the evidence clearly points to some people using care services, such as older or disabled people, experiencing poor treatment that is undignified and humiliating. At its most extreme, abusive, cruel and degrading treatment is similar to torture. This is in breach of Article 8 and Article 3 rights above (EHRC 2012).

Other laws that promote and protect the rights of people and in particular vulnerable people are the Equality Act (2010), the Convention on the Rights of Persons with Disabilities (2006), and the Mental Capacity Act (2005). The latter was amended in 2007 to incorporate the Deprivation of Liberty Safeguards (DoLs). These were further clarified in 2015 following a Supreme Court judgement (DH 2015a).

As highlighted in Chapter 2, there have been a plethora of national initiatives, polices and campaigns to address the failures of care, yet failures still persist in what Gillon (2013) describes as the '*human side*' (p.105) of care and support of the most vulnerable in our care system. Interestingly, Gillon refers to '*humanity*' (p.108), but stops short of making the link with a rights-based approach. Cornwell (2015) also points out that the provision of high quality, safe, relationship-based, compassionate care remains stubbornly elusive and suggests that what is required is to 'reinforce a positive culture, set a clear vision and ensure that staff have the practical support that is needed' (p.4). We inherit organisational cultures, which are often the legacy of past leaders' values and beliefs reflected in old structures, systems and processes (Barrett 2010). However, we have the opportunity to influence and create an organisational culture to facilitate compassionate care for the people receiving it, as well as creating positive environments within which staff can work, flourish and grow.

Before exploring what is meant by a *compassionate culture*, we need first to have a shared understanding of the concept of 'compassion'.

What is compassion?

In response to the Francis Report 2013, the DH produced *Compassion in Practice* (2012a). It articulated a shared vision, values and actions and what have subsequently become known as the 'Six Cs': care, compassion, competence, communication, courage and commitment. It defines compassion as 'how care is given through relationships based on empathy, respect and dignity – it can also be described as intelligent kindness, and is central to how people perceive their care' (p.13).

Dewar and Nolan (2013) propose that the key attributes of compassion include: recognising vulnerability and suffering; relating to the needs of others; preserving integrity; and acknowledging the person behind the illness. They go on to describe four essential characteristics of compassion:

1. a relationship based on empathy, emotional support and a real understanding and desire to relieve a person's distress, suffering or concerns;

2. effective interactions between the key people over time and across care settings;

3. staff, individuals and families being active participants in decision making; and

4. contextualised knowledge of the person and family, both individually and as members of a network of relationships.

(Dewar and Nolan 2013, p.1248)

These are particularly important attributes when we are considering an appropriate definition of compassionate care in relation to the needs of people with cognitive impairment or dementia. The characteristics of compassion accord well with Kitwood's concept of 'personhood' (1997) as discussed in Chapter 1. He reminds us that 'each person has come to who they are by a route that is uniquely their own, every stage of their journey has left its mark' (p.15). Dewar and Nolan (2013) make a similar point in highlighting that 'appreciative caring conversations' involve two dimensions: 'knowing who I am, what matters to me' (p.1250) and 'understanding how I feel' (p.1252). They go on to describe the seven essential attributes required to create the right culture within which to embed these appreciative caring conversations. These attributes are:

- **'Being courageous'** – really thinking about what it means to connect emotionally with individuals and their family carers, recognising that this requires time

- **'Connecting emotionally'** – daring to be human, inviting individuals and their carers to share their feelings and being aware of the impact of this on staff and others

- **'Being curious'** – being able to ask questions, to challenge assumptions and explore how things could be done differently

- **'Collaborating'** – finding solutions together, involving individuals, families and staff, creating a shared sense of responsibility and possibility

- **'Considering other perspectives'** – accepting difference and feeling positive about discussing these differences in an open and transparent way

- **'Compromising'** – accepting that there will not always be a consensus and therefore developing the ability to 'give and take' through discussion and reflection and

- **'Being celebratory'** – making a very conscious effort and knowing what works well and that everyone's contribution is valued.

In relation to people living with dementia, these dimensions and attributes help to acknowledge the uniqueness of the person – their route (story) to enabling them to lead meaningful and worthwhile lives, beyond the constraints placed on them by their dementia – and feature as key principles in the application and use of human rights in this context.

Adams (2009) points out that 'while dementia is often a limiting experience, many people with dementia are able to adapt and maintain purposeful and worthwhile activities and relationships, particularly in the early stages of the condition' (p.630). In his work, applying 'recovery' principles and the use of narrative approaches that take account of the person's life story enable the individual and family to:

- come to terms with their diagnosis of dementia and remain focused on who they are as a person and what they can still do

- regain a focus on what really matters to the person, what is important in keeping them connected to others and ensuring this is in keeping with their sense of wellbeing and happiness

- create a sense of hope and remain focused on making their lives count, optimising their potential at all times

- ensure that there is a focus on the individual and not seeing the person defined by their diagnosis or disability

- highlight the critical value and importance of 'meaningful relationships', taking account of what matters to the individual and thus avoiding group solutions being imposed.

It is within this context that life history and life story work have gained such prominence in the care of people with cognitive impairment and dementia (as discussed elsewhere in this book). It follows, then, that if we are to create a transformational sustainable compassionate culture, Dewar and Nolan's (2013) 'appreciative caring conversations', including their four essential characteristics of what constitutes compassion, need to be at its heart.

Creating a culture of compassionate care: embedding values and the use of people's stories at the heart of the process

Organisations are made up of individuals; our behaviour is influenced by our values and beliefs and impacts on others around us. Barrett (2010) argues that in order for whole system cultural change to be successful and sustainable, four conditions must be met: alignment between values and beliefs of individuals and their behaviours; a congruence and alignment between the organisational values and its systems, processes, policies and practices – the culture; alignment between the values of the staff and the organisation; and alignment between the vision and mission of the organisation and the sense of motivation and passion felt by staff. If these conditions are met, staff feel comfortable and valued in an organisation, knowing that they are contributing and making a positive difference on a daily basis.

It remains unclear how the ambition of the Francis Report (2013) to introduce positive values across the care system will be achieved. Francis himself stressed the need for clear, strong, ethical leadership shared at all levels, from the board to floor. The care system responded with programmes of work focusing on values, with the aim of ensuring that there was a better alignment between organisational and system values and the personal values of staff.

Despite good intentions and the development of these initiatives, there is a much quoted statistic by John Kotter (1996) that 70 per cent of all transformational change processes fail. The Life Story Network's 'Your Story Matters' training programme confirmed the necessity of securing ownership from organisational leaders to support and empower staff to change their practice as part of wider cultural change; training individuals and expecting them to be able to do this on their own is unrealistic. As a consequence, 'Your Community Matters' (Life Story Network 2013) included a one-day workshop with senior managers to ensure they understood the principles of life story work and narrative approaches, and the potential beneficial impacts on care practice. They drew up action plans to support the staff development programme, which proved significant in reassuring staff that they had the necessary permissions not only to undertake the training but also to put what they had learned into practice.

We will now explore some approaches to cultural readiness and change and suggest a model change process to illustrate an approach to creating a culture of compassionate care – embedding values by using people's stories at the heart of the process.

Approaches to cultural change

The work developed on the 'Cultural Web' (Johnson, Scholes and Whittington 1992) provides a useful framework for attempting to change the culture of an organisation. Johnson *et al.* (1992) identified six interrelated areas that make up the 'paradigm' – pattern, model or culture – of the organisation:

1. **'Rituals and routines'** – the way things are done on a day-to-day basis – the activities, events or informal habits, which reinforce things that are felt to be important about culture

2. **'Stories'** – what stories are being told and retold to current staff, new recruits or external partners, letting people know what the organisation holds to be important and acting as a way of embedding them in this 'history'

3. **'Symbols'** – the visual representation of the organisation, including logos, offices, dress code and the language used by the organisation

4. **'Power structure'** – both formal and informal – those who are in positions of power or who have informal power and influence

5. **'Organisational structure'** – including the hierarchical structure as well as some unwritten lines of power and influence that indicate whose contributions are most valued

6. **'Control systems'** – these can include systems of rewards, what is being monitored or measured in the organisation, what is important to it.

Using this framework to undertake an analysis of the existing culture and describe the future 'desired' culture enables us to focus on what changes are necessary and ensure that the policies, processes, systems and staff are all in alignment. In addition to looking at the cultural readiness of the organisation, it is important to decide which of the many change models to use in order to achieve sustainable change. Kotter's model (2012) includes eight accelerators that take account of the constant need for change and for many people to be part of the change process – what he refers to as a 'volunteer army' – rather than the selected few. The steps are also designed to work alongside and within the traditional hierarchical organisational structures – what is referred to as a 'dual operating system'. At the heart of this new system are five key principles:

- **'Change is driven by many change agents'** – not just the few selected leaders.

- **'A want-to and a go-get – not a have-to mind-set'** – with people feeling motivated, enthused and having permission to deliver the desired improvements, creating an energy about the change process.

- **'Head and heart, not just head'** – people need to see how this gives meaning and purpose to their work and have an emotional investment in creating and working in this new culture.

- **'Much more leadership, not just more management'** – this new way of working is about vision, opportunity, influence, inspired action, reflection and celebration. It is much less about project management, budgets and accountabilities.

- **'Two systems, one organisation'** – the network of change leaders must operate in and be supported by the traditional hierarchy.

Governed by these principles, Kotter believes that his new 'accelerator' model will drive collaboration and creativity and the people involved will be focused, committed and passionate.

Putting it into practice

We know that staff will not change their attitudes and behaviour merely by being 'told to do' something or by being exposed to a plethora of strategies and initiatives that reiterate this message – instead they need to 'want to' embrace this new approach through being more aware of their own values and identity and the importance of these to them as individuals. Further, they need to be provided with the time, tools, knowledge, training and development to enable them to see the linkages between their values, beliefs and behaviours and the culture that they are contributing to on a daily basis. By making changes in these areas, they will effect change in the culture across their teams.

Using Kotter's change principles and eight accelerator steps as a guide, an organisational change process might look like this:

1. **'Creating a sense of urgency around a single big opportunity'** – the organisation sets out clear principles that underpin what they do:

a. going beyond minimum standards set by other organisations

b. getting the basics of care right every time

c. doing the right thing for people – making improvements because we care about the care that we provide

d. helping staff to try improvements, learn from their mistakes, and apply what works more rapidly.

e. helping staff to try new ways of working that improve quality and outcomes whilst reducing cost.

Specific goals that an organisation such as an NHS Trust might set over a defined period in relation to dementia might be: reduce falls by x% and enable all individuals to return home from hospital to complete assessments before decisions are made about long-term care. A care home might aim to reduce the numbers of people on anti-psychotic medication, reduce the numbers of residents admitted to hospital by x%, or enable residents to die in the home rather than be admitted to hospital. Within both these contexts, initiating and fostering caring and meaningful relationships with people using the service and their carers, by getting to know their unique life stories, are vital.

2. **'Build and maintain a guiding coalition of volunteers'** – leadership from the CEO will engender a sense of enthusiasm and commitment from the staff and encourage them to volunteer to be trained in the use of narrative approaches, including life story work. This team of volunteers would then roll this training out to other defined staff, supported by a programme of coaching, mentoring and action learning.

3. **'Formulate the strategic vision and develop the change initiatives designed to deliver this'** – The project must be clearly aligned with the strategic vision and values articulated by the organisation, with a designated executive director or senior manager lead and a number of key initiatives to support its delivery.

4. **'Communicate the vision and strategy, create "buy-in" and create a buzz attracting a growing army of volunteers'** – The initial group of volunteers are trained, in self-awareness of their own values and beliefs and impact on behaviour, culture change management, the practice of using life stories and how this facilitates relationship-based care – contributing to a compassionate culture. They have to model the attitudes and behaviours they want to see in others.

5. **'Accelerate movement towards achieving the vision, by ensuring that the network and hierarchy removes any potential barriers'** – A project steering group, with executive director leadership, would receive, discuss and address any potential barriers and ensure that these are addressed expediently, enabling the adoption of the right behaviour and attitudes to be embedded in practice. In particular, staff should be given the time to get to know the individuals they are caring for.

6. **'Create visible and significant short-term wins'** – The project would identify a suite of measures to evaluate the content and delivery. The measures could include: validated tools such as the Quality of Life in Alzheimer's Disease (QOL-AD) – a brief, 13-item measure designed specifically to obtain a rating of the patient's Quality of Life from both the patient and the caregiver (Logsdon *et al.* 2002); staff surveys to measure impact; vignette interviews with people using the service, carers and staff; information from learning and reflective diaries kept by staff; and a care plan audit. The results of these measurements would be communicated widely across the organisation with the support of the organisation's communications and marketing team.

7. **'Never let up – keep learning from experience, don't declare victory too soon'** – The principle of experiential, reflective learning is a key part of the overall process, so the outcomes of regular review and course evaluations would be incorporated as the pilot is rolled out.

8. **'Institutionalise changes – embed them in everyday working practices and habits'** – The purpose of inviting volunteers from within and across the organisation is to ensure that ongoing support, challenge and reflection feature on a daily basis in their practice.

Conclusion

A transformative and sustainable shift in culture across our care system to one based on values and respectful relationships is urgently needed. As our values govern our behaviours, then it follows that in order to effect this change, the starting point has to be to look more closely at our own values. As is highlighted elsewhere in this book, the use of narrative practice (stories) is a powerful way to examine and become more aware of our values. It offers staff the opportunity to connect emotionally with individuals and their carers and underpins a person-centred approach to care.

Organisations are a collective of individuals; their values must be aligned with those of the organisation to achieve sustainable change. Staff need to want to change their attitudes and behaviour and understand that doing so will have a positive impact on the purpose and effectiveness of the work that they are doing. Our proposed organisational change model enables us to engage a network of volunteers to lead the process. Such a network creates the space for them to reflect on their own stories and become more aware of their own values and how these affect the quality of their practice. The training programme should enable them to become skilled, confident and energised in the use of stories to effect change within and across their teams. Through this process, we can drive a more compassionate culture, based on values and rights, as the bedrock of high quality care and support.

4

Equality and Diversity in Life Story Work

Polly Kaiser

If we do not know what we are going to be we cannot know what we are. Let us recognise ourselves in this old man or that old woman. It must be done if we are to take upon ourselves the entirety of our human race.

Simone de Beauvoir, *Old Age* (1970, p.12)

If you don't know who I am, how are you going to provide a particular package of care for me to deliver something? When you do not know how important my religion is to me, what language I speak, where I am coming from. How are you going to help me cope? The first step is about identity…it's absolutely fundamental.

Professor Kamlesh Patel, Chair of Mental Health Commission, *The Guardian* (2005)

Introduction

As we have seen in previous chapters, stories are important and can influence the way we see ourselves and others. The Equality Act (2010) protects people with 'protected characteristics' from discrimination. These are defined as age, disability, gender reassignment, marriage and civil partnership, religion or belief, sex and sexual orientation. However, the stories or narratives about these attributes affect the way people are perceived and treated. A prime motivation for doing life story work in dementia care is to enable the voices of people who have been traditionally marginalised and stigmatised, to be heard in more positive ways. If a person has a diagnosis of dementia and has some of these additional characteristics, telling their story and having it heard can be hard (Ekdawi and Hansen 2010) so the issue of supporting traditionally 'seldom heard' voices (Robson *et al.* 2008) within dementia itself is vital to consider. These stories are socially constructed and change over time as we see with dementia itself.

This chapter looks at equality and diversity issues in the context of life story work with people with dementia. It will give definitions of the terms used but will not focus on religion and spirituality as these are covered in more detail in Chapter 14. Whilst disability is touched on, particularly the disability of dementia, the main examples are in the areas of race, age, gender and sexuality as these have been my focus over the years.

The aim is to provide some ideas to increase confidence in having helpful conversations with the people you work with who you may perceive as different from yourself in some ways.

The discourses or 'stories' around equality and diversity have evolved as the history around us evolves. It is still evolving. When I began working in this area some 25 years ago, 'diversity' was not spoken about. Teaching and dialogue were often about race, ethnicity or people from other countries and skin colour. Later, conversations began to broaden out about 'culture and ethnicity'. However, people do not come in boxes and many people share multiple, overlapping identities: people with disabilities, people of different faiths and religions, sexuality and sexual preferences. The stories around dementia too have changed. Twenty-five years ago, I only met people with dementia on the in-patient wards or, at best, about to be admitted to them. Now, not only do I hear people with dementia speak at conferences, but I serve on committees, present talks and co-design training with them and am Facebook friends with some. Stories change and can bring about change. The stories people with dementia are telling us are changing the way people view dementia. Before looking at issues of whose story and which story, I will give some definitions.

Definitions

Age

Age can be defined in terms of chronological or biological definitions – you are 50, 30 or 70. However, like dementia and race, age is a social construct (Phillipson 2013, 2015). The stories about ageing vary through history and cohorts and across different cultures. The generation of people born in the 1950s is very different from those born in the 1920s. There are stereotypes about older people that can lead to different treatment. Ageism was a term first coined by Butler in 1963. He defined it as:

> a process of systematic stereotyping and discrimination against people because they are old – just as racism and sexism accomplish that for skin colour and gender… Ageism allows the younger generation to see older people as different from themselves: thus they suddenly cease to see their elders as human beings and thereby reduce their own fear of dread and ageing…at times ageism becomes an expedient method by which society promotes viewpoints about the aged in order to relieve itself from responsibility towards them. (Butler 1987, p.22)

Disability

The World Health Organisation defines disability as:

> an umbrella term, covering impairments, activity limitations, and participation restrictions. Impairment is a problem in body function or structure; an activity limitation is a difficulty encountered by an individual in executing a task or action; while a participation restriction is a problem experienced by an individual in involvement in life situations. It reflects the interaction between features of a person's body and features of the society in which he or she lives. Overcoming the difficulties faced by people with disabilities requires interventions to remove environmental and social barriers. (WHO n.d.)

Life story work has the potential to reduce some of the social and environmental barriers for people by promoting activity and connections and other people's understanding. Historically, life story work grew out of work with people with learning disabilities and it is equally relevant for people with learning disability and dementia. Dementia itself is now being viewed through the lens of disability, as not only does someone have the syndrome, but they also have to cope with the environment around them, which can be disabling (Marshall 2005; Jolley 2005). The Dementia Friendly Communities initiative is an attempt to begin to address this (see Chapter 10).

Race, ethnicity and culture

The terms race, ethnicity and culture are often used interchangeably:

> Race was a concept which became prevalent in the nineteenth and twentieth centuries and has largely become discredited in biological science. It is a socially constructed term which categorises groups on the basis of genetic and biological characteristics. It is an idea usually linked to notions of hierarchy, inferiority and superiority and historically justified racism. (Patel *et al.* 2000, p.30)

Race is important as it affects people with regard to how they are seen and how they may be stereotyped (Sewell 2009); and, as with age, it can lead to discrimination.

Ethnicity, on the other hand, is not deemed as fixed. It can be shifting and impermanent. Ethnicity is a term that is open to much debate and one that often causes great confusion. The word 'ethnic' is derived from the Greek word 'ethnos', and simply means 'tribe' or 'people' (Senior and Bhopal 1994). Most definitions of ethnicity imply a shared culture, religion, traditions or heritage, language and geographical origins. It is about group identification and belonging. We all have an ethnicity.

Culture can be defined as

> those sets of shared world views, meanings and adaptive behaviours derived from simultaneous membership and participation in a multiplicity of contexts – such as rural, urban, suburban, language, age, gender, cohort, family, race, ethnicity, religion, nationality, socio-economic status, employment, education, occupation, sexual orientation. (Falicov 1995)

Culture has been defined as 'the way things are done around here' (Deal and Kennedy 1982 p.4) – so that might be in a family, on a ward or in a care home as well as in wider society. Figure 4.1 shows a helpful table that is used to summarise these differences.

	Characterised by	Determined by	Perceived as
Race	Physical appearance	Genetic Ancestry	Permanent, genetic/biological
Culture	Behaviour and attitudes	Upbringing and choice	Changeable (assimilation and acculturation)
Ethnicity	Sense of belonging, group identity	Social pressure and Psychological need	Partially changeable

Figure 4.1: Race Ethnicity and Culture (Fernando 2001, p.11)

Whilst both the term BME (Black and Minority Ethnic) and Black and Asian Minority Ethnic (BAME) are commonly used, in this chapter I use Botsford's definition of BME to refer to 'both white and non-white, including Asian, group and individuals' (Botsford and Harrison Denning 2015, p.12) and recognise that it does not describe a homogenous collective (Sewell 2009).

Sexuality and sexual orientation

Sexuality is a complex and multi-dimensional concept that describes: the desire for sex, sexual activity, sexual orientation, values and beliefs, a person's self-concept and self-esteem and a sense of sensuality (Kaiser 1996; Penhollow, Young and Denny 2009). There is a great deal of stigma and taboo around thinking about and speaking about sexuality and ageing. 'Older people weren't asked in surveys about their sexual activity because everyone knew that they had none, and they were assumed to have none because nobody asked' (Comfort 1974). Older people's sexuality and sexual needs are often overlooked; and if they are addressed, individuals are assumed to be heterosexual. For many of the current generation of older people, homosexuality would have been illegal when they were younger and the stigma may remain in discussing it. Some people with dementia may be reliving a time when they were cautious and fearful. They may revert in their memories to a period before they came out or when they led very different lives. So, for example, in Victoria Metcalfe's chapter (Chapter 13) Ronald started talking about his children; Edward knew nothing about them and was distressed.

Which stories?

I'm black, and I'm brown and I am a brother, and I'm Indian and I'm Jewish and I'm Muslim. White people have told me that I am white too...after all I went to Oxford and I talk properly don't I? Wherever I go I can't fit in so I am everything. But I am nothing. I fit in but I am never at home. I am not part of a community.

Raphael Mokades (*Guardian* 2005)

Which stories do people want to talk about? If someone lives with different and potentially stigmatised labels, which aspects of themselves and their identities do they feel comfortable to share?

The aim with life story work is to enable people to feel comfortable enough to share some of their stories. As described elsewhere, sharing stories needs to be in the manner of the person's choosing; it is about helping people marginalised in communities to have a voice and to be seen and heard. A person with dementia may find it hard to tell their story, but this can be made more difficult by other aspects such as language, race, disability, sex, sexuality and class. Some of these issues about 'which story?' are discussed later, particularly in Chapters 7, 13, 14 and 17.

Invisible/visible: voiced/unvoiced

In the context of diversity, family therapists John Burnham and Alison Roper-Hall provide a useful model. They invite people to think about diversity in terms of what they call the 'social graces' or GGRRAAACCEEESSS, which include: Gender (Sexism), Geography; Race (Racism), Religion; Age (Age-ism), Ability, Appearance, Class, Culture, Ethnicity, Education, Employment, Sexuality, Sexual orientation and Spirituality (Burnham 2013; Roper-Hall 2008). Burnham goes on to point out that some of these characteristics may be visible – for example, biological sex or skin colour, while others such as religion, sexual orientation and employment are invisible. Some people may be able to speak about and 'voice' aspects of their identity, while for others these may remain, and may need to remain, 'unvoiced'. Older men who grew up when homosexuality was illegal may still feel tentative about who they share this information with. It is not our job in doing life story work to necessarily 'out' people and make them voice the unvoiced.

Past conversations may have been far from helpful. For example, Bert, an older gay man who was given aversion therapy in the 1960s to 'cure' him, was understandably a bit cautious about opening up to a care worker in his care home now. In another example, Lucy told me she had never worked with a Muslim woman before and she was anxious about 'saying the wrong thing'. We need not only the knowledge and skill but also the confidence to have conversations with people from all backgrounds if we are going to be able hear their stories. As Victoria Metcalfe discusses in Chapter 13, we also need good support and supervision. It is important, however, to be aware of one's own views and 'listen for' the story that someone may need and want to voice – even if, together, you decide it does not go into a life story book.

Stories of disability

Dementia is in itself an equality issue as so many people experience discrimination and stigma. This stigma means that it is often invisible – and even if voiced, not heard:

> People think, as soon as you mention dementia, they look at you and go there's nothing wrong with him, he's fiddling the system, they look at me and think I am fiddling the system, they don't know what is going on.

> If you say to someone, 'can you wait a couple of minutes, I've got dementia and I want to explain?' they look at you and think there is nothing wrong with you, you should be able to talk…then again you get some who go 'HOW – ARE – YOU?' and you think, 'grrr, I'm not that bad'. (Alzheimer's Society 2010, p.22)

People may have other disabilities and illnesses alongside their dementia, which can compound the difficulties they encounter – for example, Frank was blind and could not see to do a life story book as such. Instead he and his psychologist worked their way through music that was meaningful to him and created a musical life story.

Stories of gender and sexuality

It has been estimated that 6 per cent of people in the UK are gay or lesbian. This means an estimated 49,200 gay people are living with dementia in the UK. Three in every 50 people living in care homes could be gay (Béphage 2008).

> I am a lesbian and I work in a care home. I see how people are treated. We were sent on a course to think about people's sexuality and my colleagues said 'what...on top of all our other troubles we have to think about that!!'...what would it be like to be somewhere where you couldn't be yourself?[1]

This woman feels she would definitely have to keep a large part of her story unvoiced; but even when voiced, people are not always heard:

> My partner and I had been together for 25 years when she was diagnosed with Alzheimer's...when she went into hospital I kept telling them that I was her partner, but they moved her to residential care without asking me. I phoned up to see how she was and she wasn't there. (Anon)

Victor

Tom, a skilled occupational therapist, undertook some life story work with Victor. Tom was alert and open to different stories and as he listened it transpired that Victor liked to dress in women's clothes and had done so all his life. This had always been very private and, within the family, an invisible aspect of his identity, at least to his children. When his daughter helped to move him into the care home she had been so shocked that she got rid of all her father's clothes and make up. He was depressed as he could no longer express his identity and 'be him/herself'. The life story work undertaken over time by Tom with Victor helped to build up trust and allow Victor's unvoiced identity to become more safely voiced. Conversations were had with his daughter who came to accept and integrate this new information about her father and shop for the clothes he needed.

Victor had two life stories – his private one and a public one.

Reflection points

- Take a moment and think about aspects of your identity that are visible, invisible, voiced or unvoiced.

- What stories about yourself would you be happy to share now? With your friends? With work colleagues?

- If you had to go into a care home, what would be important for people to know about you or not know?

Black minority ethnic stories

The Alzheimer's Society estimates that there are 11,000 people of BME origin in the UK with a dementia. There are a range of factors affecting people from BME communities.

Mrs Malik

Mrs Malik came to England in 1969. Her husband had been here for six years already, working in the cotton mills. She had stayed at home in Pakistan with their two young children. Her husband finally called for her to come and join him. When she arrived she found it dark and cold. She could not get the food she was used to cooking with. She did not go out much as people stared at her but she eventually became friends with other women and more shops opened. She had two more children of whom she is very proud. Her two eldest sons have become lawyers, the third is a dentist and her daughter is a school teacher. Her English is not very good.

Now a widow, her extended family still lives in Pakistan and she cannot go and visit them because of her health; she has diabetes and angina. She had a heart attack two years ago and is getting more and more forgetful. She is very proud of her family; they have done well and they are busy now with their own lives. She doesn't want to bother them. She has been very active in her community and attends a lunch club, but she is beginning to forget things and she feels people are beginning to talk about her behind her back. She will not go to the doctor and she will not speak to anyone. She did ask if she could borrow a DVD about dementia and take it home to show her family, but she would not talk about it.

Mrs Malik would gladly talk about her life but was terrified about the idea that she might have dementia. Research suggests that there is a lack of awareness regarding definition and recognition of dementia in BME communities and a greater need for community education to reduce stigma and myths. Moreover, in some communities there are no words for dementia (Jutlla 2015; Seabrooke and Milne 2004).

Making Connections Not Assumptions (Pennine Care NHS Trust 2009) was a two-year piece of work I carried out with others, including Abdul Shakoor and John Newton, to encourage older South Asian women who might be suffering from mental health problems (including dementia) to seek advice and access services. The main focus was on engagement to better understand the issues and concerns of women and to develop culturally appropriate information and services. A number of narrative approaches were adopted throughout the project.

The project found that, whilst women did talk about mental health issues, dementia was still very much a taboo. These stories remained largely invisible at that time. The women said they would rather speak within their families and with their adult children about it. Language is another barrier; even if people can speak English, people with a dementia may revert back to their language of origin as the dementia progresses:

> I feel lonely because I can't speak English and I do not know how to communicate.

> I would like someone who is kind and will listen.

You may therefore need interpreters; this adds another dimension to gathering and hearing stories that needs to be considered carefully (Botsford and Harrison Denning 2015). The reversion to the language of origin also adds weight to the importance of trying to do life story work as early as possible. Creative methods such as those described in Chapter 17 may be helpful to help elicit and share stories.

The life story work undertaken with some of the women gave them confidence to share some of their stories about coming to the UK: the loneliness, the lack of foods initially, and some of the racist attitudes they encountered. Even though they knew each other well and had been coming to the luncheon club for a long time, the life story work that they did, and then shared, promoted connections between them.

They all had individual tales to tell of their journeys here but shared common ground also, often with laughter and tears.

Conclusion

The essence of life story work is eliciting and sharing stories. For people and groups who may not have been used to their stories being heard, this may take extra time and sensitivity. We cannot know everything about all the groups or cultures, but asking respectful questions can help build rapport. We need to be sensitive to a person's visible and invisible identity and not 'out' stories unless they want them to be shared.

? Reflection points

- How comfortable do you feel having conversations about sexuality, culture or disability?

- Have you experienced any problems talking about sexuality with people you have worked with?

- What challenges or barriers have you experienced with someone from a different background?

- Have you received any training or supervision in this area?

- Are you aware of any guidelines in this area?

- What would help you?

Note

1.   From *Out on Tuesday,* a Channel 4 programme broadcast in early 1989.

Part 2

Does It Work?

The Evidence Base for Life Story Work

5

Understanding the Outcomes of Life Story Work

Kate Gridley

This chapter presents findings from research funded by the National Institute for Health Research Health Services and Delivery Research Programme. The views and opinions expressed herein are those of the author and do not necessarily reflect those of the HS&DR Programme, NIHR, NHS or the Department of Health.

Introduction

This chapter is about the possible outcomes of life story work. More specifically, it is about understanding:

- what difference life story work could make for the various people involved

- how this difference could come about (the routes to outcomes)

- what methods are available to assess whether the desired changes have come about (approaches to outcome measurement) and how suitable these are.

Understanding the possible routes to achieving desired outcomes is an essential step in designing any evaluation, especially an evaluation of a complex intervention (Craig *et al.* 2008). Life story work may not seem complex. Indeed, it can be quite simple to do in the right circumstances (although it is by no means always so, as Jane McKeown and colleagues describe in Chapter 16). However, *evaluating* life story work requires an understanding not only of the potential outcomes, but also what is going on in the undeniably complex and ever changing environments in which life story work is undertaken. These usually contain some people (not easy to control) and a whole array of concurrent processes that may interact with life story work, and which may impact on how the people involved feel and act.

This chapter begins with an overview of the potential outcomes of life story work as identified through focus groups with people with dementia, family carers and care staff. We then consider how these outcomes might be achieved (the routes to outcome), before finishing with a discussion of approaches to outcome measurement and some things to think about when designing your own evaluation.

Possible outcomes of life story work

The evidence presented here comes from a study of life story work carried out by the Social Policy Research Unit (SPRU, part of the University of York) between 2012 and 2015. The aim of the study was to gain a better understanding of life story work, its costs and outcomes and approaches to measuring these, in order to assess the feasibility of a full-scale evaluation. At the time of writing, the feasibility study is still underway,[1] but the initial development work is complete, including a set of focus groups with people with dementia, family carers and dementia care staff looking at the outcomes participants felt they had experienced (or could achieve) through life story work. In the past, the outcomes measured in evaluations of healthcare interventions tended to be those considered by clinicians or academics to be of most importance, such as mortality (death) and morbidity (illness) rates (Haywood 2006). More recently, it has been shown, however, that people living with health conditions can have quite different views about which outcomes are important (Hewlett 2003). In the SPRU evaluation of life story work, we started from first principles, wishing to establish from the point of view of people with dementia (and their carers) what outcomes they felt they had experienced (or could achieve) through life story work and how these might come about.

We spoke to 73 people in total during the focus groups. Four focus group sessions were held with people with dementia, supported by Innovations in Dementia[2] involving a total of 25 participants. These were run through existing community groups and day services in order to ensure that participants felt confident in their surroundings and could be supported by known and trusted workers. Three focus groups were held with family carers recruited through Dementia UK's Uniting Carers network,[3] involving 21 participants. Finally, three groups (involving 27 participants) were held with dementia care staff and professionals with experience of life story work, recruited through the Life Story Network.[4] Below we outline the types of outcomes identified through these sessions, grouped into: 1) those that might be experienced by the individual with dementia; 2) those that offer benefits not only to the individual but to the people around them (which we call interpersonal outcomes); and 3) those that might be achieved through the impact of life story work on people who provide care.

Outcomes for the individual

Some people gain immense pleasure from talking about memories. Indeed, reminiscence activities have long been used in dementia care (Gibson 1994). Life story work can involve a specific form of reminiscence that focuses on the life history of the individual, although a person may also choose instead to focus on the here and now, or the things they look forward to. In each of the focus groups with people with dementia there were some participants who found it enjoyable to talk about memories. More specific to life story work, a number of these felt that it was important to *record* memories, so that they had them to look back on and could share them with others:

> **Researcher:** What are you going to use them [the life story books] for?
>
> **DF3R7:** [Pause] For memories.
>
> **Researcher:** For yourself?
>
> **DF3R7:** For myself, and the family, they've all seen them. It's – I think it's nice just to have a look and think – I used to look like that once!

Highlighting and celebrating past achievements was also a priority and one that appeared to bring much pleasure. Moreover, each object or photograph referred to by participants came with a story. Through storytelling, people have the opportunity to review, construct and reconstruct their own identities, both in the eyes of other people, and for themselves. Such actions are not unique to people with dementia:

> If you want to know me, then you must know my story, for my story defines who I am. And if I want to know myself, to gain insight into the meaning of my own life, then I, too, must come to know my own story… It is a story I continue to revise, and tell to myself (and sometimes to others) as I go on living. (McAdams 1993, p.11)

Yet, people with dementia may find themselves increasingly left out of conversations and storytelling (Scherrer, Ingersoll-Dayton and Spencer 2014). Life story work might therefore offer a valuable opportunity for people with dementia to continue to make and remake their identity, through helping them to communicate aspects of themselves, as this participant with dementia explained:

DF2R2: It's a very good thing.

Researcher: And why is it a good thing?

DF2R2: Because it expresses everything. I mean, I've got an album with that – at home, and I forgot to bring that.

Interviewer: But what does it express?

DF2R2: It expresses that you remember the past and the future… it's quite nice for communications, isn't it?

This benefit may be of particular significance to people with impaired speech.

Some participants were very clear that the primary purpose of life story work for them was to review their past in order to help them have a better idea of who they were today and who they might be in the future.

> …in writing this, I can't say that I'm writing it for posterity or for my children… But it is important to me, as I go through it, to set my thoughts, retrospectively, as accurately as I can recall… Because I've never really looked back at the whole of my life at any stage, and taken stock of what I've done and what I aim to do…it does make you think about your life… (DF3R3)

In this way life story work can cross over into life review (Butler 1963), and indeed life review and life story work are sometimes combined, implying that making a book might help sustain the benefits of life review (Morgan and Woods 2010).

Finally, it was suggested that life story work could provide an opportunity for people with dementia to achieve something *today*. Some of the people with dementia we spoke to were clearly very proud of the life story books they had made, seeing the process not only as an enjoyable activity but a personal challenge.

Table 5.1 summarises the outcomes identified for individuals with dementia. All of these have the potential to feed into the larger outcome of improved wellbeing or quality of life.

Table 5.1 Outcomes for individuals with dementia arising from life story work

Immediate outcomes	Overall (hypothesised) outcome
Enjoyment/pleasure	Overall quality of life
For identity	
Person is listened to/has feelings validated	
Issues resolved	
Skills maintained/independence reaffirmed	

A note of caution

It would be a mistake to assume, just because all of the outcomes in Table 5.1 were identified by focus group participants with dementia, that *all* people with dementia will necessarily experience these benefits. Good evaluation will tease out the degree to which benefit is experienced in the population you are working with, but we know just from this small sample that not everyone thought life story work was right for them; at least one person in each group said that they would not like to make a life story. For more details, see Chapter 16 on the challenges.

Interpersonal outcomes

Life story work tends to be a shared activity, and as such a number of potential outcomes were identified that went beyond the individual. Family carers and staff, for example, suggested that life story work could bring people with dementia and others (extended family, other residents in care homes) together through the identification of common ground and interests. Improved understanding may also be important to family carers themselves seeking to connect, or reconnect, with their loved ones; as one carer explained:

> I find it comforting, in a way, that we can still have some things in common... (CF2R7)

In some cases, engaging in life story work could lead to family members learning things about their loved ones that they never knew before and found interesting or were proud of:

> By...producing this album, I was getting to know her even more, and admiring her more as a person. So, for me, I think it probably had more beneficial – [laughs] and more impact for me than my mum. (CF1R3)

The risk here, of course, is that family members may uncover things that have been kept secret from them for good reason (see Chapter 16 on risks for more on this).

A number of staff thought that life story work could encourage a wider range of people to visit care home residents and hospital patients, providing new triggers for conversation and more topics to talk about. For some, the opportunities for conversation sparked by life story work may be limited by the severity of their dementia and associated communication impairments. Nevertheless, life story work might still provide a way 'in' for the families and carers of people with limited speech:

> And that's when a life story book's quite good, because they can go in. There's no speech, but they can look at the photographs...I think that life story books can bring everybody in... (CF3R3)

A number of participants felt that a life story could help others to understand better the person with dementia. As one woman put it:

the younger ones today ought to realise it, even though I'm 82, I still feel just like I did... (DF1R3)

Improved understanding could have a number of benefits. Feeling understood may in itself be important to an individual's wellbeing, and improved understanding may alter other people's attitudes and responses towards people with dementia. Tom Kitwood (1993) highlighted the significant ways in which the actions and responses of caregivers can impact on the wellbeing of people with dementia. It was explained in the focus groups that staff may form negative perceptions of patients or residents from reading their medical histories before meeting them, which could in turn affect how they act towards them. Learning about people's life stories might help to redress the balance, as this hospital occupational therapist explained:

> ...staff receive a report about who's coming in. 'Oh, we've got somebody coming in that's done this, this, this, and this,' and it immediately triggers those...negative attitudes. But...when people have arrived with a life story...once people have had a chance to look at it...the attitudes change completely. (SF1R1)

A summary of the potential interpersonal outcomes identified in this section is set out in Table 5.2.

Table 5.2 Interpersonal outcomes arising from life story work

Immediate outcomes	Overall outcomes
Highlights common ground	Improved relationships
Fosters understanding	Personhood recognised Overall quality of life
Shared enjoyment	
Assumptions challenged	

A note of caution

What is described in Table 5.2 are *potential* interpersonal outcomes identified through focus group discussions. It is important to note, however, that a number of potential challenges were also identified through these discussions, and some family carers in particular reported having significant problems when they attempted life story work.

Some found it hard, for example, if a person did not respond to images of people or things that had once been meaningful to them. Indeed, in some instances life story work had the potential to be distressing for both the person with dementia and their carer:

> ...a couple of times, people have tried to do life story work with him...but it wasn't very successful...he didn't want to go back. And very, very early on, he really didn't like looking at photographs, and particularly photographs of people who were dead. (CF2R6)

It is important in any evaluation of life story work to look out not only for the benefits, but also for the challenges and problems that people with dementia and those around them might experience.

Outcomes for care

We saw above that life story work can provide a hook for conversations and non-verbal interaction, helping to identify common ground and build relationships. It was suggested, particularly by participants in the staff and family carer focus groups, that this outcome could have the knock-on effect of influencing the way care staff view the people they work with, which in turn could improve the care they provide. As one professional explained:

> I think that process of helping people recognise the common ground...helps humanise people again. (SF3R10)

It could be argued that people receiving care should not have to be 'humanised' – surely those in the caring professions should see the people they care for as fellow human beings as a matter of course? However, it has long been recognised that receiving care can be dehumanising and that people with dementia in particular can all too often be viewed in terms of their disease first and their personhood second (Kitwood 1997). Life story work was therefore seen by participants in the staff and carer focus groups as a valuable tool with the potential to remind care staff that the people they care for are *people* first (with equally important hopes and fears, achievements and relationships as them) and the recipients of care a distant second. Seeing the person is an outcome in itself, implying respect and the recognition of shared humanity. In addition, it could help to personalise care, as this participant suggested:

> Life story work in itself is maybe the way to get to that person-centred care, because by...helping people see the person as an individual, you can move forward to then working with them as an individual... (SF1R3)

Life story work should tell us not only what a person has done and achieved, but what they would like to do, what they value, how they would like to spend their time and who with. Such information is crucial to person-centred care planning. It may also shed light on the reasons why a person with dementia reacts negatively to a certain situation or approach to care. There were numerous examples given in the focus groups of people acting in ways that confused or challenged care staff until they discovered, sometimes through life story work, that there was a perfectly rational explanation for the behaviour:

> ...one of the key factors is what somebody did for a living, what their daily routine was, you know. 'Go on, Fred, get back to bed, it's only four o'clock in the morning.' But if you were a bus driver...or a postman, you were up at that time and those are the memories that stay...it's about understanding the person, and then you can understand some of the behaviour, and it doesn't challenge then. (SF1R8)

Once something is understood, it may no longer be experienced as problematic.

Even when a person's actions cannot easily be understood or abated, life story work could be a useful tool in helping to put people at ease without recourse to medication:

> He's rattling the doors, trying to get out, and you start talking about all his achievements, 'cause he's so proud of all his achievements through his life. And immediately, he comes down and PRN [antipsychotic] medication isn't needed... (SF1R1)

Similarly, some family members found that life story work helped to calm or orientate the person they cared for:

> I think it is useful for my husband, although we don't know how much he recognises...but it's about the familiarity of it... So it

is all part of that comforting, assuring familiarity of having these things...' (CF3R4)

One effect of staff getting to know and understand the people they work with better could be that they themselves gain more satisfaction from their work. If a life story sheds light on the ways in which a staff member can meet the needs or desires of a person better, then it may be easier for them to deliver care in a way that elicits positive feedback. This in turn may motivate them to find new ways to further the person's wellbeing, as this extract indicates:

SF1R4: ...the staff do get very excited when they learn new things about people and very encouraged, and, you know, it's good for them, too.

SF1R3: And they start connecting, as well, and go...

SF1R9: 'Oh, I'll have to bring that in because I was a horse rider and she was a horse rider...' finding things in common, that's really important...

A final area of benefit could come when people move between one care setting and another. We heard above how life story work could challenge the negative assumptions of staff by revealing the person behind the dementia. This effect was felt to come not only from seeing who the person was, but also who they still are and what they can still achieve. In one hospital ward they took photographs of patients taking part in activities and sent these with the person on discharge:

...those photographs went in the life story book [made on the ward and passed on] to the residential home or the nursing home. So the care staff didn't just see Joe Bloggs who needs X, Y, and Z, but Joe Bloggs that actually can still do a bit of this and can still do a little bit of that... (PF2R2)

Table 5.3 summarises the outcomes for care identified in this section, including outcomes for care staff.

Table 5.3 Care-related outcomes arising from life story work

Immediate outcomes	Overall outcomes
Fosters understanding	Personhood recognised
Assumptions challenged	Better care Behaviour no longer experienced as
Care tailored to the needs/ preferences of the individual	challenging (problems 'solved') Improved staff satisfaction/
Calming/de-escalation	motivation
Smoother transition	

A note of caution

Many of the potential outcomes set out in this final section depend upon the actions of those providing care. While benefits for the individual may come simply from the joy of remembering or recognising achievements, improvements in care will only come if care staff take (and indeed are granted) the time and freedom to absorb life story information and use this to inform and improve the care they provide. Unfortunately, many of the family carers we met were sceptical that this always happens, and indeed several examples were given where lovingly crafted life story documents packed with useful information had been ignored, such as the following:

> I put it in her bedroom, and I just, in my naïveté, thought that they would share it… She was given dreadful antipsychotic drugs to keep her sedated, and the input from the care home was, 'She has a condition', and they ignored what I'd put together… They didn't use it at all. (CF3R7)

This is why evaluation is so important, and with this an understanding of how improvement might be achieved. It is not enough simply to produce a life story and expect it to make a difference, if the route to improvement is through the actions of busy staff who may not even realise that the life story documents exist. If, on the other hand, the outcomes anticipated are individual or achieved through interaction with family members, staff involvement may not be necessary in order to see improvements. Figure 5.1 shows the various mechanisms, immediate outcomes and broader consequences (overall outcomes) of life story work identified through our focus groups.

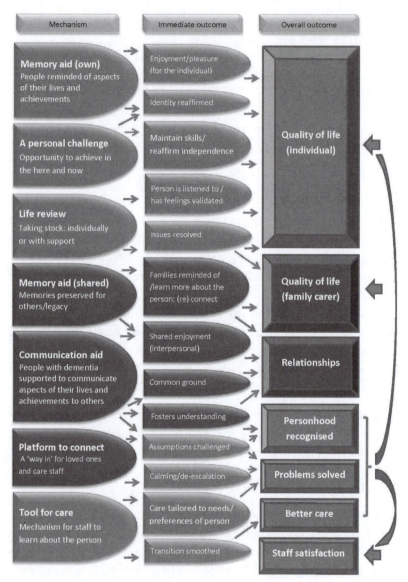

Figure 5.1 The mechanism and outcomes of life story work

Measuring the outcomes of life story work

Our study found that people with experience of life story work expect it to improve quality of life through a variety of routes. Looking at these routes might be one way to assess whether change is taking place as a result of your intervention. Are staff assumptions about people with dementia being challenged, for example? How is communication affected? What sorts of interactions are taking place? In our study, in addition to quality of life, we looked at relationships, identity, staff burnout, person-centredness and staff perceptions of people with dementia. We used a number of tools to do this, including the Approaches to Dementia Questionnaire (Lintern 2001) and the Personhood in Dementia Scale (Hunter *et al.* 2013). To measure quality of life itself we used QOL-AD (Logsdon *et al.* 2002) and DEMQOL[5] (Smith *et al.* 2007), but measuring the quality of life of people with dementia is notoriously challenging (Banerjee *et al.* 2009) and we felt that these tools did not necessarily pick up the sorts of things identified as important to people with dementia through our focus groups. Quality of life measures are designed to identify sustained changes in wellbeing using a number of general indicators such as mood and physical health. Participants are asked to assess how they have felt about these indicators over the last few days or weeks, but the benefits of life story work may be much more fleeting than this: a moment of joy, a period of calm.

More work is needed to identify ways of measuring 'in the moment benefits' such as enjoyment and sense of achievement. How do you capture a smile? We also need to think more creatively about how to measure outcomes for people who do not speak, read or write and cannot respond to quality of life questionnaires. Simply asking a person's family or care team is not enough, as proxy ratings of quality of life tend not to tally with those of people with dementia themselves (Trigg *et al.* 2011).

Various observational tools have been used to evaluate the impact of interventions with people with dementia (Algar, Woods and Windle 2014). Dementia Care Mapping (DCM) is perhaps the most widely used of these, but even DCM was originally designed as a practice development tool and has a number of limitations as a research tool (Sloane *et al.* 2007). It may be worth considering whether quantitative measurement is necessary at all, or whether a more qualitative approach, such as simply asking participants how they feel (using non-leading questions), might be more appropriate. Where communication is limited, could visual approaches such as photo-voice or video ethnography be used? As with all evaluation, it would be important to obtain consent before using these methods, but with participants' agreement they might provide a valuable means of capturing the impact of life story work, which, whilst perhaps not quantifiable, would certainly have validity.

⌖ TOP TIPS

- When evaluating any change to care, it is important to have a clear idea of *what* outcomes you expect to achieve and *how* these might come about. Life story work may have a variety of outcomes, arrived at via a range of different routes.

- Understanding these routes to outcome when evaluating life story work will help you to understand:

  - why you do or don't see a change in the outcomes you are measuring

  - what other factors could be influencing outcomes

  - what changes to the way you do life story work could contribute to (or hinder) your achievement of desired outcomes.

Notes

1. For the most up-to-date findings from this project, see the SPRU project webpage for 'Life story work with people with dementia: an evaluation' at http://bit.ly/lsDem
2. This is a community interest company. See www.innovationsindementia.org.uk/who.htm
3. This network has since been disbanded.
4. This is a community interest company. See www.lifestorynetwork.org.uk.
5 DEMQOL is the name of a quality of life measure especially designed by researchers at the Institute of Psychiatry, King's College London, for measuring the quality of life of people with dementia.

6

The Evidence Base for Life Story Work So Far

Bob Woods and Ponnusamy Subramaniam

Introduction

This chapter will help you think about the various factors involved when considering the evidence base for life story work, such as the type of intervention and the groups of people involved in the studies. It then goes on to examine the evidence itself, before describing the effects of life story work on one individual with dementia and how those effects were measured.

Defining an evidence base

Whenever psychosocial interventions are being discussed, before too long the question 'Does it work?' inevitably arises. The agenda behind the question may vary, depending on who is asking. The service commissioner may want to know whether there may be a means of improving services in a cost-effective manner, perhaps even by reducing costs. The service manager may want to decide which of a number of approaches to prioritise for training and development. The practitioner may want to be confident of a return on investment of time and energy. The service user may want to feel better in some way, to experience pleasure and enjoyment. An evidence base should aim to address all these perspectives and more, but it must be stated at the outset that there is no simple answer to this apparently simple question when we are considering complex interventions such as 'life story work'.

The intervention (not always what it says on the tin)

Although 'life story work' is perhaps a more specific term than reminiscence work or reminiscence therapy, it is perfectly possible for two interventions to share the same label and yet be quite different in practice. There may be readily recognised differences in delivery (e.g. one-to-one sessions as opposed to group work) or output of the work (e.g. a conventional life story book, compared with a memory box or a digital 'book' on a tablet or laptop). Or there may be substantive differences in approach; a life review process with an emphasis on evaluation of memories and experiences may be quite different from life story work undertaken less systematically and involving recording of a variety of stories and anecdotes. The difficulty in evaluating the evidence is that terms are often used interchangeably.

The target group

Reminiscence approaches have often been associated with work with older people. Robert Butler (1963) did much to overturn the perception that reminiscing was pathological, a negative characteristic of older people. His identification of 'life review' processes, linked to Erikson's late life stage of human development, identified one function of reminiscence as being to make sense and meaning of life, spontaneously or with the assistance of a therapist. Subsequently, reminiscence approaches were often targeted at people with dementia in particular (Norris 1986). The emphasis on autobiographical memories from earlier in life appeared to fit well with the cognitive profile of people with dementia, who are often said (not entirely accurately) to remember their childhood, but not what they had for breakfast. However, life story work has been applied extensively to other groups of people, being seen as especially valuable at times of transition, throughout the life span. Children and young people, especially those who are looked after (Willis and Holland 2009), and people with learning disabilities (Middleton and Hewitt 1999; Hussain and Raczka 1997) have benefited from life story work. It is suggested that it may be useful in reducing depression in younger people as well as older people (Hallford and Mellor 2013a) and in people with physical illnesses such as cancer (Leung 2010).

Outcomes studied (for whom?)

Choosing the appropriate outcome measures is critical if the effects of any intervention are to be captured adequately. If being used as a treatment for people who have depression, then self-report measures of mood will clearly be appropriate, whereas in the general population such measures may show little change. In people with dementia, it may be tempting to study whether memory and cognitive function improve, but it may be more relevant to evaluate the person's self-rating of quality of life and wellbeing. If cognitive function is evaluated, then changes in autobiographical memory may be more feasible than in orientation for time and place and new learning. For looked-after children or people with learning disabilities, measures of adaptation and adjustment may be most appropriate.

Complex interventions

Designing an evaluation study involves understanding and taking account of the interaction between specific approach, specific target group and desired outcomes. The approach and outcomes need to be adapted to the specific needs and features of the target group. In each case, outcomes should be chosen that are sensitive to change and where the group studied are not already scoring at a high level. The 'dosage' of the intervention should be sufficient for change to occur, in terms of the number and length of sessions and the time period over which they occur. In few instances will a one-off session suffice.

The Medical Research Council Framework for evaluation of complex interventions (see Woods and Russell 2014) indicates the importance of careful attention to such issues before carrying out a large-scale definitive evaluation. The intervention needs to be tried and tested, the target group clearly identified and the outcome measures appropriately selected. Consideration needs to be given as to how the intervention would be rolled out into routine practice if it proved to be effective – who would deliver it? What training and support would they need? It is often thought that the only definitive source of evidence for effectiveness of interventions is the randomised controlled trial (RCT), where the results of individuals randomly selected to receive the intervention are compared with those of people receiving a 'placebo' intervention or 'treatment as usual'. Social care practitioners are often wary of such study designs, viewing them as based on a medical model, and appearing to withhold treatment from many participants. Woods and Russell (2014) discuss the ethical and practical issues related to RCTs in social care research and identify a number of chance-based designs that are capable of producing high quality evidence, whilst avoiding the pitfalls that have often been highlighted. They also indicate that the results of RCTs should be viewed alongside other sources of evidence, including case studies and qualitative research. Moos and Bjorn (2006) also warn that because there is still a great deal to be learned regarding the best ways of delivering life story interventions, it would be premature to discontinue qualitative evaluations.

Overview of the evidence

A systematic review of the use of life story work in health and social care was carried out by McKeown, Clarke and Repper (2006). They identified 51 relevant publications, with most referring to older people or people with learning disabilities. Most of the papers were clinical descriptions, practice guides or theoretical accounts. Life story books were the most common approach to the work identified. They highlighted the need for more high quality research and for the views of patients and carers to be reflected more fully. Benefits for staff, in terms of attitudes, relationships and individualised care planning, were noted in several studies.

Pinquart and Forstmeier (2012) provide a more general systematic review of reminiscence work, identifying 128 controlled studies, involving more than 8000 participants. They categorised the type of work undertaken as:

- **Simple reminiscence** – the recall and sharing of selected personal and shared memories and stories.

- **Life review** – a structured, evaluative process, covering the whole life story chronologically, usually individual, seeking to integrate negative and positive memories.

- **Life review therapy** – life review with additional therapeutic elements (e.g. from cognitive therapy), usually with people with depression or other mental health difficulties, where the aim is to re-evaluate negative memories, promoting a more positive view of life.

Most studies (90) used a group format, and the majority evaluated simple reminiscence, with 37 studies offering life review and 18 life review therapy. Most of the studies (94%) involved older people. Overall, results were positive, with improvements in, for example, depression, ego-integrity, purpose in life and wellbeing. The most positive results were obtained where the target group were people with depression or chronic health difficulties, and where life review therapy was used. However, this analysis compounds different types of reminiscence work and different target groups, and so it is important to examine the evidence for each target group more specifically in relation to life story work.

Children and young people

Most of the work here has been qualitative, with few empirical studies reported. For example, Willis and Holland (2009) interviewed 12 young people aged 11–18, looked after by one local authority in South Wales. All were positive regarding their experience of life story work, which had been varied in terms of style and content, although there were a few negative comments about the process being tedious or intrusive. The process appeared to be helpful to the young person in developing aspects of their identity, and the life story books produced were generally seen as likely to be used in the future, for self-reflection or for sharing with others.

People with learning disabilities

Van Puyenbroeck and Maes (2008) reviewed the literature on reminiscence work with people with learning disabilities, drawing together work that had used terms such as 'life review', 'oral history', 'life history', 'autobiography' and 'narrative'. They identified 16 papers, 12 of which used qualitative methods, with four being descriptive. An important theme was the empowerment provided by enabling people to tell their own stories, where previously the voice of the person with a learning disability had not been heard. Life story work also contributed to person-centred care planning and was seen as especially useful in relation to transitions and loss. Improved quality of life, in terms of, for example, self-esteem, self-awareness and wellbeing, was cited in a number of the papers reviewed.

Empirical studies are now beginning to emerge in this domain. For example, Bai *et al.* (2014) evaluated the effects of a life story work intervention with 60 older adults (aged 50–90) with mild to moderate learning disabilities. Over a six-month period a comparison group took part in their usual activities, whilst those in the intervention condition took part in 16 individual or group sessions with a life story focus. Each participant developed a life story book that they were encouraged to use to share their life story and achievements. The life story book group showed a significant improvement relative to the control group in interest and pleasure and in their degree of connection to the community. Participants with better communication skills appeared to show the greatest benefit.

Depression

Most studies of reminiscence work in relation to depression have been conducted with older adults. However, Halford and Mellor (2013a) argue that its effects could be similar with younger people. A person who is depressed tends to remember negative events from the past, and the memories tend to be general rather than specific. Life story work may help the person review the balance of positive and negative memories, rather than seeing everything as dark and gloomy. It can also help problem-solving, as the person identifies how they have tackled difficult situations previously. Halford and Mellor (2013b) have now embarked on an RCT of an individual reminiscence approach, linked with cognitive therapy, to treat young adults (aged 18–25) with depression.

Reminiscence work, including life review, has consistently been found to be helpful for older depressed people (Bohlmeijer, Smit and Cuijpers 2003; Pinquart, Duberstein and Lyness 2007), with effects comparable to both pharmacological and other non-pharmacological therapies. Life review may also be helpful in preventing depression in older adults (Pot *et al.* 2010) and in improving life satisfaction and wellbeing in older adults in general (Bohlmeijer *et al.* 2007). A recent review suggests that the effects are also seen in older depressed people living in institutions (Zhang *et al.* 2015).

Dementia

Two recent reviews of the published evidence on the effects of life story work with people with dementia are available. Cotelli, Manenti and Zanetti (2012) report overall benefits in relation to mood and some areas of cognitive function, but point out that there is still relatively little evidence to draw on and suggest a number of the available studies are of poor quality. However, they do not specify the type of reminiscence work adopted. Subramaniam and Woods (2012) focused on individual reminiscence work with people with dementia, identifying five RCTs. Two studies used a life review approach, where the person with dementia was guided through their life story chronologically, with encouragement to not only recall episodes and stories, but also to evaluate memories and experiences (e.g. 'What was life like for you as a child?') In each case, a life story book was developed, capturing the person's story in pictures and words. A third study developed a life story book for each participant, but did not attempt to be evaluative or cover the span of the person's life. The remaining two studies used a general reminiscence approach, with memory triggers to prompt recall and conversation. It was evident that the three studies where a life story book was developed reported the most positive results, in relation to mood, wellbeing and aspects of cognitive function, with the two studies using the more structured life review approach having the clearest positive results. Simple reminiscence on an individual basis did not appear so effective.

The potential importance of the life story book itself was highlighted in this review, and the question may be raised as to how essential it is for it to be produced through a life review process, which, by its nature, is demanding in terms of both time and emotional effort. It is not unusual for families to produce such a book for the person with dementia on their own account, and, for example, Kellett et al. (2010) report a positive qualitative evaluation of a project where family members and care home staff work together to produce a biography of the person. Earlier, Haight et al. (2003) had evaluated the effects of involving carers in the life review process, either with the person with dementia or on their own. Carers reported reduced burden, whether the person with dementia was involved or not, but the mood of the person with dementia only showed improvement where they were actively involved.

Accordingly, Subramaniam *et al.* (2014) set out to establish what would be the effects of the carer producing the book without the involvement of the person with dementia, in comparison with the book being produced by the person with dementia through a life review process. The study took place in a small care home using an RCT. In line with previous studies, the life review process was associated with improved autobiographical memory and quality of life for the person with dementia. However, the control group, who received a life story book as a 'gift' produced by their relative, did not differ from the life review group once they had received their book. Interestingly, relatives reported an improvement in their relationship with the person with dementia after the book had been completed, irrespective of how it was developed. In addition, care home staff reported greater knowledge of the resident and more positive attitudes to dementia after the book had become available. This is consistent with the findings from the multiple case study design used by McKeown, Clarke, Ingleton, Ryan and Repper (2010), which demonstrated the potential for life story work to enhance person-centred care.

Digital life story work

Traditionally, a life story book has taken the form of an album, with photos, words and pictures, although other media such as memory boxes have also been used. A major trend currently is to use digital media and create a 'book', which may include music and video-clips and spoken narration as well as words and pictures. Subramaniam and Woods (2010) reviewed existing literature on this development in relation to people with dementia, and although the evidence mainly comprised case studies, they concluded there was evidence regarding the feasibility of the approach. They felt it raised questions regarding the balance between private and public reminiscing, and also the familiar question about the extent to which the involvement of the person with dementia was essential to beneficial outcomes. There are now numerous examples of available software and apps to assist the process, but little, if any, extensive evaluation. In the case example that follows, the person's conventional life story book was later transferred into digital format, with positive results. Computer 'supplements' have also been used in a recent study of life review therapy with depressed older adults (Preschl *et al.* 2012). These included a 'book of life' of personalised text, music and pictures, and a programme encouraging the recall of positive autobiographical memories. The combined therapy appeared to be effective in reducing depression and increasing wellbeing and self-esteem.

The effects of life story work

Gwen was a participant in the study described above (Subramaniam *et al*. 2014), and developed her life story book through a process of individual life review with the researcher, a clinical psychologist.

Gwen was aged 73 and had been living alone after her husband passed away and then had lived in residential care for just over two years due to memory difficulties. She had a mild degree of dementia. She had no children but was regularly visited by her two sisters, who were very happy to assist Gwen in this project. They provided Gwen's life history with many pictures covering her entire life. When approached regarding participation, one of her first reactions was:

> I worked in a pub for many years, I met many people...we always talk...I love to talk...sometimes too much (laughing)...I missed that...Now not many people to talk to...at least I can talk to you.

Gwen positively engaged in the life review process. She would often give responses at length for each question, triggering recall of many life experiences and important life events. Sometimes it was quite difficult for the therapist to end each session as Gwen always had something else to tell. The life review process proceeded in a chronological sequence, following a structured protocol, assisted by her many pictures.

Gwen spent a great deal of time talking about her childhood, her parents and sisters:

> My father was a wonderful man...lovely man...but with very little money...sometimes he gave money for me to buy sweets...I love prawns and crabs...my father used to go fishing with his friends and he brought fish and crabs for us and sometimes prawns if lucky.

One of Gwen's main lifetime interests was poetry. She enjoyed reading some of her poems with the therapist and chose one of her favourite poems to be included in her life story book.

Whilst Gwen enjoyed her childhood and teenage years, she perceived her first marriage as a major setback in her life:

> When I look back at my life…I'm happy about my life. However, my first marriage was horrible. The first two years of my first marriage were nice but after that things changed from bad to worse.

However she quickly moved on from the memories of the breakdown of her first marriage with pleasant memories of meeting her second husband:

> The best thing that ever happened to me in the world is meeting my husband.

When asked 'What do you think about life review?' Gwen replied:

> Oh wonderful! You bring back all my memories…nice to see them again!

On the evaluation instruments used in the project, Gwen showed improvements in quality of life, depression and autobiographical memory following the life review intervention, leading to her having her own life story book. However, six weeks later, perhaps because Gwen was physically less well, quality of life and depression scores had worsened slightly, although they were still better than at baseline. The initial improvements in autobiographical memory had also been lost by this point. The sister's ratings of her relationship with Gwen show an interesting pattern, with a dip in relationship quality overall at the end of the life review but an overall improvement from baseline, having had the life story book to share for six weeks. Overall, the book did not appear to maintain Gwen's initial improvements, but she was pleased with her life story book and would become excited if someone sat and talked with her about it.

Subsequently, Gwen and her sisters agreed to take part in making a digital life story book, in the form of a movie, from her original book. Music, songs and video clips were discussed and obtained. A few weeks later, when the initial draft of the movie was screened, Gwen sang along with the songs and was clearly excited by it:

> I stopped listening to music and songs for a very long time. All of these songs are full of memories and have a story behind it… nice! Very nice!

Gwen chose to record her own narration for the movie and although this was not easy for her, she managed by recording small sections at a time. She and her sisters were delighted with the completed movie, and Gwen said that she preferred it to the book, because the music stimulated and triggered memories. Gwen was proud of the movie:

> I enjoyed it. I have tears. This is my life in a movie and not everybody gets this. Wonderful! Best thing that ever happened to me, after meeting my husband.

The movie also triggered her sisters' memories – they had shared the same childhood and teenage life together. When they watched the movie together, they engaged in active conversation with Gwen, with laughter and evident excitement. Many stories would emerge triggered by the movie clips or pictures:

> Old pictures and songs bring back good memories. Trigger many, many memories, all very precious moments... The movie brings memories and we feel good. Sometimes it makes us feel sad (e.g. mother and father pictures). Makes us sad but also makes you happy about life...We miss our childhood life. (Gwen's sisters)

Staff reported that they felt they knew Gwen better, having seen the movie, and felt it helped their communication with her. The movie was 12 minutes long and could be played on a loop on a TV in Gwen's room in the home. Staff recorded that she watched it four or five times a week.

A month after the completion of the movie, the same questionnaires that had been used previously were administered. There were improvements on all measures, with Gwen now scoring better on all of them than at the original baseline. Quality of life scores were identical following the life review and following the availability of the movie, and autobiographical memory had improved again. Gwen's sister rated their relationship overall better than at baseline. In this case, it appeared that the digital life story book was more effective in maintaining quality of life and autobiographical memory than the conventional book, perhaps because it was more successful in engaging others to interact with Gwen – something that she enjoyed and valued greatly.

Conclusion

Life story work has attracted great interest across many different target groups, although the bulk of research is on older people. There is a need to analyse carefully research on the topic, to ascertain the type of work undertaken; reviews often include it alongside other forms of reminiscence work, without making a clear distinction.

There is now a growing evidence base, especially in relation to older people with depression and dementia, but there remains a need for careful development of approaches and outcome measures before launching into RCTs, which are more appropriate when the intervention has been fully tested, and thought given to its eventual implementation.

The development of digital life story books poses the challenge of how best to organise the mass of materials that will be available in the future – life story work will no longer consist of sorting through a small box of faded photographs, but will potentially need to select from literally thousands of items – photos, music and video, both in people's personal collections, but also online. This is an area where evaluation research is less developed, but early indications are that digital life story books may have even greater power to trigger memories and enhance relationships.

Part 3

Why Is It Important?

The Benefits of Life Story Work

7

What Life Story Work Means for People Living with Dementia

Steve Milton

Introduction

In this chapter the focus will be firmly on the benefits of life story work as defined by people with dementia themselves. People describe a range of benefits, from the chance to 'take stock' to the opportunity to communicate more effectively to others. There are also some concerns and caveats, not least about the risk that life story work might be seen as a short cut to direct communication.

A personal story

Life story work was key in enabling staff to understand the basis of my father's anxiety around the curtain rails surrounding the beds during his stay in hospital. He frequently talked about a train that was coming, often gesturing at the curtain rails as staff moved the curtains. This often made him anxious and staff were unable to respond meaningfully. We suspected that there might be a connection with his former role as a signalman in the 1950s, when he was responsible for routing trains from one track to another, not least to avoid collision. We thought there was a chance that the sight of the curtain rails, together with the sound of the curtains being moved, may have been triggering memories from that period and the strong drive on his part to take action to prevent a collision. A picture of my father in his signalman's uniform in the life story book that my mother showed to staff gave them a possible insight to his behaviour, as well as suggesting strategies for reassurance and engagement; these included engaging him in conversation before moving the curtains or talking clearly about 'the curtains' as they moved them.

What does the literature tell us about the benefits of life story work for people living with dementia?

Although much has been written about the benefits of life story work, very little of this has been from the perspective of people with dementia themselves. It is the case, however, that most studies focus upon outcomes that ultimately have potential benefit for the person with dementia: for example, outcomes primarily focused on the awareness and understanding of others of the person with dementia (Bruce and Schweitzer 2010; Hansebo and Kihlgren 2000). Much of what is broadly known as a person-centred approach to dementia is premised upon an understanding of the person's background, what makes them 'tick'and how they perceive the world. Outcomes that show improvements in awareness and understanding therefore lay a sounder foundation for approaches to support that are person-centred.

Similarly, improvements in the relationships between staff in in-patient settings and family carers (Clarke, Hanson and Ross 2003) have great potential to deliver tangible benefits to the person with dementia. Good relationships between staff and family carers can broaden understanding not only of the needs of the person with dementia, but also of the needs and perspective of the carers and staff members.

Other studies have identified benefits more directly to people with dementia, such as enjoyment (McKee *et al.* 2003) and improvements in cognition and mood (Woods *et al.* 2005). However, the majority of these studies are based on observation, rather than direct communication with people with dementia. There are limitations to observational measures, not least the fact that the person with dementia themselves has no say in either the judgements being made nor the criteria upon which the judgements are based. A study by Eledman *et al.* (2005) found little correlation between observational measures of quality of life and quality of life as reported by the person with dementia themselves. The authors found that people with dementia reported significantly better quality of life than observation measures would suggest.

So, what did people with dementia tell us about life storywork?

'It helps me when people understand about my life, about me' (Forget Me Not member)

Feeling that we are understood is important for all of us. Being able to communicate our opinions and our values and being able to have a say in decisions that affect our lives are basic human rights.

For people with dementia, the need to be understood and thereby heard and valued can present particular challenges for a variety of reasons:

- The person's ability to express themselves may be compromised by their dementia.

- They may feel inhibited by not wishing to 'impose' on others or fear that they are boring others or repeating themselves.

- Many people with dementia experience a progressive loss of key roles essential to their sense of self – for example their job, hobbies, community connections and their role within their relationships. These losses can make it even more difficult for people to maintain both their sense of who they are and their ability and motivation to communicate this to others.

- The prevailing stigma around dementia can mean that those around them may have low expectations of their ability to communicate their wishes, by virtue of their diagnosis rather than on the basis of their actual ability to communicate.

- Stigma can also mean that people become defined by their diagnosis or by aspects of their behaviour. People are not uncommonly referred to as 'sufferers' of dementia, and in some settings as 'wanderers', 'screamers' or 'wetters'. Not only are these labels highly stigmatising, but they also serve to dehumanise people to the point where their identity can seem entirely submerged.

- Many people with dementia in care settings are often supported by people with very different life experiences, not least by virtue of age.

- It is not uncommon for people with more advanced dementia, or who may face challenges in communication for other reasons, to be in care settings – especially acute care settings – where very little is known about them.

In these situations, life story work can provide both a framework and tools for the person with dementia to communicate themselves to others.

Many people with dementia talked about the role life story work can play in enabling them to maintain, reinforce and communicate their identity:

> I think it [life story work] has been good especially for the kids as I think they thought I had always just pottered round the garden. I think they see me differently now, and it has given rise to lots of questions from them as well. (Forget Me Not member)

> I think I did it first to give my family something to remember me by, and because I think there were things in my life I have never told them about. (Ken Clasper, Advisory Group member)

People also talked about the benefits of being understood in the here and now, but could also see how it might help them to maintain their personhood in the future, perhaps beyond the point when they could communicate it to others.

> It's fine at the moment, but it might get to the stage when I find it more difficult to express myself. I will want to make sure that people know about the things that have happened in my life... and maybe see me as more than the old lady in the corner. (Forget Me Not member)

The notion of 'self' or 'personhood' is notoriously difficult to pin down. Tom Kitwood (1997) described personhood as 'a standing or status that is bestowed upon one human being, by others, in the context of relationship and social being. It implies recognition, respect and trust' (p.8).

To adopt a person-centred approach to supporting a person with dementia means to make every effort to understand how the person with dementia ticks, how they see themselves, their world, and their place within it. It is about *who they are*.

I also thought that should I ever lose the ability to communicate about my past, this [memory] box would be of help to those working with me – it would help them to learn more about me and see me as a person – and maybe change their perspective of me. (Larry Gardiner, Advisory Group member)

It will be of help if I go into a place where people don't know me and I can't tell them or can't communicate with them. (Ken Clasper, Advisory Group member)

Each of our personal identities is shaped by our experiences to some extent. Not only are people with dementia sometimes challenged in their ability to communicate their life experiences, but they are also often supported by people whose own experiences are very different, not least because of the frequent age gap or, increasingly, because of different cultural or ethnic backgrounds.

For example, younger care workers might struggle to comprehend why someone might be amassing large collections of napkins, cutlery or sugar cubes in their room. Learning that the woman in question was responsible for a large number of younger siblings during rationing after war may allow the worker to understand that what he is witnessing may be the result of a formative period of thrift, rather than simple acquisitiveness.

As well as supporting their identity, especially in situations where that might be under threat, people also recognised the usefulness of life story work to enable them to make sure that others know about their practical needs and preferences. Indeed, for some participants, this was the only function of life story work with which they were familiar.

However, there were also concerns about situations in which the presence of a life story product could actually result in poor care and further erosion of personhood. The greatest fear for the majority of participants was that – especially in situations where the dementia is more advanced – a life story product might be used in place of continued communication.

This danger is likely to be at its greatest in situations such as the following:

- Care staff or family members use a life story book as a convenient shortcut to the person's needs and preferences.

- There is another persistently held belief, especially about people with more advanced dementia, that the 'person' has gone.

- Even if the person is not viewed as 'absent', there may be a belief that the person has lost capacity to make choices, either globally or in respect of specific issues, simply because they are different from the choices outlined in their life story.

In this situation the carer might genuinely believe that:

- the person with dementia is unable to coherently or consistently express their wishes and needs

- the person with dementia described in the 'book' is the 'true' representation of personhood, and their views outweigh those that are being expressed by the person as they are now.

It is important that Life Story Work is seen as a process and not as a one-off. You are a different person at 20 or 30 or 40 and what you like changes over time. In fact, you might be a very different person at 51 than you were at 50. The danger is, especially if life story work is done at a very early stage, which it should be of course – that the person becomes set in stone for the rest of their lives. Let me give you an example. I always loved cricket – I always was a Somerset boy – it was a real obsession. But you know, something has happened, and I just couldn't be less interested. Now I can tell you that now of course – but if in the future you were relying on my 'life history' to tell you what I like, then I'd end up getting dragged along to cricket all the time – I'd hate it. So talk to me, my life isn't over yet. (Brian Hennell, Advisory Group member)

What right has the today me got to tell tomorrow me what to do? Haha, can you imagine if the 16-year-old you was deciding what you should wear in the morning? Hahaha. (Forget Me Not member)

Others recognised that unless done well, life story work can engender a sense of finality, that useful life is over – as much a symbol of redundancy as a carriage clock on the mantelpiece of the newly retired.

The past is important – but sometimes it [life story work] can make you feel that's all there is, and I don't want to feel that way. People with dementia get that message often enough, that they are through, that their life is behind them, and you know it's not true don't you... (Brian Hennell, Advisory Group member)

My taste has changed, now I like curry and rock music! (Ken Clasper, Advisory Group member)

'It gives me something to talk about'

People with dementia have told us that some people seem to be at a loss for what to say:

Some people didn't know what to say to me when I first got diagnosed, either that, or it was the only thing they could talk about. (Forget Me Not member)

I tell you what – I am so bored with talking about my dementia. (Participant in Innovations in Dementia Film project)

Similarly, people with dementia can feel they have little to talk about, or lack the confidence to engage, especially if they are starting to experience problems with recall, concentration or using or understanding speech. Life story work can provide a focus and structure for conversation, both during the course of the work itself, and through the resources that are produced as a result.

...doing (the book) was great – it gave me a chance to talk about the things that had happened to me, good and bad without feeling like I was boring people, it was my time to speak... (Forget Me Not member)

When my grandchildren come – sometimes they ask to see the book – they like seeing pictures of their mum and dad when they were their age and how naughty they were sometimes. (Forget Me Not member)

'It gives me a chance to think about who I am and what I am about'

This might sound a bit daft, but I never really thought about what my values were, what I believe in or that sort of thing – it really pulled me up – I had honestly never actively thought about it. (Advisory Group member)

The chance afforded by life story work to take stock, look forward as well as back and think about what is important was mentioned by a number of participants and is also a common theme in conversations with other people with dementia:

> Since I had my diagnosis, alright, some things are more difficult of course they are, but you know what? I think I understand myself better, I know myself better, as I've had a real chance to think about what is most important to me – and that's my relationships…it's love. (Forget Me Not member)

This comment is highly significant, as the focus shifts from the need for a timely diagnosis, towards how people with dementia are supported post-diagnosis to develop a narrative about their lives that will enable them to live well with dementia.

'It might help me to remember me'

Those of us without dementia can easily take for granted our ready access and recall of our personal story, the events and people that have shaped our lives and how we in turn have shaped and shared the lives of others and the world we live in.

> I got involved in a memory box project because I thought it would be nice to have something to look at, and back on, later. (Larry Gardiner, Advisory Group member)

Looking back over the past can be a pleasurable, reassuring and reaffirming experience for most of us. Many of us will have had the experience of finding an old photograph or other object that reminds us of something we had forgotten, and which in turn triggers other memories.

> The more I remember, the more I remember, if that makes sense. (Forget Me Not member)

For people with dementia, the ability to remember and connect with the past becomes increasingly challenging but never more important, not least as a way of connecting with and making sense of the present. Life story work can not only serve as a way of capturing memories, but also of stimulating the recall of memories thought to have been long-forgotten.

Last but not least…it can be really enjoyable!

> For me it was enjoyable, and helped my recall. (Advisory Group member)

Many people with dementia describe how much pleasure the process of creating and working on their life story is. People mention not only the pleasure of remembering, but also the re-kindling of connections, of companionship and forging of new relationships.

> I think there were things we had all forgotten – we had such a laugh! (Forget Me Not member)

These are stimulated both by the initial process of building the story and creating the 'resources' but also in their continued use and refinement.

Some other concerns

We have already discussed concerns about the potential misuse of life story work. People with dementia were also conscious of other potential pitfalls.

Not all memories and life experiences are positive and this presents significant challenges, which are discussed in more detail in Chapter 16. The issue of potentially distressing memories was significant for many group members, though there was a range of opinions on how this should be addressed:

> It might also be that you end up thinking about or discussing things that are really upsetting for you – so the person needs to be really sensitive to that – and again make sure that stuff in your bottom drawer stays there. (Ken Clasper, Advisory Group member)

> Maybe you could sit down at the beginning and work out what those areas might be – and family might help to work out what they are. (Advisory Group member)

Others were conscious of a sense of regret for times past, rather than unpleasant memories:

> It makes me shiver and shake [to look at these photos], it's just regret that it's gone. (Focus Group participant)

Many stressed the importance of making sure that the person has the freedom, and consistent re-minders of the freedom if necessary, to only talk about what they wanted to talk about.One member of the Advisory Group, Larry Gardiner, had different views on the exploration of *'difficult'* areas and felt that it would be beneficial to individuals if they were able to express and explore uncomfortable episodes in their life:

> There should be no untouchable part of a person's life – IF someone wants to bring something up. (Larry Gardiner, Advisory Group member)

Larry explained that for him, the difficult experiences of his life could have an impact on him later in his dementia, especially if he were not allowed to explore them. Larry's feelings are commonly reflected in experiences of behaviour that others find 'challenging' in people with later stage dementia, and which many believe are linked to earlier, often unresolved trauma.The skills and sensitivity needed on the part of those undertaking life story work were recognised by participants:

> I think the person needs to be really skilled and sensitive so that they can determine whether this is a place that the person wants to go. (Advisory Group member)

Conclusions

Life story work means different things to different people. For some it is about enjoyment, about the company of others and the ability to enjoy shared experiences. For others it is about creating and maintaining identity in a world in which it sometimes seems one's place is becoming increasingly less clear. Some find that there is a strong psychotherapeutic element, while others take the opportunity to review where they have been, who they are and what they believe is most important in life.

It is clear that people with dementia themselves find life story work valuable across a range of domains. With an increasing emphasis on post-diagnostic support, ways need to be found to enable and support people with dementia to build a different narrative if they are truly to live well with dementia.

The life review aspect of life story work, in particular, has significant potential in supporting people to reflect on their lives and on their values and to think constructively and creatively about ways of living and being that can sustain them into the future.

On that note, this quote is worth revisiting:

> ...I've had a real chance to think about what is most important to me – and that's my relationships...it's love. (Forget Me Not member)

☼ TOP TIPS

- Remember that life story work is ongoing, and people change.

- Don't allow the presence of a life story book to circumvent the need for ongoing communication – the book it is not a substitute.

- Before you start, find out if there are 'no-go areas' for the person with dementia, and be prepared to review and renew this as you go.

- Life story work will mean different things to different people; don't start out with assumptions about individuals.

Acknowledgements

The author would like thank the members of the York Life Story Research Virtual Advisory Group and Forget Me Not Centre in Swindon, whose views inform this chapter.

8

The Benefits of Life Story Work for Family Carers

A Personal Perspective

Jean Tottie, former carer

In this chapter I will tell you of my experience as a carer of the benefits of life story work, report on the success of a training programme for family carers and offer some tips about doing life story work with a relative or friend.

Our story

I was struggling as a carer with my Dad's diagnosis of dementia in February 2006. I was juggling work demands and trying to support my Dad as best I could. It was a stressful time. So much seemed to be about loss...loss of memories, loss of driving licence, loss of independence. So I was excited when, as a judge for the Care Services Improvement Partnership (CSIP) national awards, I came across the Oldham Life Story group. Life story work seemed to be about what people *can* do and what they were proud of, not what they could *not* do. I was even more astounded to find that this existed on my Dad's doorstep...but that we had to go all the way to London to find out about it.

When Dad was diagnosed with mixed dementia the family's aim was to support him living at home as he was fiercely independent. Giving up his car was a major blow. He had no insight into his condition and I immediately became his advocate, as the only other family member was my brother some distance away.

He had been a widower for six years and was very active:

- He walked round the country park every morning in all weathers.

- He went dancing at least once a week.

- He pottered in the garden – a lifelong passion.

- He continued doing his painting – or so he thought.

- He continued with most of his household chores, but in truth my husband and I were doing more and more on our frequent visits.

I made shopping a social occasion, encouraging him to maintain his routine. However, Dad's dementia advanced quite rapidly, particularly as he was having minor vascular events, which advanced his cognitive decline markedly. I quickly realised that he would need more support at home.

Through the Oldham Life Story Group, we were offered the opportunity for a psychology student (Steve) to work with Dad to create his life story. We didn't know anything about life stories but Dad said 'why not?' Steve started to visit Dad most weeks for about three months and they quickly hit it off, though I had to remind Dad, using his calendar as well as a phone call, to expect Steve to call on the agreed day. Occasionally Dad had gone out! After two or three visits Dad said to me, 'Why have they chosen me?' I would reply, 'Don't you think you've had an interesting life Dad?' It seemed to satisfy him, but I really did believe it was true.

Steve worked with Dad, talking about his life and even going with him on his walks so they could take photos to include in his book. He took photos of some of Dad's paintings and of his work portfolio as a technical illustrator which he was so proud of. He also found a picture on the internet of the ship Dad had served on in the navy. All I was asked to do was to confirm significant dates such as weddings and dates of birth of family members. Dad wasn't sure where all his family photos were kept, so I had the task of finding appropriate ones for him to include.

At the end of the three months, Dad was presented with a loose-leaf copy of his life story book and I was given a CD of it so that we could continue to make additions. I was proud of my dad and it was good to see his achievements together in one book. Dad was proud too.

We agreed we would go through it together the following week and see what we might add; but when I arrived, the book was nowhere to be seen and Dad did not know where it might be. I worked out that he had been to his weekly dance, so I called his friend up. Apparently

Dad had been so proud of his life story book that he wanted them all to see it, so it was being passed around the group. I had to retrieve it to add some more pictures.

It was clear that Dad had enjoyed the process of putting his life story together with Steve and was very pleased with the outcome. He clearly felt valued that a stranger was showing an interest in what he had done with his life. It helped me as a carer to know Dad was not alone – it reduced his social isolation. Another unexpected outcome was that it helped to ground him in his routine. Life story work is not just about the past but also the present and the future. It was helpful for Dad to talk about his routines and keep them alive in him.

Dad's dementia deteriorated quite rapidly and he surprised me by agreeing to a short stay of respite in a care home near to his childhood home. I told the manager that Dad had his life story book and, despite the placement only being planned for two weeks, the staff read it. They understood what his interests were and so immediately bought him some artists' materials to use. In fact, Dad did not return home but agreed to move to a care home nearer to me. He visited it first with us. As I had told the manager a bit about his life story, she only talked to Dad, because she had discovered that they had something in common – rugby!

Within the first week of Dad moving to live there, all the care staff had taken time to sit with him, read his life story and make a connection, whether it was painting, gardening or where he had holidayed. He had also shared it with other residents! It was Dad's book and it stayed with him in his room.

From the day Dad moved in to that home the quality of his life and our lives improved immeasurably. We could concentrate on spending quality time together without worrying about all his care needs and all the chores that go with it. The fact that the care staff read Dad's life story with him meant that they quickly got to know him as a person. I could see that he was treated as an individual who had led an interesting life and I became a partner in his care from the day he was admitted. He quickly made new friends. Through this knowledge the care home staff really understood the sort of man my Dad was – gentle, proud, smart and always interested in other people. This was reflected in the dignified care he and I received in his last few days of life.

Prior to Dad arriving at the home, the staff had had no experience of life story work but soon realised the value of it to them. They asked my advice about how to approach the families of the other residents to start doing their life stories.

Initially I just saw the advantage of life story work for Dad: it helped to keep him connected to others and to be as independent as possible in his routine. I could also see how it would be helpful when the time came for residential care. In my busyness of helping Dad I could only see the benefits for him. Later, I was surprised how it benefited me. It validated my views about my dad and confirmed what sort of a man he was. Others saw my Dad as I saw him. And that was reassuring.

Through my experience I could see the benefits of life story work for Dad, for me and for the care home staff. It had transformed his life as a care home resident into one that was of value and interest to others, as well as affirming for him what he had done with his life and helping him to keep hold of his memories. That is why I was keen to support the setting up of the Life Story Network Community Interest Company (CQC) so that many more people with dementia and their family carers can enjoy the same benefits. I am passionate about supporting family carers to remain connected through life story work.

'Family Carers Matter' at Life Story Network

At the Life Story Network we piloted our first Family Carers Matter course in 2012 with a group of carers recruited from Uniting Carers at Dementia UK. This received positive feedback and we continued to refine the course over the subsequent two years: first, with Tyne and Wear Care Alliance, funded by Skills for Care to provide training to family carers in three boroughs; and then with Greater Manchester West NHS Trust with carers in Bolton, Salford and Trafford.

The course is run over two short days with a gap of about four weeks so that carers can reflect on the first day and get started. We concentrate on communication, relationships and rapport and how life story work can help families remain connected. The training aims not only to promote emotional wellbeing for people living with dementia, by enabling them to reconnect with earlier episodes of their lives, but also to improve relationships between the carer and the person being cared for through the shared experience of developing the life story together and providing a focus for conversations that are enjoyable and make sense to both parties.

We have worked with Hartlepool Carers to deliver this course to two cohorts of 12 carers. The aim is also to recruit volunteers from the courses who would be trained and coached to become supporters of Life Story Network Associates by delivering more courses to carers in their locality, thus building in some sustainability. In order to demonstrate impact of the training, over and above the regular evaluations and feedback from participants, we used the Adult Carer Quality of Life Survey (AC-QoL) (Elwick *et al.* 2010) before and after the course. This showed that carers gained a great deal from the course both in terms of their own wellbeing and their relationship with the person being cared for (Life Story Network 2014).

On average, those who attended the training felt as though their life was on hold (because of caring) 'some of the time' after the course, rather than 'a lot of the time' before the course. In particular, carers suggested that the training enabled them to do something for themselves, which also benefited the person with dementia.

In addition, following the training, attendees felt satisfied with their life as a carer 'a lot of the time', rather than 'some of the time', which was the case beforehand. In particular, participants reported that they now found spending time with their loved one 'a pleasure rather than a chore'. Sharing experiences and ideas with other carers enabled many to see their caring role with a 'fresh pair of eyes'. Developing an understanding of the benefits of life story work also enabled carers to identify what they wanted to gain from the carer relationship: 'It has made me realise the things I want to find out about my mum's life before it's too late.'

Participants suggested that it helped them to understand that some of the more challenging behaviours exhibited by those with dementia are not intentional or wilful. In particular, finding new ways of communicating reduced carers' frustrations and improved their tolerance of their loved ones' behaviour. One carer said they would try to approach their mother in a different way rather than become frustrated by the difficulties of talking to her.

An example of this was shown by Ann.

Ann's story

Prior to the course Ann had never heard of life story work but the Dementia Support Worker at a local carers' centre had recommended she attend.

Ann attended the pre-course meeting with us and was clearly very stressed. In talking to her she explained how her father's Alzheimer's had developed very suddenly in his early 60s and resulted in him being admitted to a care home. Ann told me that she was really struggling in communicating with her father when she visited and that she felt she had to talk and bombarded him with questions. I advised that the course focused on communication and relationships and felt that she would benefit from attending. Ann, a single mum with two teenage daughters, had been a care worker for 25 years and was the primary carer for her dad.

After attending Day One of the 'Family Carers Matter' programme, Ann changed her approach when talking with her father and started to create a memory box. On Day Two, Ann arrived walking tall, smiling, visibly less stressed and proud that she had started a memory box. At lunchtime she shared this with everyone present, explaining how each item in the box had meaning and relevance for her father. She said she now left the home after visits smiling!

When asked what she had learned from Day One Ann said:

> How to talk. I saw it work with another resident where I work – I'd advised another careworker what to do with a resident and it worked so I thought 'I can use this with Dad – I can communicate.' It's nice to go home and think it was a better visit today and go home with a smile. It was a pleasure to see him. *We've found each other again.*

This theme of connection and reconnection has emerged again and again in our work with other family carers:

> I'll look again at him as my husband. Today reminded me of what I had; made me re-evaluate my thinking – he is still with me as my husband.

> It made us talk more.

> We just started chatting.

> I had forgotten that my mum loved to go shopping – we went shopping and she bought six new outfits!

My mum has come back to me as the mum I know and love.

Time flies. I spent nearly two hours looking at photos with Mum and she's so much happier. There was no sorrow as she thought, just tears of laughter. Her sense of humour has surprised me; she's just let go.

Valerie's story

I was very hesitant to come on life story workshops. I thought it was about endings – about helping us to let the person die…about letting go…it was so reassuring to come and find out it was just the opposite…not letting go but to kick-start momentum. It was hard to persuade the rest of the family at first. 'We know who she is?!' they said. But it had never occurred to me that Mum might have dreams and hopes and that was important.

If I'm honest, I was treating Mum like a two-year-old. We started going through the old papers and photo albums with her… I connected with her…it bought back my memories too.

The older grandchildren were finding it difficult, but they are connecting with her too…helping her to choose her clothes and sit with her with an album and have a conversation and a laugh. It's like a revolving door at her house now with family visiting. It's changed me – I'm visiting more. I'm not just talking about doctors and appointments.

I can feel the difference it has made to my relationship with Mum. And she has noticed the difference too: holding my hand she said to me, 'I like the new you'.

Through supporting more carers to see the value of life story work, I came to envy those carers who were lucky enough to have this training, because it clearly enriched their relationship with the family member with dementia. I wish that I had had that opportunity and not been on the periphery of the process with my Dad.

Whilst doing it together brings advantages, this is not always possible. There seem to be myths developing about how to do life story work and that there is a 'best' way. A carer recently told me about how she was told she *had* to do it with her father, but because he did not want to do it she felt unable to share important snippets about his life with the care home. So unlike Ken (see Chapter 1), who did just that in relation to his wife, this daughter was left not knowing what she should do. It is important to emphasise there is no right or wrong way to do life story work. As explained in Chapter 1, it depends on the purpose. If the purpose is to improve communication and relationships, it might be vital to do it together. If the purpose is to inform care staff about preference and things that might influence care, a family member could write that up in a page or two or a member of staff could write a one-page profile together with the resident. The purpose will influence the process and the product at the end.

? Reflection points

- Think about why you want to do life story work. Think about the purpose. Is it as a legacy for the family? Is it to inform care staff about preferences? Is it to find out more about yourself or your loved one?

- You may want to produce several life stories for different purposes. One carer I know of has done at least five different ones for his wife.

The future

Family carers are the largest workforce in dementia care and need support to do the job they have found themselves in without any choosing. Life story work can make their caring role more pleasurable and help them to maintain their relationships so that they can care for longer before perhaps considering other options.

Family carers are also a valuable asset to the community where staffing is tight in community and residential services. Why not harness the potential of family carers to work with staff in health and social care to create life stories for the benefit of the person with dementia, the carer and any staff – as well as themselves?

⬙ TOP TIPS

- Make a start, give it a try and start small. It doesn't have to be a linear process, so you don't have to start from childhood and work up to the present. You can start with something that is triggered as a memory, such as a photo from a happy holiday. Gather those golden moments or nuggets and don't worry about the order at the start.

- Don't focus on the end product but more on the process of doing the life story – both for the person you're caring for and yourself.

- A list of topics can help to provide some structure to gathering information, such as where born, school, work and hobbies. Start with what the person you're caring for wants to tell you; be led by them rather than by a list of questions. Remember, it's not an interrogation for a family history, more of a chat. One carer dubbed these as 'hoover moments'. Prior to the Family Carers Matter course she would be stressed and busy doing cleaning and chores. When she came back on Day Two, she said that now, if her mum started a story or anecdote, she would switch the hoover off, listen and jot things down.

- Get the person's own version of events rather than try to correct them. Does it really matter that it may not be completely accurate? Better that it is something they're happy with.

- Aim to include the person you're caring for as much as possible in telling their own story. Sometimes this can be difficult and you may also need to find other people, such as relatives, friends or work colleagues. Often younger members of the family (e.g. grandchildren) can be helpful, as they can be less cautious when asking questions but are genuinely curious and interested.

- Even if the person you're caring for appears unable to contribute to their own story, do everything you can to keep them involved. Notice their facial expressions when they encounter photographs, objects and smells or give accounts of their life. If you find out a snippet of information can you engage them in telling you more about it? Can they make choices on what book to choose, what to decorate their memory box with? Can you work out which objects are their favourite, and which textures or smells they prefer?

9

The Benefits of Life Story Work for Paid Staff

Lesley Jones and Gillian Drummond

Introduction

We are two Registered Mental Health Nurses and have many years' experience in working with people with dementia within NHS settings. Throughout our careers we have always striven to ensure that people with dementia are seen as people first. Our own belief is that a life story approach should be the 'bedrock' of working and offering care to people with dementia. This underpins this chapter, coupled with nearly 20 years' experience in using this approach as a foundation from which we base our own person-focused practice.

This chapter will focus on the benefits that a life story approach and life story work can enable from a nursing and care staff perspective within one's day-to-day caregiving practice. The information in this chapter is relevant to a wide range of health and social care roles across a variety of settings. Throughout the chapter, examples from practice will be used to illustrate the value of life story work. We will conclude with some top tips in relation to the advantages for staff of using this approach.

Who are the staff?

During the course of their illness, people with dementia will come into contact with and receive support, help and interventions from a number of different staff across a range of care providers, both statutory and voluntary. This contact may be varied and wide-ranging.

Contact may be short and time-limited or continue for a longer period. It may include contact with, for example, home care, day centres, residential and nursing home staff, doctors, nurses, social workers, occupational therapists, memory assessment teams and community mental health teams.

Irrespective of the level of contact, be that transient or longer term, it is our belief that all staff should have at the forefront of their minds that the person comes first, then the illness. The rest of this chapter will provide evidence to support this philosophy and the benefits that this approach brings for staff.

Context of caregiving in dementia

Recent years have seen an increase in the awareness and recognition of dementia. This in turn has resulted in a wealth of supporting policy and guidance: for example, NICE/SCIE Dementia Guideline (2006), NICE Quality Standard (NICE/SCIE2010), the National Dementia Strategy (DH 2009a) and The Prime Minister's Challenge on Dementia (DH 2012b, 2015b). The central tenet of the dementia care-related policy and guidance is that the assessment and delivery of care for the person with dementia should be provided by skilled staff who are able to take into account the life experiences and social circumstances of the individual and their family. This focus should ensure that the person with dementia is a person first and foremost, and that assessment and care delivery are based on their individual needs.

Sadly, in many instances the health and social care provision for older people, including people with dementia, has been the source of numerous concerns in relation to undignified and poor care. As Anna Gaughan discusses in Chapter 3, this has resulted in a number of national inquiries and reviews, such as The Rowan Report (Commission for Health Improvement 2003) and The Mid-Staffordshire hospitals inquiry (Francis 2013). In response, there have been a number of initiatives aiming to promote compassionate and person-focused nursing care – for example, *Compassion in Practice* (DH 2012a) and *Making a Difference in Dementia Care: Nursing Vision and Strategy* (DH 2013a).

What all these developments have in common is a drive for care to be based on the person, who has their own unique perspectives, values and life experience. Despite this, it can be argued that when an older person is a recipient of care, staff may still cease to view them as a person with a past, present and future; instead they are seen as someone with an 'illness' or a range of 'difficulties' or 'problems'. This is particularly the case in dementia care, where it is all too easy for the person to become 'lost' due to cognitive difficulties, with care delivered based on an illness and deficit-focused 'medical model'.

The concept of person-centred care stems from the work of Kitwood (1997). His work is centred on the maintenance of 'personhood', which is defined thus: 'A standing or status that is bestowed upon one human being, by others, in the contact of relationship and social being. It implies recognition, respect and trust' (Kitwood 1997, p.8). The importance of valuing the person with dementia and understanding their life story are central tenets of the concept of person-centred care.

The person first: How life story work helps in caregiving

Irrespective of the staff's caregiving role or setting – for example, day centre staff, dementia nurse or domiciliary caregiver – the guiding principles of care are based on the following:

- assessment
- planning of care
- delivery of care
- reviewing effectiveness of care.

We will now discuss how the use of life story work can benefit each of these areas.

Assessment

The concept of using life story work as a means of identifying social and welfare needs of older people can be traced back to Malcolm Johnson (1976). He argued that all too often the assessment of an older person was made from the viewpoint of the professional, with the emphasis being on identification of problems as opposed to strengths and capabilities.

Based on this belief, he proposed an alternative known as the biographical approach. Central to this approach was the biographical interview in which older people were encouraged to reconstruct their past lives so that their current needs and preoccupations could be better understood. Johnson advocated that this approach would enable care to be planned *with* the person and not *to* them. It would also prevent the assessment of the older person being made from the standpoint of the professional and therefore encourage the recognition of strengths and capabilities as opposed to just problem identification. One can argue that this early work of Johnson helped to lay the foundation of the evolution of life story work with older people and people with dementia.

The use of life story work at the assessment stage promotes the concept of working with the person rather than the illness from the beginning of the therapeutic relationship, thereby instilling a collaborative approach and ensuring that the individual is engaged and central to the process. This puts the relationship with staff on a more fulfilling, but sometimes challenging, footing as the worker begins to understand the person as a unique individual.

Listening to the individual's story enables staff to increase their understanding of them and use this information as the basis for person-centred intervention (Russell and Timmons 2009). In a study undertaken by Clarke *et al.* (2003), which explored the use of biographical approaches to encourage person-centred care, staff using the approach in a nursing home reported that collecting biographical information helped 'gain a more dynamic and complete picture' and that knowing the person's life story enabled staff to find out more about residents' needs and behaviours (Clarke *et al.* 2003). Adopting an approach based on the use of life story can also give an insight into how the person understands and makes sense of their dementia in the context of their life history (Keady, Williams and Hughes-Roberts 2005).

Using life story at the assessment phase enables care to be planned 'with' the person rather than 'for' them. The case example below will demonstrate this.

Using life story in the assessment process

Emily is 70 years old and has never married. Three years ago she was diagnosed with Alzheimer's disease. Up until four weeks ago she was living at home with support from her neighbours. Over the previous three months Emily had on a number of occasions been found by the police in the middle of the night walking the streets in her nightwear. Four weeks ago Emily agreed to intermediate care for a period of assessment as her GP had expressed concerns regarding her health and wellbeing. On admission to the intermediate care facility, care staff undertook their usual assessment – a series of questions that focused upon medical history, medication and which areas Emily required help with.

Since admission Emily had been very quiet and withdrawn; she refused to join in group activities and would tell staff to leave her alone. She constantly asked to return to her room and was refusing to let staff assist her with her personal care needs. Staff were experiencing difficulty in establishing a caring relationship with Emily and they perceived her to be unfriendly and standoffish.

One day Emily's nephew turned up to see her and care staff mentioned their concerns. He was able to tell them that Emily had always been a quiet lady who preferred hobbies such as needlecraft and listening to classical music. This conversation made the care staff realise how little they knew about Emily as a person. This prompted one of the staff to talk to Emily about her life story, leading to a number of changes to Emily's care – for instance, Emily was offered her meals in her own room as opposed to the dining room, and instead of group activities Emily was offered one-to-one activities such as listening to classical music. Over the forthcoming weeks Emily responded well to these changes and began to talk and engage more with staff. Staff found that, instead of avoiding Emily because they did not know how to engage with her, they actively sought her company.

If the initial assessment had focused upon Emily's life story, this plan of care could have been implemented much sooner and enabled staff to have developed an empathetic and caring relationship with Emily much earlier.

Planning of care

In undertaking an assessment based on the principles of life story it can be assumed that the resulting plan of care will be grounded in the strengths, values and uniqueness of the individual. As opposed to a standardised care plan, the plan of care should be tailored to the individual.

Using life story approach enables staff to promote goals that are based on the context of the person and their history and also ensure that as practitioners we are aware of the areas that the individual does not wish to address. This can enable the person to be seen as an individual, therefore promoting effective engagement, collaboration and relationship-based care that is more likely to succeed.

Using this approach ensures that care planning is holistic and embraces the bio-psychosocial and personal aspects of the individual. This is of particular relevance to people in long-term care.

Using life story in planning care

Joyce is an 86-year-old with dementia, who was born with a cleft lip and palate. Joyce lives in a care home and has been referred to the Community Mental Health Team as she was displaying aggressive behaviour when in the dining room at mealtimes. When the Community Psychiatric Nurse visited to assess her needs, she focused on Joyce's life history. Joyce was able to explain that she has always been embarrassed by her cleft lip, particularly when eating and drinking, and for most of her life has avoided eating in front of other people. Once the care staff knew this crucial part of Joyce's life, they were able to include this in her plan of care and enable her to eat in a private area. As a result of this change, all aggressive behaviour ceased.

Delivery of care

Adopting life story-based practices in providing care can shape the way that interventions are delivered so that they are meaningful and personal to that individual, rather than based primarily on routine and standard practices in the care setting.

Person-centred and dignified care cannot be delivered unless staff listen to and understand the person they are caring for. When a life story approach is adopted, the information learned about the person can be used to inform care delivery directly. This results in care being more individualised and person-centred, as the staff will have a greater understanding of the person (Russell and Timmons 2009).

This approach to care delivery can be empowering for the person with dementia as by telling their story they are being actively involved in shaping the care they receive, thereby enabling care to be undertaken 'with them' as opposed to 'to them'. Listening to the story of a person with dementia helps us to understand the person and see them as an individual and is key to treating that person with the dignity that they deserve.

In a systematic review of the literature on life story work, McKeown *et al.* (2006) concluded that staff valued life story as a means to get to know and understand the person and that this led to improved care practices. It can also improve communication in caregiving interventions; for example, when carrying out personal care tasks, engaging in meaningful and relevant conversation rather than working in silence or – worse still – talking to a colleague over a person. Knowing the person and not just the details of their illness can also help to explain behaviour that may previously have been seen as challenging. For example, a retired general nurse may constantly check other patient IV infusions while a patient on a medical ward themselves.

The life story act in itself can also be the intervention. An example of this would be to use aspects of an individual's life story to distract, reassure and engage with them if they were becoming anxious or distressed.

Joan

Using life story as an intervention was used with Joan, who was admitted to a mental health dementia assessment ward under Section 2 of the Mental Health Act 1983. In the afternoon, Joan would become increasingly distressed, wanting to leave the ward. She would try to open doors, bang on doors and windows and become agitated. She did not respond to verbal explanations as to why she could not leave the ward, and on a number of occasions such was the degree of her distress and agitation, staff had to give her 'as required' medication to help reduce her agitation.

The use of a life story approach identified that Joan had always kept a number of cats. Joan's cats were a big part of her life – she was a successful breeder and had won a number of cat shows. She also worked on a voluntary basis for the Cats Protection League.

One day when Joan wanted to leave and was becoming upset, a staff member who knew of her interest in cats engaged with Joan by showing her pictures of cats on an iPad. This intervention successfully diverted her. Joan become animated and interested in the pictures and began sharing her stories with the staff member. This approach was incorporated into Joan's care plan and staff used this intervention each afternoon. This resulted in Joan no longer becoming distressed and requiring medication, and her afternoons were spent in purposeful, engaged and enjoyable activity, resulting in a more satisfying and rewarding experience for staff as well as for Joan.

Reviewing effectiveness of care

Reviewing the effectiveness of care when supporting people living with advanced dementia can present challenges. The reason for this is often linked to changes in the individual's cognitive processes and verbal communication skills. However, it is still important that care is reviewed to ensure that it continues to meet the needs of the person.

Attempts at communication by people with advanced dementia can often be perceived as behaviours that challenge. The reason for this is that instead of communicating needs, wants and hopes verbally these are often communicated by the person's behaviour. For example, the person constantly walking and opening doors may be looking for the toilet. It is therefore important that the underlying cause for the behaviour is explored and that approaches adopted to meet the person's needs are reviewed.

A number of models have been developed that facilitate the assessment of the possible causes of challenging behaviour, identify person-centred interventions and facilitate a review of effectiveness of care delivered. These models use a needs-led approach and multiple pathways to assessment (Bird and Moniz-Cook 2008; James *et al.* 2007), using two types of information: the person's life story, personality, physical and mental health information; and an in-depth description of the behaviours that challenge (Keady and Jones 2010). Needs-led approaches are underpinned by the belief that behaviour is a form of communicating an unmet need. The use of life story is the bedrock of such models.

The case example below illustrates how such a model was implemented to identify interventions and review care.

John

John is a married man, aged 72, with a diagnosis of dementia. John was admitted to the ward for an assessment because at home his wife was struggling to meet his personal care needs as he was becoming resistive to care interventions. In addition, his sleep pattern was disturbed and there had been occasions where he had failed to recognise his wife, believing her to be a burglar. In these instances he had tried to throw her out of the house in the middle of the night.

Staff on the ward observed that John's sleep pattern was disrupted: he was awake most of the night and constantly walking up and down trying to access other people's bedrooms. When the staff tried to stop him entering other bedrooms, he became angry and started shouting that he would get the police as he believed that the staff and other patients were intruders. On a number of occasions John had physical altercations with staff and fellow patients when he refused to leave their bedrooms. During the daytime he was spending long periods of time sleeping and when staff tried to wake him he would become angry and resistive to care interventions. Staff were becoming increasingly worried about the risks John's behaviour presented to himself, the staff and other patients.

A needs-led case review was attended by all members of the multidisciplinary team and John's family. When exploring John's life history it transpired that all of his working life he was a security guard and used to patrol a warehouse checking that doors were secure. All his work was carried out on night shifts when buildings were unoccupied. John's family also informed the team that he had always been a strong-willed and independent man, preferring to work through things himself before asking for help. This information enabled the reviewing team to begin to understand John's behaviour and adapt his plan of care on the ward. Changes included giving John a clipboard and a set of unused keys and accompanying him each night to check the building. Once John had performed his 'security check', staff invited him to join them in a tea break. On personal care interventions, staff used only verbal prompts, giving John extra time and the autonomy to meet his own personal care needs.

Two weeks after this plan of care had been implemented the team met to review. There had been no further incidents of John becoming angry or resistive. Staff found that after he had checked the building and had his tea break with them he would start to fall asleep in the chair and could be coaxed into bed with the reassurance that his shift was over.

This case example highlights the importance of using life story work in planning and evaluating care and how it can be used to understand behaviours in the context of the person's life.

What are the benefits for staff?

The use of a life story approach when working with people with dementia may initially seem to equate to extra time and work. However, our experience leads us to believe that this is time well spent. Adopting a life story approach has the potential not only to have a positive impact on the person with dementia but also to bring numerous staff benefits such as those described below.

Having a greater undertaking of the person you are looking after, rather than seeing them only as a set of symptoms or problems to be dealt with, leads to greater job satisfaction and a belief that the care being delivered is valued and having a positive impact. Subramaniam *et al.* (2014) suggest that challenging staff assumptions about the person with dementia can lead to a change in staff attitudes.

In the long term, the use of life story work can save time for staff as it enables care and interventions to be planned with the person in the context of their lived life. As a result, there is a greater chance that interventions and care packages will be acceptable to the person and tailored to their needs. It may therefore reduce the amount of time spent on reviewing ineffective interventions and care packages. It ensures that care and treatment decisions remain in the context of what the person would want, where they are in the illness trajectory and what is in their best interests.

Life story work can facilitate the use of creative approaches to care that also promote people's strengths. Additionally, their new knowledge of the patient enables staff to engage in conversation based on what is meaningful to the person. This in turn can help reduce the resistance to care often encountered when supporting people with advanced dementia. Life story work has the potential to improve therapeutic relationships with the individuals being cared for, making interactions and interventions more positive and enjoyable from the perspective of both the individual and the staff team. This in turn has the potential to reduce complaints as care interventions are planned with greater understanding of the person. Complaints are known to reduce staff morale and motivation. Similarly, life story work enables improved involvement and relationships with relatives and carers, which can increase their confidence in the care that their loved ones are receiving.

Knowing the person reduces negative labelling and stereotypical assumptions and encourages staff to undertake positive risk taking as they have a greater understanding of the person in the context of their lived life, current situation and future hopes. It makes difficult conversations easier to initiate and sustain in the light of the person's background, history and known values.

As the case examples have demonstrated, life story work provides a framework to explore behaviours that are perceived to be challenging by staff. Our experience of using this approach with care teams has resulted in: greater consistency of care; improved communication with the person and between team members; a greater understanding of why certain behaviour may be being displayed; and what the person may be trying to communicate. In turn, on occasions, this has resulted in medication not being used as an intervention to help manage a behaviour as staff have understood the reasons why the behaviour is occurring and have been able to use non-pharmacological interventions instead. Increased understanding of why behaviours may occur and tailored individualised interventions aimed at meeting a person's needs also resulted in a reduction in the amount of reported incidents. The use of a life story approach in exploring behaviours that may be displayed by a person with dementia enabled the staff to develop a greater understanding of the person and their lived life and how this may affect their present and future.

Finally, we have found that life story work increased staff morale and motivation and increased job satisfaction. We have heard staff saying proudly that they now know their patients and have a far greater understanding of who they are as individual people. They want to spend time with people to talk with them as part of their care and treatment plans, as opposed to just engaging in order to undertake task-orientated care.

Conclusion

This chapter has demonstrated through the use of case examples the importance and value of using a life story approach in the assessment, planning, implementation and evaluation of care. It has highlighted how the use of life story work can keep the person at the heart of care delivery. The following anonymous staff feedback illustrates this:

Knowing the life story of a person really helps with caregiving.

I see the patient as a person now, not just an illness.

I understand now how the past can still impact on the present.

We believe that a life story approach should be the foundation of caregiving and not the 'icing on the cake'.

⋅ϙ⋅ TOP TIPS

Adoption of a life story approach through the above phases of care will:

- enable needs to be assessed, care to be planned and interventions to be delivered in the context of the person and their life

- challenge staff's assumptions about the person to help change attitudes

- promote the person and not the illness

- identify strengths, hopes and dreams to counterbalance deficits, needs and losses that we normally focus upon

- reduce task-driven care

- promote an understanding of an individual's behaviour and presentation, which in turn may reduce the need to resort to medication and increase the use of non-pharmacological individualised interventions

- improve the caregiving relationship as staff will know more about the person

- provide opportunities for engagement, meaningful conversations and shared enjoyment

- keep the person at the centre of care.

Part 4

How Can We Use It?

The Practicalities of Life Story Work in Various Settings

10

Communities, Housing and Life Stories

Keeping People Connected

Ruth Eley, Polly Kaiser, John Shaw and Pat Broster

Introduction

This chapter will explore how life story work can be used to build community understanding of people with dementia and the role of housing in helping people stay connected. It will explore the concept of dementia-friendly communities and some of the essential ingredients that enable the participation of people with dementia as active citizens. It will describe the importance of collective memory and the idea that communities too have stories that can help strengthen people's identity and sense of self.

Jack's story

During a visit with a local health group to an extra care housing scheme for people living with dementia, we were introduced to Jack, who was living independently in his flat. He did not engage in any conversation, but as we toured the housing scheme he allowed our small group to view his flat.

As we looked around, he sat and watched the television, uninterested in what was going on around him. We asked the scheme manager about the frequency of buses and how people could get out and about. One person in the group mentioned that he worked on the railways all of his working life. Jack immediately picked up on this and entered into a detailed conversation about his job and career on the railways and mentioned particular people who they might both know. Jack was keen to stay in touch and to pick up on the conversations connected with the railways. It was obvious that Jack had enjoyed his years at work, that he felt a sense of worth and that this formed a really important part of his life. Until this conversation, the scheme manager and other residents in his small community had no idea about Jack's career. All they knew about Jack was that he had dementia and liked to smoke sporadically.

Communities and people with dementia

As part of their Dementia without Walls programme, the Joseph Rowntree Foundation explored how York might become a more dementia-friendly city. The project drew on the lived experiences of people living with dementia who were trying to carry on their lives as normally as possible, despite their diagnosis. The report (Crampton *et al.* 2012) highlighted what worked well for people with dementia and what could be improved. It formulated the Four Cornerstones model – People, Place, Resources and Networks – to assist in assessing how dementia friendly a community is.

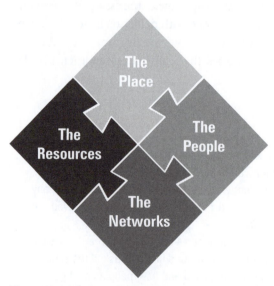

Figure 10.1: The Four Cornerstones

The focus was on people's lives *in the round*, in which health and social care play only small parts. The definition of a dementia-friendly community, formulated by people with dementia themselves in this and in earlier work (Local Government Association 2012) was one that enabled them, inter alia, to 'maintain the social networks that made them feel still part of their community' (Crampton *et al.* 2012, p.4). The concept used an asset-based approach and built on what people can still do, rather than what they can't. It was clear from the York project that a combination of factors – as in the Four Cornerstones – is essential if a community is to claim to be dementia friendly. An accessible environment with excellent signage is of limited value if people working in it are unkind, ignorant or impatient and if people with dementia are not encouraged or supported to join in everyday activities such as going to the theatre, eating out or playing golf. Being dementia friendly is only half of the story; empowering and enabling people with dementia to be confident participants in their local communities are just as important.

The role of housing

Social housing provides mainstream and supported housing for rent. Registered social landlords (RSLs), who manage millions of social houses across the UK, have a major part to play in helping people to live independently for longer. Housing staff are well placed to identify people who may be struggling with memory loss or other cognitive deficits and to encourage them to seek help. Sometimes the first a housing officer or manager of a supported scheme will know of difficulties is when other tenants complain of disruptive behaviour such as getting up in the night or knocking on doors searching for someone, which they perceive as anti-social, leading in turn to a punitive approach – a breach of the tenancy agreement with potential eviction – rather than a supportive one that enables the individual concerned to access advice and help.

Using their approach to life story work as a whole, the Life Story Network decided to explore the contribution of housing providers to the development of dementia-friendly communities. Initially working with one RSL, the Life Story Network trained a specialist team working with older people, other housing staff, tenants and a group of older people in dementia awareness and an introduction to life story work.

Feedback was positive and the model was developed further in *Your Community Matters* (Life Story Network 2013). This project, funded by the Department of Health, aimed to facilitate and develop the capacity and capability of local communities to improve their support to people living with dementia and their families. This was one of three project themes, the others being exploring the concept of the care home as a community hub and offering life story work training to the home care sector. Three Merseyside RSLs expressed interest. The training was adapted to ensure it met the needs of the housing staff, volunteers and tenants concerned, focusing on dementia awareness through getting to know the person with dementia and using a life story approach to establish and develop relationships with them and their family. Some of the tenants participated in the training because they wanted to find out more about dementia and be able to challenge the negative and hostile attitudes of their co-tenants, whilst others wanted to be able to better support family members with dementia. Feedback from participants included the following:

> I feel much better equipped to offer my help and support to anyone with dementia in the future.

> This training helps with ensuring that the wider community has a better understanding about the issues people with dementia face and that they have interesting back stories to tell, that may have similarities with our own.

> I now have confidence to have conversations with older people.

The project demonstrated that life story work approaches have a definite role to play in helping to keep people connected with their community – be that a neighbourhood, a housing scheme or a faith group. One of the RSLs reported that 'The Life Story Network have delivered training sessions to groups of our tenant volunteers who will be spreading the awareness to their neighbours and to groups of family carers' (Life Story Network 2013, p.8).

Keeping connected is important for our health. The effects of social isolation on older people and the importance of networks are well documented. Marmot (2010, p.137) noted:

> Social networks and social participation act as protective factors against dementia or cognitive decline over the age of 65. Individuals who are

socially isolated are between two and five times more likely than those with strong social ties to die prematurely. Social networks have a larger impact on the risk of mortality than on the risk of developing disease, that is, it is not so much that social networks stop you from getting ill, but that they help you to recover when you do get ill.

Evans and Vallelly (2007) examined the social wellbeing of frail older people living in extra care housing and concluded that some tenants, such as those who have cognitive impairments or limited contact with family and friends, are at particular risk of social exclusion. They found that opportunities for a social life independent of the housing scheme and activities covering a wide range of interests and abilities were some of the elements important for the social wellbeing of tenants.

The workplace

Work is important in our lives. Not only does it provide us with an income to support ourselves and our families, but it is often where we make friends or meet our partners; and for many it can be where we feel valued and achieve some status and success. When we meet new people, we often start our conversations with information about where we work, or where we used to work, as a way of making connections and exploring common ground. During a visit to a day centre for people with dementia, one of the authors sat and talked to the members about where they lived, which quickly generated information about where they had worked. It soon became apparent that some of them had worked in the same textile mills – many of which had closed and disappeared from the landscape – and they were able to share stories of their working lives, especially about how hard they had to work and the long hours involved. The memories were not all rosy, but they provided the members a means of connecting and strengthening rapport with each other. It was clear from the reactions of the staff that they were unaware of these connections and these rich lives. A follow-up conversation with them helped them to realise the potential opportunities for enjoyable activities based on undertaking life story work with individuals or groups of members who were interested.

The importance of the stories of place and home

The concept of 'home' is much more than bricks and mortar. We intuitively know from our own personal experience and relationships within our local communities that our concepts of 'home', 'identity', 'personhood' and 'wellbeing' are inextricably linked. The very idea of home is inseparable from our sense of self, and our sense of identity: 'Our home is our base, a place that roots us to the earth, to the city or the landscape; it gives us permanence and stability and allows us to build a life around it and within it' (Heathcote 2014, Introduction). For some people with dementia, returning to the home that they remember – rather than where they live now, which may have ceased to be familiar – can be an urgent need that those caring for them may not always recognise. So-called 'wandering' may actually be actively seeking that home and safe place of comfort. It is important for us to understand the perspective of someone with a dementia searching for 'home'.

? Reflection points

- Where was home?
- What did home mean to you?
- When you think of home, what comes to mind?

Betty

For Betty, home was Salford. She had grown up there. She had lived there with her mother and father. Her home had all her memories in. She had friends and was known in her neighbourhood. When asked, 'What do you think of when you think of home?', she replied – quick as a flash – 'Home-made chicken soup'. For Betty, home was about comfort, connections and continuity – things we all value but that are even more vital for a person with a dementia who needs to feel safe.

Connecting stories from place, home and life experiences underpins our identity and helps to develop our values in life to make us who we are. Home is the anchor that gives us our sense of belonging; and whilst our 'tribes' old and new reflect societal developments, our storyline and roots of home can be strong. Some people may have memories of bad experiences – in particular, places that were meant to be 'home' but that turned out to be far from the comforting and secure environments that most of us experience – and it is equally vital for us to know this.

Edna

Edna's home had been cold and she had grown up in poverty. Her family had often 'flitted' (i.e. moved out at night before paying the rent they could not afford as her father had drunk all his wages) and she had experienced physical violence from her parents. Edna took a long time to feel safe in the nursing home. It was difficult for her to trust people and she found personal care particularly challenging. Once the care home manager understood something of Edna's background, she was able to rota fewer carers to look after her, so that some continuity and trust could develop.

Irrespective of the content of our early lives, it is important for us to recognise in ourselves and others the emotional echoes that so influence us. It may be even more necessary that we have some understanding of this for a person with a dementia.

Communities have stories too

Gone
Buried
Covered by the dust of defeat –
Or so the conquerors believed
But there is nothing that can
Be hidden from the mind
Nothing that memory cannot
Reach or touch or call back.'

Don Mattera (1987)

Whilst communities can develop as they grow, some have been displaced to benefit minority groups who often hold the balance of power. For example, the Highland Clearances began at the end of the eighteenth century when landowners realised they could make more money from the land by high-volume sheep farming than by the traditional crofting that had been a feature of the landscape for generations. Sheep were not dependent on crops and did not look to the landlord for support when harvests failed. Thousands of families were displaced. Faced with destitution, and assisted by government sponsorship aimed at swelling the colonies, many people took the emigration route, sailing to Canada, America, Australia and New Zealand. As with Irish emigrants, their heritage remained immensely important to them, and as well as personal items, they took with them the traditions of music and storytelling.

More recently, the apartheid regime in South Africa implemented its policy of designating specific areas for different communities, securing areas of high economic value for the whites and displacing other ethnic groups many miles away to townships with few basic amenities and no employment. District Six, a multi-racial community in Cape Town in close proximity to the port, was identified by the government as a valuable area to be developed. It was labelled as crime-ridden and deemed a slum area unfit for habitation. In 1966 the Group Areas Act – a consolidation and extension of earlier legislation – was enacted and District Six was declared a whites-only area. Removals began in 1968 and by 1982 more than 60,000 people had been 'relocated' to an area called Cape Flats, a township complex some 25km from District Six. The old dwellings were destroyed by fleets of bulldozers, with only places of worship left behind. The area was never developed, however, and following the fall of the apartheid regime some residents started to return. The District Six Museum was established in 1994 and features a large street map that covers the ground floor. Former residents have placed handwritten notes on it to remember and record where their families had once lived. Another area contains histories and life stories of families from the old District Six as well as explanations of how life was lived and the subsequent destruction of the area. The result is not only the life stories about individuals but also the story of the former community: District Six's website includes the quotation 'No matter where we are, we are here' (Mrs Abrahams, taken from the memory cloth 1994), reflecting the strength of association with place and community experienced by the former residents.

Urban renewal and relocation of communities

With a post-war push for economic regeneration, better housing and health were developed alongside key industrial sites. Examples include the Speke and Halewood housing developments in Liverpool to support industrial complexes such as Dunlops and Fords. In Manchester, over a third of residents were moved out from inner city areas to overspill estates on the outskirts of the city. Hattersley and Gamesley were two council estates built in the former borough of Hyde, now part of Tameside borough. In 2005, Hattersley residents were encouraged to meet together to share their memories of living in Manchester and their experiences of building a new community. This led to the Mancunian Reunion project, which collects memories from residents of Hattersley and other overspill estates. Now a local charity, they hold social events and organise outings to significant locations in the collective memory.[1]

Wilmott and Young (1957/1986) set out to find research evidence to support more radical housing policies from the Labour Party, based on the needs and experiences of the working classes. Unexpectedly their study in Bethnal Green stumbled upon a highly articulated network of kinship relations that enabled them to widen their research beyond housing into a more detailed study of a post-war working-class community in East London that was being dislocated through clearance and rehousing programmes. People were located to the outer suburbs. Housing policy during the 1950s and 1960s was to build flats rather than houses. Local authority architects and planners had come under the influence of the modern movement, led by Le Corbusier, to build 'cities in the air' and were, in part, reacting against the urban sprawl of the 1930s. Financial subsidies offered by central government increased with the height of the blocks. The flats were unpopular with residents, but they saw them as the only route to get into better housing, so believed they had little choice. Flats were 'universally detested by those in them and they created an environment in which it was difficult for social networks to be re-established' (Wilmot and Young, p.xxi, new introduction to 1986 edition). Young people rehoused from Bethnal Green were cut off from their families and the support that they provided. Twenty-five years later, Holme (1981) found that fewer people in Bethnal Green had relatives living nearby than in 1955, with 'a greater isolation from the surrounding community' (pp.137–41). In their introduction to the new edition, Wilmott and Young concluded that although kinship networks were more dispersed than they used to be, nonetheless kinship remained an important force in most people's lives and was 'in particular, still overwhelmingly the main source of informal care and support' (p.xxiii).

Like Manchester and London, Liverpool had its own housing clearance programme, leading to similar dispersions of communities and a fragmentation of connections and networks.

Peggy's story

Peggy Hulme, the grandmother of one of the authors, saw herself, along with her husband and young family, relocated to the outskirts of Liverpool in the 1950s as part of this clearance programme. Over time, Peggy established new friendships and together with her family and their neighbours created a new community in their new location. As good as this was, the ties with the old neighbourhood and friends that she had lost as a result of the relocation remained. For many years, right up to a few weeks before she died in 2014, Peggy would visit a church in the centre of Liverpool. Whilst the religious activity was important, Peggy had other reasons for maintaining her links with the church. It was located in the city centre district from which she had moved, and there she was able to meet regularly with a number of old friends from that old 1950s neighbourhood. Following the church service, they would retire to the café room and spend up to two hours together. They did not just share memories about the old times but also talked about life now and news they had heard about other old friends and neighbours. Relocation and the passing of time had not weakened the bond between Peggy and her friends, a bond that had been built over many years as part of a community and strengthened by the many stories told over days, weeks and years. Peggy was known here. Her story mattered.

The story of Peggy and her friends confirms that community is much more than a physical place: it is about life and the people who pass through that life. Community is the people and their stories. Although the physical evidence of these former communities has changed considerably – and in some cases disappeared completely – the stories of individuals and families, their life challenges and successes, what they have done or been a part of and their many friends and neighbours are the ingredients that make up communities. Life story work is a practical tool to enable people to bring their memories together, not only helping to identify and affirm who they are as individuals but also to tell the stories of their communities.

Conclusion

The opportunities that were part of everyday life to meet, talk, listen and share are disappearing through the changing workplace and the fragmentation and diversity of local communities. With the demise of the larger employers since the 1990s, people have had to be more mobile to secure work. Furthermore, developments in technology enable people to work remotely from home or in more isolated environments.

Social housing is under threat from the welfare reforms being introduced at the time of writing that challenge the whole concept of housing provision for those who are unable to compete in the private market, be that for owner occupiers or tenants. The twenty-first century is witnessing further mass displacement of people, with few possessions and personal reminders of where they have come from other than their memories and stories.

Life histories are as important now as they were to our ancestors, but the opportunities to capture them and those of the communities with which they are associated have diminished. There is less reliance on enduring paper documents and photographs and much greater use of social media and electronic communication that is instantaneous and often public – the lines between what is private and what is available for all to see are becoming increasingly blurred. Reliance on social media and electronic communication may mean that in the absence of hard copies of letters and photographs, for example, precious moments may be difficult to retrieve or lost for ever. In this context, life story work becomes especially important as a way of gaining some understanding of individual preferences, likes and dislikes. It helps us to establish rapport, share experiences and make sense of people's lives and how they have shaped aspirations and choices. It helps individuals to stay connected with their families, friends, neighbourhoods and communities, which is especially important for people with dementia who may be less able to communicate their needs and wishes and make sense of their surroundings. Without these connections, care and support can be random, ad hoc and even harmful. Not everyone is as lucky as Peggy. For a person with dementia, life story work helps them to see that their story matters, that connections can still be made, and for others to recognise that it matters too.

Note

1 Mancunian Reunion, see http://mancunianreunion.org.uk/MRindex.html

11

Introducing Life Story Work into a Memory Service

The Benefits

Joanne Sutton

Introduction

This chapter will discuss the establishment and subsequent findings from a project looking at the introduction of life story work into a memory service. The aim was to introduce life story work as a means of collecting information about a person in a way that focused on them as an individual whilst protecting their dignity and respecting their human rights. It was used as a framework to identify, highlight and build on an individual's strengths to enable them to adjust to a diagnosis of dementia. It will show the benefits realised by individuals with dementia and their family carers. It will demonstrate some clear benefits to staff of utilising this approach, along with top tips.

Context

Memory clinics were established with the aim of supporting people to receive an early diagnosis of dementia and psychological help and support (Moniz-Cook and Woods 1998). Unfortunately, many clinics have not delivered this and have functioned within a purely medical model where only the recognised neurological damage to the brain is taken into account. Wright and Lindesay (1995, cited in Moniz-Cook *et al.* 1998) surveyed 20 memory clinics and found that the emphasis was mostly on research for drug trials and instigating treatment with the anti-dementia drugs, rather than offering psychological support and other interventions.

Over the past decade national policy has continually recognised the need for improvements in dementia care, in particular the information and psychological support offered to people being given a diagnosis and to their carers. Standards produced by NICE/SCIE in 2006 stated: 'By learning about each person with dementia as an individual, with his or her own history and background, care and support can be designed to be more appropriate to individual needs…' (NICE/SCIE 2006, p.71).

Where previous policy had recognised and advocated generic psychosocial interventions, these standards went further by recommending interventions that specifically related to knowing the individual and their unique biography. Since then, recognising and knowing the person, not just the dementia, has been a consistent message in national policies on dementia.

I am aware that older people have had fascinating lives and feel quite strongly that their stories should not be lost. As a manager I have seen the penny drop with staff when they hear about someone's life and the difference that this makes when the person becomes more than 'just a patient'. The project convinced me of the potential of this tool to help change the culture into one that is more person-centred, where we see people not just in terms of their dementia, but in the context of their whole lives, with all their strengths and abilities.

Methodology

In order to inform the project and give some indication of what the possible findings may be, a literature review was undertaken. This focused on the research question: 'How does the introduction of life story work into a memory service benefit individuals with dementia and their carers?'

The project entailed working with a group of people with dementia and a group of carers of people with dementia to explore the use of a life story approach and its benefit to both groups. The life story approach was delivered within a framework that recognises people's individuality and emphasises the importance of relationships and a person-centred approach to care. Staff, a group of carers and a group of individuals with dementia took part in some workshops that introduced them to the principles of life story work.

For the purposes of the project, anyone currently known to the memory service who had a diagnosis of dementia, or was the carer of an individual with dementia, was offered the opportunity to be involved.

Initially the project was seeking to recruit approximately eight carers and eight people with dementia to participate. Eight carers and seven people with dementia consented to participate in the project following the initial meeting to appraise them of what the project was about and what it would entail. Unfortunately, for personal reasons five of the carers and three of the people with dementia dropped out during the project, resulting in the evaluation being based on the experience of three carers and four people with dementia.

All participants were in the early stages of dementia or were carers, and all were judged to be able to give informed consent by means of a capacity assessment. This was revisited at every contact with the individual to ensure continued informed consent. Following on from the workshops, the carers who had taken part were visited every four weeks by staff from the memory service over a period of three months. The purpose of these visits was to support them in undertaking life story work with the person with dementia whom they were caring for. The people with dementia were visited at similar intervals by staff from the service to support them in undertaking life story work. The carer of the person was invited to take part in these visits with the permission of the individual.

The participants decided how or if they wanted to produce something in a life story format from these sessions.

For the purposes of consistency and to allow for the formation of therapeutic relationships, the same member of staff worked with the participants throughout the duration of the project.

Impact on the individual with dementia, their family carers and staff

All individuals receiving a diagnosis of dementia experience it differently. It is important to note that the experience is heavily influenced by the individual's innate personality and their strengths, abilities and preferences through life (Kitwood 1997). However, the impact of a diagnosis on carers should not be marginalised as this can have a significant effect on the individual who has received a diagnosis.

It can either help or hinder the process (Steeman *et al.* 2006). The psychological welfare of the family carer is as important as that of the individual if they are to continue to care.

In order to demonstrate the benefits of engagement in life story work for the individual, their family carers and staff, a number of outcome measures were utilised, along with qualitative data collected from interviews. Only the qualitative data are reported on in this chapter. All these data were examined to identify themes relating to benefits for the different groups. These themes are discussed below.

Valuing the person as an individual

Valuing the person and maintaining their personhood are integral parts of whether the person with dementia has a positive experience (Killick and Allen 2001; Kitwood 1997; Sabat 2001). Evidence from the data collected from this project suggests that the introduction of life story work into a memory service increases the satisfaction of people with dementia in that staff know and care for them as people.

It is clear that being seen as an individual and being valued as a person are important and seen as the cornerstones of person-centred care. This project shows that involvement in life story work enhances this feeling of individuality and value for both people with dementia and their family carers. One carer stated:

> It has given me hope that support can be creative and individual and not just a packet of pills.

Another carer stated that she felt her husband had gained much from being involved in life story work but that she was just happy:

> that people were listening to him and taking him as a person seriously.

McKeown, Clarke, Ingleton, Ryan and Repper (2010) asserted that life story work helps staff to see the person with dementia beyond being a patient. Staff involved in the project supported the view that life story work is a vehicle to knowing and valuing the person. One member of staff stated:

> Life stories provide a valuable insight into the life of someone, especially when they have difficulty in sharing the information

themselves. As a nurse it has been really interesting to me to understand what's important to people and how this affects their behaviour. It has helped me to build up relationships with people by facilitating communication. It definitely supports the delivery of person-centred care by focusing on the person and not the problem.

These sentiments were echoed by another staff member, who felt that life story work had helped to:

break down barriers – enhance relationships – you are privileged to know the person's strengths – you can use them to support them both now and in the future. You know what's important to people.

This belief that knowing people helps to support them appropriately is the essence of person-centred care; and the fact that life story work helps to do this is a common theme in research (Keady *et al.* 2005; McKeown *et al.* 2006; Thompson 2010, 2011).

Clarke *et al.* (2003, p.704) stated: 'Listening to a person's life story is a powerful way of showing that they are valued as an individual and may also have a cathartic value.' However, central to this project was the process of life story work, placing the emphasis on the relationships and conversations about significant aspects of the individual's life rather than on a task to produce a product. Our task in a memory service is to assess and diagnose – the specification for the commissioned service leaves only limited time with individual patients.

This focus on the approach keeps the process person-centred as it seeks to highlight strengths and not weaknesses, and it helps all parties to look to the future. It moves life story work from being purely an intervention tool or template to an approach to a whole systems culture of care, based on relationships but focusing on individuals and what is important to them. The knowledge of the person gained by staff by undertaking life story work is essential to the ability to work with people in a meaningful, person-centred way.

Keady *et al.* (2005) argues that the way in which each individual deals with and constructs a diagnosis of dementia is different. As staff we must accept that an understanding of the person's unique experiences is integral to providing appropriate support. Keady and colleagues suggest that life story work is an effective way of working alongside people and their carers. In support of this argument, staff involved in the project stated that life story work had helped them to 'engage with people, to assist in their care, now and in the future'. Nolan *et al.* (2006) cited in McKeown, Clarke, Ingleton, Ryan and Repper (2010) discussed this need to know a person's biography in order to be able to contextualise the present. They stated that this was important for a sense of continuity and in achieving relationship-centred care. Utilising this life story approach to an individual's care in the project allowed staff to have meaningful conversations with people in ways that were supportive of their wishes and rights as a person.

Our findings suggest that all three groups involved in life story work agreed that it increased staff's understanding of people with dementia as individuals and enabled their thoughts and views to be valued. This ultimately led to a greater satisfaction with the service in terms of their treatment as individuals.

Better quality of life and increased wellbeing

As well as supporting personhood and valuing a person as an individual being integral to a positive experience of dementia, it is essential to maintain a person's sense of wellbeing (Cook 2008). High levels of wellbeing mean that we are more able to respond to difficult circumstances and to engage constructively with other people and the world around us. Engagement at this level improves our quality of life and so the two are intrinsically linked.

Findings from this project suggest that involvement of individuals in life story work improves their quality of life. All the people with dementia whose quality of life was measured pre and post intervention showed an improvement in scores overall, with three out of four showing an improvement in their life as a whole. Two out of four also reported a subjective improvement in their memory. This could be due to life story work increasing their awareness of their memory and utilising their recall of memories to engage in the process.

They were also reported to show significant increases in factors that would be seen to constitute an improvement in wellbeing – for example, greater engagement.

One gentleman with dementia was described by his wife as being 'much more settled and animated. He has become so involved he doesn't even miss me if I am not here.' This sentiment was echoed by a participant with dementia who stated:

in the months before taking part in this I haven't felt competent – doing this makes me feel good.

Such feelings of wellbeing and pride are seen as being important to the person with dementia in maintaining a sense of worth and significance (Nolan *et al.* 2006, cited in McKeown, Clarke, Ingleton, Ryan and Repper 2010; Sabat and Harre 1992).

People involved in life story work in this project showed improvements in validated outcome measures that directly correlated to an increase in their wellbeing. Most carers had a greater sense of competence overall following involvement in life story work than before it. This would suggest that life story work for these carers had a beneficial impact.

'I have a future'

This theme came through quite strongly during interviews, primarily from the individuals with dementia. Depression, grief, loss of hope, anger and frustration are all responses reported by individuals receiving a diagnosis of dementia (Kasl-Godfrey and Gatz 2000). Loss of hope was directly related to loss of function and anticipated disability and a sense that life as they knew it had finished. This belief is often shared by carers who feel that the person they knew will be lost to them.

A positive outcome of involvement in life story work for both the individual and their family carers is evidence that these beliefs are challenged. One carer stated that being involved in the life story work had made her realise that 'the old person was still in there'.

Another carer talked of how his view of dementia had changed, that he had learnt that dementia is not always 'destructive' and that the future can be bright. An individual with dementia talked about how he had not wanted to live when he learned of his condition but that life story work and his involvement in the project had given him 'hope'.

Reconnecting as a couple

Listening and conversing are key components of life story work as they are the basis of developing good relationships that are fundamental to delivering high quality, person-centred care. As well as having positive implications for relationships between staff and people with dementia and their carers, this project suggests that this is an identified benefit for the relationships between the person with dementia and their spouse. This view is supported in literature, where it was found that using a life story approach with couples improves their communication and strengthens their identity as a couple (Scherrer *et al.* 2014).

Findings from our interviews suggest that relationships significantly improved during the process of undertaking life story work. One gentleman with dementia stated:

> Me and my wife have got together to do this – it's brought us back together.

This view was further supported by comments from carers such as:

> It's helped me communicate with my wife again.

The ability to communicate as a couple following a diagnosis of dementia is critical to the care relationship and is significant in terms of carer stress and burden experienced (Haight *et al.* 2003). Molyneux *et al.* (2011, cited in Scherrer *et al.* 2014) suggest that following a diagnosis of dementia, couples need to do a great deal of 'identity work' to maintain their relationship. They suggest that life story work is a means for couples to explore their past together and reaffirm their strengths so they can move forward and deal with challenges in the future. In support of this, one carer stated:

> We have shared our memories and now we can plan for the future. We have accepted the future will be different but we still have one.

A number of the benefits to family carers overlap with those to the person with dementia – for example, reconnecting as a couple. Comments from carers suggested that prior to involvement in life story work they felt they had lost the person they knew, but that following it they had a renewed sense of togetherness:

> We are telling her story together, it's our story. It is very emotional sometimes but it is making us stronger.

Clarke *et al.* (2003) suggested caution with life story work as it can evoke painful memories. However, interviews with the participants in this project suggest that this does not need to be a bar to undertaking life story work, as even painful memories can lead to positive outcomes. Jane McKeown and colleagues explore this further in Chapter 16.

Improving relationships

A benefit to family carers reported in the literature review was that involvement in life story work strengthened their relationships with staff. Little evidence was found to support this in the project. Carers did not report a higher level of satisfaction with their treatment as an individual by staff post intervention, nor did they report a higher degree of confidence in their ability to talk to staff. However, scores in these areas were high pre intervention so possibly this would account for the lack of demonstrable improvement. In contrast, feedback from staff suggested that they felt relationships were improved as it 'breaks down barriers – enhances relationships'.

Job satisfaction

A major benefit to staff suggested by those involved was that undertaking life story work with people significantly increased their job satisfaction.

One member of staff commented:

> It gives me so much satisfaction, when people tell their story. A glow comes from them – they come to life.

Another commented:

> As a member of staff it is good to look at spending time with people to enhance their wellbeing instead of just thinking about targets.

Oldham Memory Service

Oldham has had a local life story group since 2003. At that time Age UK Oldham offered a service producing life story books for care home residents. Life stories were also done in a dementia day hospital. Since that time life story training has been co-delivered by a family carer and can be accessed by family carers.

The commissioning of memory services has evolved alongside the policy initiative of dementia-friendly communities. After the national life story training programme 'Your Story Matters' (Life Story Network, 2012a) was rolled out, Age UK Oldham extended life story work to include people living in their own homes and in their enhanced luncheon club service in the community.

The Oldham Memory Service offers an eight-week rolling post-diagnostic programme for people with dementia and their carers to attend. A session on life story work has been included since the pilot group in 2009 and subsequently since the full service was commissioned in 2013. As part of this re-commissioned service a speech and language therapist and assistant support life story work with people newly diagnosed. People may hear about life story work through the post-diagnostic group and then can be supported by the speech and language therapist to participate.

Alternatively, the speech and language therapist can see people in the community who are referred for communication support, which often leads to the making of a life story book. This is regardless of where the person lives in the Oldham area, be it in a residential care setting or their own home. The speech and language therapist often gathers new referrals from the many support groups in the Oldham area, which are run by the Memory Service and also by Making Space, another voluntary sector organisation.

The Care Home Liaison Team also supports people in residential and nursing homes in producing life story books.

Workers and volunteers from Age UK Oldham can provide support depending on where a person attends.

Conclusion

Although the resources to continue the project were not forthcoming, there are several positive outcomes that have influenced our practice. We include an awareness session about life story in our post-diagnostic group, which everyone, including those with a diagnosis of vascular dementia, can attend. Our learning from the process of undertaking life story work has informed the development of our initial assessment documentation, so that it is much more about who the person is, focusing on their assets, strengths and skills. The revised documentation helps us to see the person as a whole. We have found that the narrative approaches we use are helping us to bring about wider cultural change that promotes real person-centred care. We don't just talk about it but make sure we do it, which these two quotations illustrate:

> Life stories provide a valuable insight into the life of someone, especially when they have difficulty in sharing this information themselves. As a nurse, it's interesting to understand the meaning behind what people say and their behaviour and helps me to build up a relationship with that person by facilitating communication. It definitely supports the delivery of person-centred care by focusing on the person and not the problem! (Member of staff)

> Jack always loved people and talking. Poetry in particular holds a special place in his heart. What struck me was how animated he became after getting involved in this work. It was like someone flicked a switch! He has been able to review and pull all of his favourite poems together. It has been a long time since I have seen him like this. It is like he has a glow over him and purpose!

☀️ TOP TIPS

- Life story work should be undertaken with both the individual with dementia and their family carer.

- It should focus on strengths not weaknesses.

- It is the process and *not* the final product that is important.

- It is about meaningful conversations that are respectful of the individual and their human rights.

- Life story work is an ongoing process and not a one-off exercise.

- It provides a framework for high quality, person-centred care.

12

Life Story Work for People with Dementia in Acute General Hospitals

An Alternative Model for Care?

Rachel Thompson

Introduction

Whilst the use of life story work to support person-centred care is becoming more popular, it remains a relatively new concept in acute general hospitals. This chapter considers how life story work may be used within such settings where medical models usually predominate. Although perhaps not life story work in its truest sense, there is an increasing use of personal profiles to inform the care of people with dementia and/or delirium. Whilst challenges remain in providing person-centred care within general hospitals, the gathering of biographical information to help promote a more holistic approach to care, should be welcomed. The use of personal profiles may go some way to increase understanding of the person and improved individualised care, but implementation and benefits are yet to be evaluated. As the benefits of life story work are recognised and evidence grows, it is anticipated that life story work will become more widely understood and used to inform the care of the growing number of older people and people with dementia in general hospitals as well as other settings.

Why life story work matters to me

Life story work provides a fantastic tool for developing meaningful relationships, which for me is at the heart of good nursing care. Learning about the richness of others' lives – the things they have done, the people who matter to them, their joys and sorrows, their likes and dislikes – is perhaps one of the most interesting and rewarding things we can ever do.

I have seen life story work transform care in many settings – from a gentleman in a continuing care unit who had not spoken for months, singing his favourite song to his wife, to a lady in a general hospital accepting life-saving treatment after refusing for three days, because the nurse found out she loved listening to the radio. I have seen life story work change staff attitudes, improve relationships with relatives and help make people's care meaningful. We should never stop asking, listening and learning about each other. Life story work encourages us to remember this.

Challenges in acute general hospital settings

The challenges faced by older people and those with dementia and their families during an acute admission to a general hospital have been well documented (Alzheimer's Society 2009; Moyle *et al.* 2008; NHS Confederation 2010). Acute general hospitals are busy places in which the care usually focuses on medical needs as opposed to psychosocial needs. Care is based on assessing and treating people so they can be discharged as quickly as possible. This relies on people being able to express their own wishes, and understand and cooperate with their treatment. However, for people with dementia this may not always be possible; and if not accounted for or understood, detrimental consequences may occur for both the person and their family.

Admission to hospital can be traumatic due to the physical and emotional demands placed on people. For people with dementia, who may have reduced resilience and coping mechanisms, this may be particularly stressful. The environment itself is likely to be unfamiliar and disorientating and the person may find it difficult to communicate their needs. In addition, people with dementia may be at greater risk of decline as a consequence of their hospitalisation. Studies have shown that following admission to hospital, people with dementia experience longer lengths of stay, malnutrition, functional decline, falls and higher mortality rates compared to those without dementia (Archibald 2006; Gladman *et al* 2012; Mecocci *et al.* 2005; Sampson *et al.* 2009).

Hospital admission can also be extremely distressing for family carers and friends. A number of studies have shown family carers often feel disempowered and report feeling dissatisfied when excluded from decisions about care, treatment and discharge (Clissett *et al.* 2013; Jurgens *et al.* 2012; Whittamore *et al.* 2013). If essential information is not communicated with and from family carers, this can result in poor outcomes for the person for dementia. The *Counting the Cost* report (Alzheimer's Society 2009) highlighted that more than half of the carers who responded to their survey felt hospital admission had a detrimental effect on the person's symptoms of dementia.

Poor detection and/or little understanding of the needs of people with dementia can lead to inadequate and poor care. For example, people with dementia may be at risk of having pain un-recognised and undertreated. This may result in distressed behaviour and be treated inappropriately with antipsychotic or sedative medication. If someone has difficulty communicating their needs, they may become incontinent, have inadequate nutrition or not comply with treatment. Bridges and Wilkinson (2011) reported that people with dementia admitted to a hospital ward are likely to be more vulnerable to thirst, fear and over-stimulation than those without cognitive impairment.

Until recently, staff working in general hospital settings in the UK have had very little preparation and/or support to care for people with dementia and/or delirium. The attitudes and understanding of staff, as well as the culture of care in which they work, are significant contributing factors to the delivery of care. In a study of the care of older people in an acute care setting, Cowdell (2010) found the attitude of staff was often one of de-valuing people with dementia. This may be as a result of a culture of care that tends to focus on physical needs, routines and meeting compliance targets (Anna Gaughan explores this in greater detail in Chapter 3). Consequently, meeting the individual needs of people with dementia, including understanding their psychosocial needs, is likely to get overlooked or not be prioritised. Indeed, people with dementia may be viewed as a 'nuisance' or not suitable for an acute care setting (Moyle *et al.* 2008; Tadd *et al.* 2011). As such, the delivery of person-centred care is hampered by a number of factors and may feel an unachievable goal within this setting, unless significant changes are made (Dewing and Dijk 2014).

It is in this challenging context that the use of personal profiles to gather information, which highlight the psychosocial needs of patients, may have something promising to offer. Increased use of these tools in acute general hospitals and their potential for supporting person-centred care will be examined in more detail in the next section.

As the number of older people and those with cognitive difficulties increase within the hospital population, it is imperative that environments of care are adapted to meet the complex needs of this vulnerable group. Recent national strategies for dementia care have all included a focus on improving hospital care for people with dementia, and a variety of initiatives have been introduced to support this ambition. These have included a range of education and training opportunities, specialist staff (including mental health liaison), improvements in identification, specialist wards, environmental changes and new approaches to care. A project supported by the Royal College of Nursing (RCN) and Department of Health in 2011 identified a number of elements required to support good dementia care based on findings from surveys of people with dementia, family carers and practitioners. This included the need to provide individualised care and recommended the routine gathering of personal life story information (Thompson and Heath 2013).

Whilst a number of positive initiatives are underway to improve the way care is provided for people with dementia in hospital, providing individualised care remains a challenge. An evaluation of a development programme supported by the RCN demonstrated that significant improvements can be achieved, but that these require investment in clinical leaders, practice development approaches and addressing organisational culture (Evans *et al.* 2015; Thompson 2015a).

Despite all the initiatives to improve care, it is fair to say that these have not yet been widely adopted or well evaluated. A review by Dewing and Dijk (2014) concludes that a tension remains between the priorities for existing co-morbidities within acute care and the ability to deliver person-centred care. Whilst the adoption of life story work approaches may not address the wider challenges of changing the system in which people are cared for, they may go some way to supporting improvements in understanding and changing attitudes.

Life story work and personal profiles

In order to examine how personal profiles (the term I am using to include personal communication or patient passports) and life story approaches might contribute to the delivery of person-centred care in acute general care settings, it is useful to explore the origins and their relationship to life story work. As previously mentioned, personal profiles are perhaps not life story work in its truest sense. They do, however, provide a collation of personal and biographical information that is aimed at providing staff with a summary of the person's psychosocial needs. Other multimedia approaches, incorporating life story information, are also beginning to be adopted within acute care settings.

Definitions of life story work are considered in the introduction, but that offered by Murphy (2000) describes life story work as 'the recording of individual information to produce a tangible product such as a life story book, story board or multimedia resource to inform care delivery'. This definition may come closer to many people's understanding of how life story work is used in practice, including within acute general settings.

McKeown *et al.* (2010) suggest that life story work enhances person-centred care by allowing nurses to make the link between past and present, which can promote understanding of the person's preferences for care. Life story work can also help in understanding the meaning behind what people say and how they behave, reinforce identity and facilitate communication (Bruce and Schweitzer 2010). Life stories can provide a valuable insight into the life of someone, especially when they have difficulty in sharing this information themselves. Knowing how to use information from the person's biography to help stimulate and provoke memories to calm the individual can be particularly helpful in unfamiliar situations. However, most of the research has focused on the benefits of life story work within care home and/or community-based settings as opposed to acute general hospital settings.

So, how do personal profiles and other forms of life story work differ in the acute general hospital setting and can the same benefits be realised?

As highlighted previously, hospital care is geared towards fast and effective responses with assessment and treatment of the presenting co-morbid condition in order to expedite discharge. However, people with dementia often experience longer stays than those without dementia and may be moved several times between wards and departments during their stay. As a result they meet multiple staff in a system that is often geared towards routines and medical interventions as opposed to meeting psychosocial needs. People may be additionally compromised in their ability to communicate their needs due to delirium and/or other physical illness, making coping mechanisms less robust. All of this can make it difficult for staff to get to know the person and their family and to develop meaningful relationships, which are important ingredients for life story work.

In response to these challenges, personal profiles were developed and are now being widely adopted in acute care settings. These profiles provide a short summary of the individual's biography and preferences, which is easy to access. Aimed at helping staff develop a better understanding of the person as an individual, they offer a simple and practical solution to facilitate individualised and person-centred care. However, their use and implementation have not been well evaluated.

Personal profiles are not a new initiative and similar approaches have been developed to support the care of people with learning disabilities. Indeed, the hospital passport has been used for some time for people with learning disabilities who are admitted to hospital. The use of hospital passports was recommended in the Department of Health progress report on learning disabilities care, *Six Lives* (DH 2013c), plus the *1000 Lives Plus* report (NHS Wales 2014) on improving hospital care for people with learning disabilities. As with dementia care, a number of reports (Mencap 2007; Michael 2008) have highlighted poor experiences and poor health outcomes for people with learning disabilities using general hospital services. As with people with dementia, the quality of healthcare experience is adversely affected by poor communication, fear and distress from being in an unfamiliar environment and lack of appropriate support (Cumella and Martin 2004). A variety of one-page patient passports were developed in a drive to provide continuity of care, to empower individuals and enhance relationships between those involved in care. Information from the hospital passport is used to enable 'reasonable adjustments', which may mean providing additional and alternative methods of support to achieve a positive outcome. Brodrick *et al.* (2011) suggest that in order to be effective, patient passports need to be simple and concise, supported by a coordinated approach across services and informed by patient and public involvement. Such learning and advice are undoubtedly useful in relation to personal profiles in dementia care.

The *This is Me* (Alzheimer's Society 2013) document was one of the first examples of personal profiles to be widely used for people with dementia in acute general hospital settings. It was originally developed by the Northumberland Acute Care and Dementia Group and was formally adopted by the Alzheimer's Society in 2009 with endorsement by the RCN. The leaflet was updated in 2013 to incorporate information such as taking medication and advance care plans and designed to encourage the sharing of information between care homes and hospitals.

Over the last few years a range of similar versions and/or formats has been developed as clinicians have worked towards supporting individualised care for people with a range of communication difficulties, including people with delirium, learning disability and sensory impairments. Although by no means exhaustive, some of the examples developed in the UK include the following:

- 'This Is Me' – supported by the Alzheimer's Society and the RCN for use with people with dementia in acute general hospitals

- 'Getting to Know Me' – introduced by Alzheimer Scotland and Scottish Government for use across Scotland

- 'See Who I Am' – Bradford Teaching Hospital, NHS Foundation Trust

- 'All About Me' – Pabulum Blue Book – Age UK, Norfolk.

Whilst varying in format, name and design, these documents share many principles around the intention and types of information they include. Broadly, the topics covered are outlined below; and whilst family and friends may provide information, they are designed where possible for the person to complete themselves:

- name (including preferred name)

- carer/person who knows you (the person with dementia) best

- family/friends/pets who are important

- life so far; including jobs, hobbies, background, etc.

- routines, including things that may upset or relax you

- personal preferences for food, drink, sleep medication, self-care

- mobility

- communication needs, including hearing and vision

- other information (e.g. important personal possessions, advance plans).

In an attempt to share key information with a range of staff, including non-clinical personnel, even shorter versions of personal profiles are becoming more popular. These short leaflets are designed to provide an 'at a glance' version of the personal profile and are reported to be particularly useful for staff such as porters, hostesses and domiciliary care staff. Examples of these are:

- 'Forget Me Not' – developed by St. Helens and Knowsley Teaching hospitals NHS Trust and widely adopted by a number of other hospitals across England

- 'Getting to Know Me' – developed by University of Manchester, Royal Bolton Hospital NHS Foundation Trust and Greater Manchester West Mental Health NHS Foundation Trust as part of a training pack to support people with dementia in general hospitals.

These leaflets generally include the following headings:

- name (including preferred name)

- background/place of birth

- people who are important

- occupation

- important life events

- preferences and dislikes for food/drink/sleep/activity

- things to support communication and personal care.

Whilst these formats do not include a process of life review as described within life story work, they can provide a valuable, accessible summary of important information to support a better understanding of the person and their needs. As Murphy and Moyes (1997) recommend, assessment for the best method or tool should be considered in the context of the person's circumstances. In relation to acute care settings the most practical tool may indeed be a shorter version, which is easier to complete during a short stay and more likely to be accessed and used by staff. Disadvantages, however, may be that they provide just a glimpse of the person's biography and individual needs rather than a complete life story. They also run the risk of over-simplifying and/or mis-representing the richness and depth of a person's complex history, and recorded preferences may change over time.

Implementation in practice

For those people who are more cognitively impaired, have communication difficulties or are more compromised due to an acute illness, it may be the family carer who is primarily involved in providing life story information. Family carers are an invaluable source of information, and life story work can facilitate involvement in the person's care. However, it is always important to consider the rights and wishes of the person in sharing personal information. This requires an understanding of mental capacity, as supported by legislation that sets out the need to assess capacity properly and to ensure decision making is supported for as long as possible. As with any approach to life story work, it is important that the Mental Capacity Act 2005 Code of Practice (Office of Public Guardian 2014) or relevant legislation is followed so that the information shared is in the person's best interests and reflects their true preferences.

Learning from the adoption of hospital passports for people with learning disabilities should also be considered, including how new approaches to care are introduced, understood and supported in practice. This requires good leadership, training and education of staff, engagement of stakeholders (including people with dementia and their carers) as well as access to resources. In an evaluation of a life story project within mental health acute and continuing care settings (Thompson 2010, 2011), it was found that a systematic approach, skilled facilitation and involvement of staff were crucial to successful implementation. This included training in the use of life story work, support from Admiral Nurses (dementia nurse specialists) and involvement of all staff, including clinical leaders, in its implementation.

Understanding the benefits

As personal profiles are still a relatively new approach in acute care settings, it is difficult to know if they are able to achieve the same benefits attributed to other forms of life story work. Additionally, they have been adopted using a wide variety of formats and methods and no primary studies are currently available. However, anecdotally and in practice, personal profiles are proving to be very popular. This is clearly illustrated in comments gathered from staff within a recent feasibility study of their experience of using personal profiles for people with dementia in an acute care setting (Thompson 2015b):

> It enhances your enjoyment of being a nurse, because it enhances the care you can give the patient, because you know something about them. (Referring to 'This Is Me')

> I have seen them work really well. Having that important information when somebody is not able to communicate, we can work with them and ensure that we're giving them what they would want if they were in their home environment. (Referring to 'Forget Me Not')

Within the RCN project on improving dementia care in hospital, a survey of professionals found individualised care planning and using life story information were cited by 57 per cent as being highly significant to supporting change (Employment Research/RCN 2011a). Within the same project, from a survey of almost 1500 family carers and people with dementia (Employment Research/RCN 2011b), 41 per cent were familiar with the 'This Is Me' document and half of these had used it to support care. A number of similar documents were also identified, such as the learning disabilities passport, 'Remember Me', 'Who I Am' and life story books.

Conclusion

Although a variety of personal profiles have been developed and adopted across the UK for dementia care, there has been little research on their effectiveness use in practice and implementation. Whilst there is some evidence within learning disabilities that the use of hospital passports can be instrumental in improving the experience of care, research is still limited. Following an evaluation of a specialist mental health/medical unit for people with dementia and/or delirium, Whittamore *et al.* (2013) suggest that the use of personal profile documents may contribute to improving communication and information sharing between family carers and staff. Findings of a feasibility study on the use of personal profiles for people with dementia by the author of this chapter (Thompson 2015b) indicated variation in the way templates are implemented and used by staff. However, identified benefits included improving understanding of the person, developing partnerships with families and improving the experience of care. Implementation was assisted by using a simple, concise format, including biographical details, and by directly involving family carers and patients. Other instrumental factors included facilitating understanding of the intervention, encouraging shared ownership, adopting a shared approach and support from specialists or leaders. Further studies are recommended to identify views of patients and family carers and to compare different formats.

In the meantime, developments in practice suggest the adoption of personal profiles is popular and well received. Based on a review of the literature and scoping of current practice, the following tips are offered to support the use of life story information in providing person-centred, individualised care for people with dementia in acute general hospital settings.

⚡ TOP TIPS

- Determine if the person with dementia already has a life story book or personal profile and, if relevant, ensure this is shared with the person's consent.

- Ensure a consistent approach to the format of personal profiles and seek to adopt those used in other similar settings.

- Discuss the purpose of the gathering of personal life story information with the individual, where possible, and with their family carer and clarify its use (i.e. to improve communication and provide individualised care).

- Assess the person's capacity to share information and ensure that information is in the person's best interests.

- Involve the person and their family carers in gathering relevant information and ensure it is accurate and will support the person's care.

- Provide education and training and involve all staff in understanding the benefits of implementing and using personal profiles in practice.

- Provide clear information and resources to support its use in practice and ensure a copy is kept in patient records in case of re-admission.

- Ensure the profile is kept in an easily accessible and visible place (i.e. near the bedside).

- Provide clear leadership and ongoing support in the continued use of personal profiles and life story information to promote the delivery of person-centred care.

- Regularly review and gather feedback from all those involved, including people with dementia and family carers.

13

Life Story Work in Care Homes
Victoria Metcalfe

Introduction

This chapter is about creating life stories with and for people living with dementia in care homes. It discusses the importance of strong leadership and how life story work can lead to more fulfilling lives for residents as well as increased job satisfaction for staff. The chapter includes real-life examples of positive outcomes for residents, staff and families and highlights some of the challenges and obstacles you may encounter in undertaking life story work.

A personal story

Very early in my career I had a chance encounter with a man called Colin, aged 32, his wife and very young family. At that time Colin was not diagnosed with dementia but he did go on to receive a diagnosis. His experience deeply affected my career journey. I was shocked by the lack of empathy, understanding and support available for Colin – who was very angry – and his family, who were confused by what was happening to them all. Colin felt no one was listening and he was afraid for his and his family's future as he saw himself as their provider and protector. Colin needed his voice to be heard. I spent time getting to know them all as individuals and by listening to Colin and focusing on his abilities he became less angry and more willing to talk. We started to develop a scrapbook to tell his story to other professionals, but as our journey together continued the book became Colin and his family's story. Quite simply, Colin's story ensured that those around him did not lose sight of him as a man, husband and father. As his family was so young, his story more than 25 years on is still a treasured family item as it provides an insight into all aspects of his life.

The care home sector

It is estimated that more than 376,000 older people live in approximately 10,300 care homes in the UK – a population that will increase significantly over the next 20 years as the number of people in the UK aged over 85 doubles (Warmington, Afridi and Foreman 2014). That represents a lot of potential relationships and many stories to be told.

Like people, care homes come in all shapes and sizes and all look different. Although architecture and design are important, what makes a care home great is the quality of the relationships between the people involved: those living and working in it and those visiting it. The National Dementia Strategy (DH 2009a, p.59) suggested that excellent care homes:

> generally pay close attention to staff management, staff training and development and person-centred care planning... They provide purposeful activities that relate to individual preferences...actively involve relatives and friends in the care of residents and develop strong links with and involvement in local communities.

Over 25 years of working with and for people living with dementia have taught me that it is not only essential to learn about the condition, but also vital to learn about the people involved: those receiving care, those giving care – both paid and unpaid – and those visiting. People cannot give what they do not receive; valuing each other is key to creating meaningful lasting relationships, and great leadership and quality relations are key to a great care home. The Joseph Rowntree Foundation's 'Better Life' programme has highlighted that older people with high support needs want, among other things, personal relationships, good relationships with carers and social interaction (Katz *et al.* 2011). A further report highlighted that, in order for older people to enjoy a good quality of life, we must overcome the challenge of negative stereotypes and ageist assumptions and ensure that support is founded in rewarding and positive relationships (Joseph Rowntree Foundation 2014). John Kennedy (2014) concluded in his inquiry into care homes that 'it's all about people and relationships'.

Over the years in my work with care teams, the same perceived big issue has arisen: 'Sounds great but we don't have enough time.' This reflects the misconception that a person's life story is additional work to do: a time-consuming project or a lengthy interview to be conducted, which is not the case.

The importance of strong leadership

I am less likely to hear such protestations where the leadership is great. So what is great leadership? Great leaders walk the talk. In my experience, leadership is not only a job title; it is a personal characteristic. Effective leaders lead by example, have high expectations and are creative. In care homes where the development of every resident's life story is everyday practice, leaders spend their time building a relationship-centred environment of trust to ensure all relationships are authentic, balanced and valued. They constantly reinforce the importance of knowing each other well and support their team to feel confident by finding time and giving permission to create life stories. These leaders empower their teams to find solutions to difficulties in managing time and stimulate innovation.

Developing a person's life story is a journey. Staff may need encouragement to realise how much they already know themselves about the people they care for and to apply some simple techniques to gain rich and valuable information to form a picture of the whole person. Good care is built on good quality relationships, so the more the care team know about the person, the better the care relationship will be. It is important that staff use every interaction as an opportunity to make the connection to develop the relationship and learn about the person. This does not have to be a separate 'add on' activity but can be included in the necessary everyday tasks such as helping people get washed and dressed. Like all relationships, this takes time and requires nurturing.

Using life story work in care homes

When starting a life story, it is essential to seek consent from the person living with dementia or, where appropriate, a family member or advocate. A person's capacity to give consent may fluctuate over time so this must be revisited from time to time.

Life story has a beginning, is ongoing and should also include the person's future wishes and hopes. A life story can only become a living reality if it is added to so that it grows, and is only valuable if information gathered is acted upon.

Sandra

Liz was a new member of staff. During a supervision session the care home manager suggested that Liz should spend time reading through the life stories of the group of residents she was mainly caring for to start to really get to know them. Liz started with Sandra, who had lived at the care home for some time but had become quiet and withdrawn.

Repeated through Sandra's life story was the mention of her love of horses – her father had been a coalman and had a horse. Liz used this information to initiate conversation. Sandra's face lit up with memories of Albert the horse and the mischief she got up to as a child. Liz added all the wonderful stories to Sandra's story, which enabled other team members to use the information similarly to get to know her.

Developing a person's life story, often including others along the way, can provide much valuable information such as when the person likes to get up, what they like to eat, who their family and friends are and their hobbies and interests. It can help explain why a person behaves in a certain way today and remind others that people who cannot communicate verbally still have something really important to say and can make a contribution.

Everyone has a past, a present and a future and everyone has a story to tell. Creating and hearing a person's story brings many benefits for everyone involved. For example, a life story can help grandchildren understand that an older person was once just like them with a long future before them, often with similar hopes and worries. It also encourages a shared experience of learning about each other together. It can help adult children understand why a person's past experiences can impact on how the person behaves now. It also provides an activity to be enjoyed together when conversation might otherwise be limited.

For all involved, life story work provides a continued narrative between the past, the present and the future in every relationship. It helps care teams to see beyond the illness or medical condition and focus on the uniqueness of the individual, to plan and deliver true personalised care and improve the person's daily lived experience.

It helps others to recognise and value the abilities of the person, rather than focusing on losses, and enables the staff team to support them to continue the pattern of their life by honouring their preferences. It also helps others to engage in meaningful conversations to provide comfort, pleasure and happiness.

Both Colin and his wife, previously mentioned, had difficult childhoods; and even when they met and fell in love, their families made it hard for them to be together. They vowed that their own son would only know stability and love. As Colin's journey through dementia progressed, his anxiety for his family's welfare increased. This could result in very angry outbursts. As his life story was so rich in information, the team around him knew his distress could be reduced and he would be comforted if he was reassured they were well and safe, using his life story information.

Some examples of common themes and dilemmas and how to tackle them

Commencing a person's life story is not a one-off event and certainly not an interview

The care home manager had found a life story template on the internet. This could have been a great starting point as a foundation to start and grow a person's life story, but this is not how it was used.

At the staff meeting everyone agreed life stories were a good idea but felt they had no extra time to do this. So the manager juggled the rota to allow 30 extra minutes for each team member to conduct three life stories with three residents – she had worked out it would only take 11 days for all 60 residents to have a completed life story. She missed the point completely, seeing it as yet another care task and focusing on a product, rather than building up rapport and relationships to help deliver better care.

Life story work is not a chronological task. Start at the point in their life that makes sense to the individual

Peter

Peter had lived at the care home for several weeks after an emergency placement from hospital following a fire at his home. Peter was very confused and furious as he believed the care team had stolen his house and possessions and would shout this out every time someone passed him. Precious, the team leader, was the only person Peter would allow near him. Over the weeks and months, with gentle support and clear explanations, Peter accepted his house was gone, although he would still occasionally become angry and shout at people.

As Peter was beginning to settle in, Precious talked to him about his life and he agreed he would like to talk about, share and record some of the good times. Peter's story was called 'The Good Times'.

Precious used any time they had together, such as walking along the corridor or helping Peter to get washed or dressed, to develop his 'good times' story. It was soon evident that Peter only wanted to talk about his career in the army.

From the information he provided, Precious and the team learned that Peter had been a drill sergeant and that when he shouted it did not necessarily mean he was angry; it was just his usual way of communicating. Following his retirement from the army, Peter's life had been very challenging, emotionally and socially. The staff also learned that he preferred the company of men – but Precious was OK!

This approach is in stark contrast to that of getting 60 life stories 'done' in 11 days. Here Peter's story was a part of conversations that were fed into his care plan. It also helped staff to develop greater empathy and understanding of him.

Use a pace that suits the individual

George

George moved into the care home from a long stay emergency hospital admission following a stroke and a diagnosis of vascular dementia. It was taking quite a while for George to settle as he was reluctant to receive the care and support he needed; he would become angry and shout at female carers who passed him. He also waved his arm about which looked quite threatening, so other residents started to avoid him. The care team were very concerned that not only was he unhappy but also becoming more and more isolated.

The activity coordinator, Carl, was skilled and experienced in developing life stories and started including Gorge in all small group activities, as a way of forming a relationship with him. Initially George did not take part but gradually he started to take an interest. Over a period of months, Carl and George formed a positive relationship, with George referring to Carl as his friend.

Carl then started talking to George about his life and how together they could record and develop his life story. Although George was interested he felt there was not much to tell. However, what developed was a personal story, rich with adventure and information, starting with George at the age of 14 running away to sea and travelling the world, working with a core group of men until he was 58 years old.

The care team were amazed at the information. It helped explain his frustration with his disability and his reluctance to accept female care and support. The story took nine months to start and is still being developed. Today George is much happier. He is understood and he has connections and friendships.

One memory may naturally lead to another – but not necessarily in chronological order

Connie

Connie had lived at the care home for some time, and as she lived through her journey of dementia the care team found it increasingly difficult to find activities and interests to occupy her. Dorothy, Connie's daughter, mentioned that she had been writing her mum's life story at home and had amassed a huge amount of information. It was suggested that it might be interesting for Connie to see and could provide important information to improve her everyday living experience.

Dorothy brought in the life story, which was actually a detailed family tree. The care team helped Connie and Dorothy to scan and photocopy many photographs to develop a poster-style life story, based on a wonderful image of a tree with family members, their names and significant events.

The care team learnt that Connie had been a great lover of the outdoors, particularly wildlife. During a conversation, Connie mentioned how much she missed feeding the birds. This was quickly remedied with bird feeders being filled and placed in several easy-to-view places in the garden.

When Dorothy first saw the poster, she was initially unhappy with the tree as some names, events and times were incorrect. When the care team explained this was Connie's representation of her family and important events in her life, Dorothy stopped trying to correct Connie and they enjoyed together the conversations triggered by the poster.

As Jane McKeown and colleagues discuss in Chapter 16, genealogy is about facts and dates, but life story work is about feelings, values and beliefs. This was Connie's story – it was her perspective that mattered.

We get on better with some people than others. This is no different in a care home

Marie

Marie had lived in the care home for several months and, when asked, stated that she was settling in well. However, she never left her room and rarely spoke. Several care staff felt she might be feeling isolated and lonely. They tried many strategies, including cajoling and persuading Marie to join group activities and special events, but Marie always returned to her room as soon as she could.

At a team meeting a housekeeper, Terry, mentioned how chatty Marie was. Much to the amazement of the rest of the team, he went on to describe Marie's many happy memories of her time as a professional dog groomer in France. The team were astonished and asked Terry if he could, with Marie's permission, start a life story. Marie was unsure about commencing a life story but she was keen to make a scrapbook of her life.

It is really important not to worry about what a person's story is called.

What started as a scrapbook full of dog breed pictures soon developed into a wonderful story of Marie's life and what was really important to her – for example, her preference for being alone, having always been single and worked by herself. Staff also learned of her love of animals, especially her beloved poodles; and, importantly, how much she missed her radio, which had gone missing in hospital.

Today she has a radio, which she listens to all day every day, and a huge collection of pictures of her beloved dogs. The team always have something to talk about as they now know her well. Most importantly, although they always let Marie know about activities or special events, they now know that if Marie says 'no thank you' it is because that is her preference.

Some people do not want to talk about some aspects of their life

Sanjay

Sanjay had lived at the care home for some time. He was a gentle, quiet man who had always appeared happy and cheerful. His family visited daily and were always greeted with a big warm smile. Over time, as Sanjay's journey through dementia progressed, his behaviour changed and he appeared sad. He also became more reluctant to accept the care support he needed. The team felt worried and were struggling, so they talked this through with Gerry, who was a long-term volunteer. He had always had a great rapport with Sanjay, who he felt seemed bored unless he had someone with him.

Following some training, Gerry suggested he started a life story with Sanjay. Gerry talked to Sanjay and his family and they were all very happy to do this. Family members provided a wealth of information and an array of photographs of special occasions and other family members. Gerry spent more time with Sanjay talking about the people in his family and what was important to him. One day, during their usual time together, Sanjay suddenly became increasingly distressed and agitated and threw the life story album onto the floor.

It took several members of staff to support Sanjay to feel calm and safe. Gerry was upset when he realised that each time he tried to show Sanjay photographs of his wedding, he had missed the building distress this was causing. Following a discussion with Sanjay's family, the photographs were removed. It transpired that the wedding photographs were of Sanjay's first wife, who was killed in a terrible accident one year after their marriage.

Today Sanjay is happier and enjoys looking through his album when he does not have his family visiting, and the care team feel they know him so much better.

You may discover something private about the person and this may trigger sad feelings or memories for you

Stan

Stan had lived at the care home for some time and was popular with the other residents. He was often referred to as 'a bit of a dandy' by the others due to his love of brightly coloured waistcoats and bow ties.

One of the care team, Margaret, got on really well with Stan. They had lots in common: they were from the same area and had even gone to the same school, albeit years apart, and loved a bet on the horses.

Following a training session, Margaret jumped at the chance to start Stan's life story and when she discussed this with Stan and explained it to him, he was delighted too. He had no family or visitors, but due to the quality of his and Margaret's relationship there was lots of information already gained from their conversations together.

Stan's life story developed and even Margaret, who felt she knew Stan well, was amazed at how much she did not know, including how he hated coffee, which he had been drinking every day since he moved into the care home. From this knowledge the team changed the elevenses coffee routine to 'What would you like to drink?' This was a small change with a significant response: Stan was not the only person who did not like coffee.

One afternoon when the gardening club members were potting seedlings, Margaret asked a general question to the group: 'Who had a garden, growing up?' Stan confided to Margaret very quietly that not only did he not have a garden, but he did not even have a proper house. Puzzled, Margaret discreetly asked, 'Where did you live?' Stan went on to describe his very difficult and often brutal upbringing in children's homes in the 1940s. Margaret waited for a natural break in the conversation and moved the conversation to Stan's lifetime job as a bus driver and the often funny encounters he loved to recall.

Margaret had also been brought up in the care system and had very distressing memories of this. Margaret told her manager about what happened when talking to Stan and her upbringing in care homes. The manager supported Margaret to understand that feeling upset is a reasonable and normal reaction. Sometimes you may not be the right person to support a resident; Stan might need to talk about his feelings, and letting her know that this had happened was the right thing to do. Later that day, the manager used a quiet time as an opportunity to talk to Stan about his early life. Stan discussed some of his experiences but did not elaborate. The following week, Stan sought out the manager to talk again about his experiences.

Be aware that some people may disclose information that is so personal that even those close to them do not know about it

Ronald

Ronald had lived at the care home for over a year, having previously been cared for at home by his partner, Edward, for three years. He was very settled and quite a cheery person. Edward visited daily and after seeing another resident record their was very enthusiastic to record Ronald's. Following information and support on the different methods and approaches, they both felt images and pictures would form the best basis of Ronald's story.

Edward was very artistic and what developed over many months was a beautiful album full of images and drawings that were significant and important to Ronald as the story progressed of their life together.

One day, Edward appeared to become very upset. The care team immediately went to him to offer support. Edward explained that Ronald had mentioned his children, but Edward did not know that Ronald had any children. Ronald was also distressed as he could not understand why Edward was upset.

Over time, Edward dealt with the newly learned information and accepted this part of Ronald's life long before they met. They both continued to add to Ronald's story, which evolved to be Ronald's and Edward's story.

Act on the information

Joseph

Joseph was very quiet and withdrawn when he moved into the care home. The team felt, having discussed developing a life story with Joseph, that this would be a good time to start to get to know him and each other well.

David, a care worker, started using their time together when he was supporting Joseph to shave or have a bath to talk about his life. Joseph had never married but had a large circle of friends, especially when he was younger, and his great interest was trainspotting.

David did not know anything about trainspotting so Joseph spent their time together educating him.

The care team worked together to support Joseph to visit the local train station which he greatly enjoyed. They also used an iPad to access pictures and information, which Joseph thought was magical. David found some train hobby magazines in a local charity shop. Joseph was delighted and today he spends most of his time occupied with his beloved train books and magazines.

Conclusions

Life stories can take many forms and information can be as interesting and diverse as we all are. Creating a person's life story can be a satisfying and enriching experience for all involved, particularly so in a care home, where people may arrive with little information about their previous lives.

The process of developing a person's life story does not have to be a chore or seen as a one-off project; it should be created at a pace comfortable for the person and be a pleasurable and enjoyable experience for all involved. The process of developing the life story, through the relationship with the individual, is as important as the finished product.

This links to the ideas in Chapter 19 about thinking about the Purpose, the Process and the Product. Our purpose in care homes is to get to know the person and to provide the best care we can. Staff are often good at the process of learning about a person's life – but they do not always see the relevance of it and we do not always collate it into a life story. The Product might be a one-page profile (Sanderson 2016), a family, tree as with Connie, or a book, as with Stan; or it might just inform the care we give, like getting Marie her bird feeder and radio. That is a key point – it is no good having beautiful life story books or products if the information gathered is not acted on in some way to improve the care people receive – even if it is just the simple act of sitting down and looking at it with a resident.

Crucial to creating the right culture where life story work can flourish is good leadership. Great leaders lead by example, have high expectations, are creative, possess a sense of ownership in excellence and continually strive for quality improvement. They spend time with their teams illustrating their principles and their vision.

They explain to everyone the importance of their own talents in achieving this and help to nurture these through coaching and mentoring. They give regular, robust supervision and debriefing sessions and provide continuous learning and opportunities for skill development. Great leaders are kind and compassionate and set the tone and culture by their actions – their hearts are full of love.

☀ TOP TIPS

- Good relationships are key: the better the rapport, the richer the information will be.

- Some memories can be deeply distressing or private, so be sensitive to signs that the person is becoming upset or agitated.

- Undertaking life story work is a continuous process, not a one-off event. It should be enjoyable for everyone involved.

- Don't rush the process – work at the pace that suits the individual.

- Watch out for non-verbal signs of distress in the person to gauge how they are responding to the conversation (as with Sanjay) and change the focus back to safer ground.

- If you find a person's story triggers upsetting memories for you, listen respectfully, move back to safer ground and seek supervision and support. You may need someone else to support you in the work.

- Use the information you gather to inform and improve the care you are providing.

14

Spirituality, Religion and Life Story Work
Polly Kaiser

We are not human beings seeking to be spiritual, rather spiritual beings striving to become human.

Teilhard de Chardin, in Furey (1993, p.138)

We live with a depth of spirituality rather than cognition that you can connect with us at a deep level through touch, eye contact, smiles… Spirituality is…not simply what religion we practice; it is what has given us meaning in our lives. Our garden, art, pets, the familiar ritual of religion. It is important to help us to reconnect with what has given us meaning as we journey deeper into the centre of our being, into our spirit.

Bryden, *Dancing with Dementia* (2005, p.123)

Introduction
This chapter aims to illustrate the importance of spirituality in life story work, irrespective of whether people have particular religious backgrounds or not. It will describe the overall context and give relevant definitions of both spirituality and religion. It draws on the words and ideas of people with dementia, showing the impact on them when this work is undertaken. It acknowledges that this can be a challenging area of conversation, particularly for people who have no particular faith background or for whom these backgrounds have not been supportive. Spirituality can be seen within the wider context of the importance of identity, person-centred care and purpose.

As we have already seen, life story work is a tool to help us to have conversations about who we are and what is important to us. Some of these conversations are about what helps us be comfortable in our skins and feel safe. For some people, their faith and religious practice may help; for others it might be other spiritual experiences, such as a walk in the woods, listening to music or stroking a cat. It may be that some of these form part of your conversations already. For many people, however, venturing into this territory can seem fraught with potential difficulty and it may just feel safer 'not to go there'. Although understandable, this is a mistake; such conversations have the potential to help us to understand people and help them feel safe. I hope that you will be able to connect with some of the ideas here to open up other avenues of conversation. The chapter includes practical ideas and tips to get started.[1]

Definitions
What do we mean by spirituality?

Spirituality may mean different things to those who believe in God and those who don't. Either way, we are often compelled to ask ourselves about the meaning and purpose of life. Spirituality is a more all-embracing concept than religion. One metaphor describes spirituality as a journey, with religions as different modes of transport. There are many definitions. As Frogatt and Moffitt (1997, p.225) note: 'defining spirituality is always tricky. In this context we mean a search for that which gives zest, energy, meaning and identity to a person's life in relation to other people and to the wider world.'

Life story work honours identity. Christine Bryden, who has dementia and has done so much to enlighten others about the condition, suggests that an individual's faith, religion or spirituality, however it is expressed, may be a significant element of identity (Bryden 2005). It is important that families, friends and paid staff caring for an individual with dementia are able to communicate this, not only to talk about those aspects of the person's life but also to promote practices that can respect and honour the person's beliefs.

Sometimes we worry that people may be offended if they are asked about their religious or spiritual beliefs, but usually people are happy to talk about them. Whilst formal religious teachings may lead to difficulties for some people, confidence is growing in the benefits to both physical and mental health of spiritual beliefs and practices (Gilbert 2011).

Peter Gilbert's work (2003) shows how important spirituality is in the overall field of mental health. His visual aid to help people think about it fits well into the overall framework of Kitwood's model of personhood (see Figure 14.1).

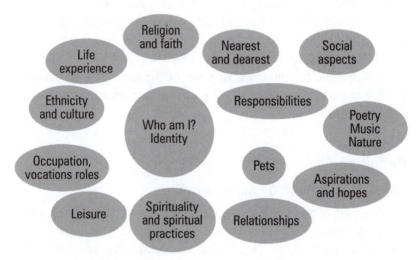

Figure 14.1: Spirituality and Identity

Hannah

Hannah had grown up in a Jewish family and had married a doctor. However, she was never a very religious woman and after she divorced became even less so. She had become estranged from most of her family. She had studied literature, was a teacher and loved poetry and nature. She missed her cat when she went into the care home but gained some pleasure in watching the birds outside her bedroom window and looking at the flowers that grew in the pot there. She felt safe and soothed when someone could read her poetry. When this was not possible, she had some audio tapes of poetry that she could listen to.

It took a while for the staff to find out about Hannah and that she gained her sense of spiritual connection via nature and poetry – not her religion. Through the use of life story work and Peter Gilbert's framework, some of her spiritual needs could be recognised and honoured.

Patrick

Patrick still lived in the Franciscan religious community he had joined as a young adult. The rhythms of prayer and work remained pretty much unchanged. What reassured him when he was distressed was to sit outside by the fish pond and recite his rosary. As his speech began to falter, he could still be found there fingering his precious beads and murmuring the intonation of his well-known prayers.

Spirituality can be particularly important for people at times of emotional stress, such as illness or bereavement (Royal College of Psychiatrists 2009); it can be of vital importance and might be an untapped asset or strength for a person (Koenig, McCullough and Larson 2001; Levin 2001).

Spirituality may be viewed as an expression of an individual's essential humanity, of how we live our lives and deal with crises. For anyone using a person-centred approach, it is an essential element in the assessment, support and recovery of those we want to help. You don't have to be religious to have a sense of spirituality. Spirituality can help people feel calm and connected to themselves and others. It can develop a sense of worth and value and can give us inner strength and peace. For Hannah, the poetry connected her to a sense of herself. She felt staff recognised what helped her, and the familiarity of the words gave her a sense of peace. It also helped the staff have a particular relationship and connection with her. Patrick found the familiarity of saying his rosary and holding the beads calming and reassuring.

What do we mean by religion?

All religions provide a world view, often acted out in stories, teachings, symbols, rites, rituals, sacraments and gatherings of the like-minded in communities that have a sense of mutual obligation. Religion creates a framework where people can make sense of their lives and their daily experiences. Religion can help people, but can also sometimes be a source of distress. It is helpful if caregivers can talk with someone with a dementia to find out whether their religion is important to them and whether it may help or, on the other hand, disturb them. We should not make assumptions based on the box for 'Religion' ticked by an individual. Hannah would not have appreciated a rabbi coming to visit, although she did discuss the possibility.

Some religions are quite culture bound, so it helps if care staff can make themselves aware of some simple taboos. There are some beliefs and practices that will be particular to specific faith communities, but the precise interpretation and patterns of adherence may be different for each individual. For example, some people from particular religions (e.g. Sikhism) may regard having a bath as grossly unpleasant and will wish to shower instead.

Religious belief can affect how people wash, the way they wipe or clean the kitchen, how they display love and affection, what they read, watch or listen to and how they use their time – for example, some people will read scriptures at particular times of the day. The most important thing to remember is that religious prohibitions or preferences may be so integrated into the sense of self that any breach or deviation will feel like an emotional assault.

Peter Gilbert (2003) suggested that it is impossible to know everything about the intricacies of people's faiths, but that it is important to understand and respect what is important to them, especially when caring for someone at the end of their life.

Why are spirituality and life story work relevant? How might spirituality and life story work be important for a person with dementia?

Research has shown that people with early-stage dementia find spirituality, and its associated meanings, important in coping with their diagnosis and its consequences (Katsuno 2003). Christine Bryden has spoken about the importance of spirituality in her life. She says that for her and others with a dementia it is the relationships and connection that are crucial' (Bryden 2005). This was so for Hannah with her poetry and for Patrick with his rosary. For many people, their expression might be far removed from the traditional practices of religion (Kevern 2011). This can be seen in the increasing practice of mindfulness.

Mindfulness has become increasingly popular and there is a growing evidence base for its effectiveness (Strauss *et al.* 2014). Mindfulness is a mental state achieved by focusing one's awareness on the present moment, while calmly acknowledging and accepting one's feelings, thoughts and bodily sensations. It is used as a therapeutic technique and is recommended in NICE guidance to help with relapse prevention for depression (NICE 2011). It has particular relevance for people with dementia as it focuses on the present moment. A pilot study exploring this (Litherland and Robertson 2014) found people benefited from this approach.

> It didn't come immediately, but there's been a progression. The more I do the more I get from it, the more I get 'within myself'. It's good. But you must do it at home. When I'm at home my meditation is my time. It's calming. Otherwise my mind is racing all the time with all the mistakes I make. It helps with stress – forgetfulness is very stressful. I can step out of worries or anger and go to my little stream. (p.32)

As discussed elsewhere in this book, life story work is often seen as just reminiscence; but while reminiscence may play a part, it is not the full picture. The approaches described by contributors to this book also point to the importance of living well in the present and aspiring to future hopes.

Ken Clasper is living with dementia and was an Expert by Experience in the 'Your Story Matters' programme run by the Life Story Network (Life Story Network 2012b). For him, life story is important in communicating about himself and his faith and spirituality.

Ken Clasper's story

Most people these days are encouraged to write their life story, once they have been diagnosed with dementia, although this is better done in the early stages of the illness.

This life story tells the reader, whether it is a family member or a member of nursing or care staff, who we are, and where we came from, what we did in life, what we enjoyed in life, including our religions, if indeed we are religious, our hobbies and things we get so much pleasure out of.

My own took off and became addictive, as the gates opened and the memories flooded back, usually at times when I could not write them down. For example, all staff may learn that the person loved spending quiet time outdoors, visiting gardens. In this situation, the care provider should work hard to facilitate access to this type of environment.

Only with time can care staff come to understand what a person is trying to say, and to grasp the expressions – so often non-verbal – that have a possible spiritual meaning. This includes encouraging care staff to take an interest in the life story of the person with dementia, and make links to possible spiritual needs.

A good quality of life is something we all cherish.

An important and vital aspect of the life story approach is the importance of the relationship, empathy, knowing the person and what might give them purpose.

How might spirituality and life story work be important for family carers?

For family carers, the ability of others to enter the world of the person with dementia is vital. How can we do that if we do not know what brings them meaning, purpose, joy and connection? This may include looking at the sunset, listening to the birds or hearing a beautiful piece of Rachmaninov. Joyce cared for her mother with a dementia and had life story training from the Oldham Life Story Group. Despite being a nurse, she said that this was invaluable in helping her recognise the signs and symptoms of her mother's dementia:

So when my mother's dementia progressed, and she eventually had to go into a home, doing her life story seemed like the obvious thing to do. I wouldn't have thought about it without the course.

Joyce and Olive's story

Mum used to go to a Baptist church which had Anglican connections. When she moved into the care home her room had a view of the Anglican Church she used to go to. Her life story helped others around her to know about her spirituality and faith. She worked in a munitions factory during the war...when she was young and going to the munitions factory, she was very nervy and scared. One night she had a dream of the 'light of the world' [a painting by Holman Hunt]. She did not know what this meant and asked her aunty Violet...who lived with them. My mum was worried that she would die...but her aunty reassured her that it meant God was with her. From that moment on she had a sense of God's presence in her life. That is in her memory book. I grew up knowing that was an important moment in her life. It was one that it was important staff could remind her of and she could connect to when she saw the picture of the painting. *It reminded her of something that sustained her.*

It helped the staff to know that her faith was important to her. It helped me... I have added to it...it helped the people left behind.

The life story book itself helped her spirituality, she could see the pictures and photographs and it calmed her. It is important to know what faith, if any, a person has. It helped staff to be more aware and it helps with end of life care. *It kept Mum connected to important aspects of her faith.*

These are both examples from Christian religious tradition, as these are the people I have known and worked with. As illustrated in Chapter 4, it is apparent that regular prayer is important for the older Muslim women in the 'Making Connections Not Assumptions' project.

How might spirituality and life story work be important for staff?

Sometimes staff may not feel confident to talk about spirituality, faith or religion. Some fear it will be seen as preaching. It is good to be aware of what feels right for you. If an individual does not seem to want to talk to you, then maybe someone else might feel more comfortable discussing the topic. Within a care setting there may be a chaplain, imam or rabbi who visits and can provide support, or perhaps there are volunteers from a local faith community. It is important that, wherever a person with dementia is, they feel they can have these conversations if they need to or want to. However, you should not leave it entirely to the chaplain. The essential task is to be alert to what a person may need or value. You may already be doing a lot to address their spiritual needs. Sitting out on a fine, sunny day or helping someone to feed the birds or watch the sun set may enable a spiritual experience for some people.

For Joyce it was very important for the staff to understand the significance of Holman Hunt's painting for her mother. Further, it was a tool to help soothe and calm Olive, and one she had used all her life.

It is important to know what faith, if any, a person has. It helped staff to be more aware and it helps with end of life care. (Joyce)

☼ TOP TIPS

This section is broken down into several areas. First, there are some ideas about how to begin a conversation with someone about their spirituality and faith, then suggestions for how you might continue to explore this. Finally, I suggest the sort of activities and practices that might support spirituality.

Starting the conversation: Useful questions

- What helps you most when things are difficult, or when times are hard?

- What helps you to feel good?

- Do you have a faith tradition?

- What is your church or faith community?

- How important is faith to you?

- How do your religious and spiritual beliefs apply to your health?

- How might we help address your spiritual needs (for example, when facing big problems, major losses or important challenges)?

Continuing to explore with the person

If a person values this conversation, exploring spiritual faith and belief is a gradual process and may take time, so this may vary depending on where you work. Practical ideas might include:

- asking a person about their spiritual and/or religious needs throughout their care and treatment, including at reviews of their care and support plans

- helping a person with dementia to identify those aspects of life that provide them with meaning, hope, value and purpose

- providing good access to relevant and appropriate spiritual and/or religious resources

- offering or making available safe spaces where people with dementia can pray, meditate, worship or practise their spiritual faith when they wish to

- providing opportunities for a person to discuss their spirituality or religion with others if they want to

- building strong and effective links with spiritual or religious groups in the local community.

Particular practices that might support spirituality

These include:

- practices of the body: relaxation, exercise, yoga, walking and singing

- practices of the mind: meditation, prayer, mindfulness, reading or being read to

- religious practices from particular faith traditions.

Conclusion

The subject of spirituality may at first seem a challenging one. It is important not to impose one's own ideas and evangelise. A person may wish to talk about such matters, particularly as they approach the end of their life (see more about this in Chapter 15). So, an awareness of spirituality and having these conversations are essential within the realm of delivering person-centred care and developing a life story. There has been a growing interest in spirituality, ageing and dementia in recent years (Goldsmith 2004; Jewell 2011; MacKinlay 2010). This chapter has focused on the benefits and practicalities of using life story work to explore spirituality from the perspective of people with a dementia themselves as well as that of family carers. We have seen that it is important not only to be able to broach it with people but also to respond to a person's need for connection and meaning – in the present moment.

Note

1. This chapter draws on material first written by the author for the 'Let's Respect' toolkit for care homes, originally published by the National Mental Health Development Unit and now available at www.lifestorynetwork.org.uk/resources/shared-practice

15

Using Life Story Work in End of Life Care

Polly Kaiser

Neither the sun nor death can be looked at steadily.

François de la Rochefoucauld 1613–1680

How people die remains in the memory of those who live on.

Dame Cicely Saunders – Founder
of the Modern Hospice Movement

Michael's story

Michael died, aged 97, in the village in Ireland where he was born and brought up. Everybody knew him. He didn't need a life story – he had carried the life story of the village in his head. Not only did he know everyone, he had known the parents and grandparents of everybody. He didn't need an end of life care plan or a funeral plan. Everybody knew what was expected and everybody played their part. In many places and cultures where religious practices and traditions are observed, ceremonies, rites and rituals support people dying and those who are left afterwards. The ceremonies and structures provide the scaffold and support for what is needed and what is expected.

Introduction

Few of us will die like Michael – we may, if we are lucky, die with family and friends around us. They may know what we want – they may not. We may have never thought about it ourselves. A census carried out by the Dying Matters Coalition (2009) found that whilst 68 per cent of the public reported that they are comfortable talking about death, less than a third have actually discussed their wishes around dying. As the seventeenth-century quotation from François de la Rochefoucauld above indicates, people find it difficult to think about death and dying and therefore to talk about it. This is not just a modern phenomenon. This is an area known for its taboos, and given that many of us find it hard to have conversations about the topic, it can be even more challenging in dementia care, where communication is likely to be compromised.

This chapter looks at how life story work may help in a number of key ways, namely: helping to have conversations; to begin to record preferences; helping the person to be remembered, in particular through re-membering practices; and legacy. The very idea behind these makes an assumption that there is such a thing as a 'good death' and that it is important that our wishes about how we wish to die are communicated. It is fascinating to think that years ago a 'good death' meant that anyone could come into the space around the person – neighbours and strangers received communion as a dying person was given the last rites. What is now deemed a private affair was once very public (Aries 1982). Death, dying and bereavement are socially constructed, and practices change throughout time and cultures (Aries 1982). They vary between and within families.

The term 'end of life care' (EOLC) is a relatively modern one. The UK government's first EOLC programme was established only in 2004 and a national strategy was published in 2008. EOLC is not only for patients in the final hours or days of their lives, but is more broadly the care of all those with a terminal illness or terminal condition that has become advanced, progressive and incurable. 'End of life care aims to help people live as well as possible and to die with dignity' (Marie Curie 2014). These ideas have come from the hospice movement started by Dame Cecily Saunders when she opened Saint Christopher's hospice in 1967. The idea of palliative care and combating 'total pain' – that is, not just the physical but the psychological and spiritual pain – was revolutionary at the time. It was developed as a counter to the increasing medicalisation of death. The idea of a 'good death' thus has its origin in here, where open communication, relief of symptoms, individual dignity, respect and acceptance of death are prominent features (Bradbury 2000; McNamara 2003; Seymour 1999). Yet it is not always clear what the components of a good death might be. Common themes that emerge from good death narratives are: 'a death free from pain, *the sense of a life well lived*, and *a sense of community*. The use of story in palliative care provided an opportunity to *create meaning* and to heal for both the teller and the listener' [my emphasis] (De Jong and Clarke 2009, pp.61–67). Certainly, Michael had a sense of a life well lived and a sense of community. There are different ideas about what a good death might be and these have evolved over time (Bélanger 2011). Religion, culture and secularism influence ideas about the good death.

It has been shown that people highly value attention to spirituality – in particular, the importance of coming to peace with God and praying. However, Steinhauser *et al.* (2000) found that for some people it was more important to resolve faith issues with themselves rather than to take part in social, organised or interpersonal expressions of spirituality. This was certainly the case for both my parents – they each had their own faith and did not see the need for priests or last rites. Each made their peace with family and friends in their own different ways.

This emphasises the point that it is not sufficient to work with religious leaders; we also have to help a person have a conversation about what is important to them and to consider the issues discussed in Chapters 4 and 14.

There is no one definition of a 'good death'. However, whether it be personal or professional, most readers may be able to recall an individual who has not received good EOLC.

? Reflection points

- Can you bring to mind someone you know who had a good death? What made it a good death?

- Can you bring to mind someone who had a bad death? What made it a bad death?

EOLC is a dynamic process that is negotiated and renegotiated among patients, families and healthcare professionals. It cannot be assumed that wishes expressed at diagnosis are those still pertinent on a person's death bed. That is why knowing the person and ongoing communication with them are so vital.

Why is end of life care important for people living with dementia?

The period when someone with dementia is approaching the end of their life is inevitably difficult and emotional and they have the right to dignity and a 'good death'.

(Alzheimer's Society 2014b)

Many people with a dementia will need 24-hour care at the end of their lives, but as the National Dementia Strategy in England (DH 2009a) pointed out, there are inadequacies around EOLC for people with dementia in terms of pain relief and access to hospice care (Sampson *et al.* 2006).

People with dementia face particular challenges. They tend to have multiple co-morbidities that complicate the progression of dementia and identification of the dying phase. Coordinating drugs and treatments can be challenging. Pain relief, cancer treatment and interference of different drugs can wreak havoc on a person, as carer June Hennel describes:

> For others affected by dementia I dream that the horrors of comorbidity be better recognised. Instead of consultants working in their own specialist silos, we need patients to be treated holistically... every person at the end of life deserves as much care and attention as we give to bring babies into the world. (Hennell 2015, p.155)

A person with dementia might not be able to verbalise their need for pain relief and their general needs for comfort and care. A particular feature of dementia is that an individual's communication skills deteriorate so that their ability to express their views and wishes is lost at an earlier stage than other life-limiting conditions (National End of Life Care Programme 2010). Dementia patients are unlikely to have any assessment of spiritual needs before death or documentation of any known religious beliefs (Sampson *et al.* 2009).

There is a major mismatch between people's preferences for where they would like to die and the actual place of death. The Health Care

Commission (2007) found that whilst most people reported that they would like to die at home, only 18 per cent did so. Only 4 per cent of people died in hospices whilst the majority (58 per cent) died in hospitals. Advances are being made with EOLC but 54 per cent of complaints in hospitals are related to the care of the dying.

If people are to have a choice about where and how they die, they need to be supported to talk about this. Given the cultural taboos around such conversations, it is not surprising that this is a challenge. For someone with dementia, it might be important to have conversations when they can still express their wishes but this is not always easy for family, friends and staff. It has been shown, however, that people with advanced dementia are perfectly willing to discuss the topic of death and EOLC, albeit in a truncated or metaphorical style. Importantly, their views may not remain the same. It is important not just to talk about the subject early on but to continue the conversations as the illness progresses.

How can life story work and narrative approaches help?

As has been described earlier in this book (Chapter 1), life story work is not just the production of a book, album or video of a person's life. It is also a set of curious conversations about a person's life, their achievements, preferences, values and future hopes. In this context it seems that the tools of life story work and wider narrative practices are potentially helpful vehicles to begin to have conversations about end of life care. 'Stories are not material to be analysed; they are relationships to be entered' (Frank 2000, p.200). Within the palliative care field it is important to:

- be sensitive to the person's feelings

- help the person to be remembered

- encourage the person to tell you what they're afraid of, even if it's hard to talk about

- not dismiss your own fears; they are important too.

(Adapted from Dr. Darrell Owens, founder and director of the palliative care consult service at Harborview Medical Center)

Life story work can help in a number of ways: helping to have conversations, recording wishes and preferences, helping the person to be remembered and helping with a legacy.

Helping to have conversations

There are no hard and fast rules for talking about dying. Much may depend on a person's religious and cultural background as well as their personal history. It is important to take your cue from the other person and not assume that people don't want to talk – often they do.

People can be encouraged to talk more about their feelings by asking things like:

- How are you feeling?

- Is there anything you want to talk about?

- Is there one thing particularly frightening you?

- Is there anything that helps you feel calm?

This last question is particularly important. As a person's dementia progresses, their ability to self- soothe tends to decrease. They are more reliant on others to recognise signs of distress and to bring comfort. Each person will have different needs around this and it is vital to know a person well to know what will help to calm them. In Chapter 17, Maria describes John Osborne's 'Sound Track To My Life' – the music that one person finds soothing will be different for someone else. What cheers one person up might have sad connotations for another. Smells, tastes and food, as well as music, can be equally emotional, evocative and important. In the Introduction, Ken Holt's story illustrated how Alice would sometimes stay in her clothes and not want to get undressed at night-time. This was because in her head she was back in the war, fearful and wanting to be ready to run to the air raid shelter. Through the life story Ken produced for her, staff became aware of this and knew what she needed.

Knowing this background is important, as a further example from my practice illustrates:

Margaret

Margaret had grown up in Liverpool during the war. She remembered rationing and it was always important for her to have food available. Dinner was so early at the care home she would ask her daughter to bring her fresh fruit – particularly bananas, which she enjoyed eating.

Narrative approaches are collaborative and it is important to check things out with the person:

- How is this conversation going for you?

- Should we keep talking about this or would you be more interested in…?

- I was wondering if you would be more interested in me asking you some more about this or whether we should focus on X, Y or Z? [X, Y, Z being other options].

(Morgan 2000)

Recording wishes and preferences

Life story work can be a helpful place to begin to record preferences, not just about comfort and calm but about what a person might want near the end of their life. Would they want family or friends to be present? Would they want the last rites, or some other marker? According to Hedtke (2003) some useful pointers to consider might be:

- In my family when someone is dying we prefer… (describes what a person hopes to have happen)

- Where we come from… (helps tell about cultural customs and practices)

- In my religion… (helps them to describe religious traditions they may have).

Such questions start with the person and build out to family and culture. Just because someone is a Catholic does not mean they want to see a priest for their last rites, as the example of Mary illustrates:

Mary

Mary had grown up Catholic but had lapsed from the organised Church after her divorce. She was still very spiritual and connected with friends who were nuns and went on retreats. When she was dying she expressed a strong wish that no priests were to be called. Her daughter, recognising her mother's spirituality and family traditions, spoke about this with her local priest, who gave her his holy chrism oil to anoint her mother. Her mother was very thankful for this.

Re-membering practices

As discussed in Chapter 1, much of the theoretical underpinning of life story work comes from a social constructionist view about the importance of relationship and that 'identity is not so much an achievement of mind but rather of relationship' (Hedtke 2003 p.58).

Re-membering practices, within narrative therapy, are not about reminiscing but about relationships and witnessing the effects of those relationships and connections. The idea and term was developed by Michael White (1988, 1997). He was heavily influenced by Barbara Myerhoff, an anthropologist who worked with older Jewish people in southern California. They had suffered great losses as a result of the Holocaust, and Myerhoff (1980, 1982) noted how they continued to honour and remember, maintaining memories in the present:

> To signify this special type of recollection, the term 're-membering' may be used, calling attention to the reaggregation of members, the figures who belong to one's life story, one's prior selves, as well as significant others who are part of the story. Re-membering then, is a purposive, significant unification, quite different from the passive, continuous fragmentary flickerings of images and feelings that accompany other activities in the normal flow of consciousness. (Myerhoff 1982, p.111)

This is a special type of re-collecting of people who have been important in the person's life: people in their life story who belong to their 'club of life' (White 1997 p.22).

These figures and identities do not have to be directly known in order to be identified as significant to people's lives. For example, they may be the authors of books that have been significant or characters in movies or comics. These figures do not have to be people.

For example, they may be the stuffed toys of a person's childhood or a favourite pet (Russell and Carey 2004). Julian Barnes, interviewed by Blake Morrison, summed up the idea beautifully when talking about his grief over his wife's death: 'the fact that someone is dead may mean that they are not alive, but doesn't mean that they do not exist' (*Guardian* 2013).

Whilst White's earlier work was about having different conversations with people who were bereaved (White 1988), Hedtke has extended this to work with the dying. For example:

- How would you wish to be remembered?

- What stories, strengths and attributes would you like to pass on?

- What do you think people love and find valuable about you?

- Who else might know about this?

It is important to ask 'questions to generate affirming and resourceful memories of this time for future times of reflection and re-membering' (Hedtke 2003, pp.51–59).

Such conversations are challenging for the listener: 'A story told aloud…is of course more than a text. It is an event. When it is done properly, the listener is more than a mere passive receiver or validator, he [or she] is changed' (Myerhoff 1980, p.27). It is not enough that a story is written and kept in a drawer: they need to be heard and are 'relationships to be entered' (Frank 2000, p.200).

Conversations about death and dying can be challenging and taboo subjects but they are very powerful in helping the person who is dying and for those left behind.

Legacy

In my clinical practice, many carers who have done a life story comment on the value of it as a legacy for the family:

> I found out things about Mum I had never known before.

> It is really good that the grandchildren know about my mum and her life in Jamaica before she came here…they love the stories she tells them and the clothes and fashions – we have laughed lot about those.

This is lovely as my granddaughter will probably not know my mum and through this she will be able to have a sense of her.

It was really helpful when my dad died – we gave it to the vicar and it made the funeral much more personal.

Dawn Johnson (Cohen *at al.* 2008) carried out a qualitative study of life story work as part of her doctorate in clinical psychology. She examined the roles and meanings of life story books done by Age UK volunteers among older people and carers in care homes in Oldham. She found that an important part was 'Leaving a Part of Self Behind' and was of an existential value:

Beyond strengthening the familiar actual relationships, in several cases the life story book was perceived in terms of leaving something behind, which is 'there permanently'. (Woman in care home)

and something to

'hand down to my family.' (Woman in care home)

In that sense, the book is seen as a monument, a living witness to the older person's life; or, as one daughter put it:

You can carry on and on with it can't you, you've always got that, something you don't think of doing. Some people do but it is nice and that will be there to be kept.

Similarly, another daughter noted that:

My brother and sister live in Spain so I sent them a copy as well and other family, so now it's in Norwich, Wales, it's all over, because we've got this extended family, all of a sudden…they all want copies of it to show their children, of their great great grandma, their great grandma so…

The story continues…

Conclusion

This chapter has looked at the background terminology of EOLC. It has discussed the idea of a 'good death' and the legacy from the hospice movement. It is a challenging area of care with many taboos and difficulties involved in talking about it. These challenges are magnified with someone with dementia, where co-morbidities, difficulties in predicting progression and timing of end of life and increasing communication difficulties render it more complex. It is hoped that some of the ideas around life story work and narrative practices, particularly re-membering practices, can help. Whilst the taboos and challenges remain, the benefits for the person, families and care staff are numerous. Dame Cecily's words: 'How people die remains in the memory of those who live on' are as relevant for staff as they are for family carers (Jones 2010).

☀ TOP TIPS

- There are various ways to talk about dying – find the one that suits you and the person concerned.

- It is important to take your cue from the other person.

- Don't assume people don't want to talk. Often people do.

- They may well change their minds about what they want for themselves so you need to keep on talking and listening.

- Focus on their achievements, relationships and values.

- Ask them what brings them comfort and sustenance.

16

Identifying and Overcoming Challenges in Life Story Work

Jane McKeown, Kate Gridley
and Nada Savitch

Introduction

The use of life story work with people with dementia and their families can be an enjoyable experience for all concerned. However, there can also be challenges and it is important that these are understood so that they can be avoided, minimised or managed in a sensitive way.

This chapter explores some of the potential issues that can arise, drawing on the research literature as well as the practical experiences of people living with dementia, family carers and care staff using life story work. With an awareness of possible issues and with effective training and supervision in using life story work, many of the potential challenges can be avoided or overcome.

At the end of the chapter the reader will:

- appreciate the range of challenges that can occur when undertaking life story work.

Understand the importance of consent and privacy

- be in a better position to minimise and where necessary respond to upsetting memories

- appreciate the importance of the person with dementia 'owning' their story

- understand the importance of the life story record and its use with people with dementia.

Initial concerns about undertaking life story work

Before starting out with life story work, it is helpful to be aware of some of the initial concerns and/or feelings that have been raised by the person with dementia, family carers and care staff whom we have worked with. Such concerns/questions may include:

For the person with dementia

- Who will see it?

- Do I have to say everything about my life?

- Will I upset anyone with what I say?

- Does making a life story of my past memories mean that my present and future wishes may be disregarded?

For family carers

- Will it upset my relative?

- I'm not sure it will help my relative in any way.

- The time is just not right, there are too many other things going on.

Care staff

- Will we be perceived as prying or seeming too nosy?

- What if we uncover family secrets?

- How will we find the time?

- The person doesn't have the capacity to consent.

These concerns should be listened to and taken seriously. However, many can be alleviated by providing information about what life story work is and what it isn't. From their research into the use of life story work McKeown *et al.* (2015) identify a range of ways in which it may be used or perceived:

- for the person with dementia to tell their story – as a way to be heard or for therapeutic benefits

- as a tool to use with the person with dementia as part of care

- as therapeutic for family members – participating and reviewing life

- to help staff to understand and care for the person

- as a way of expressing experience of condition and/or services

- as a legacy

- to assist in transition between care environments.

It can be helpful to have these in mind when responding to concerns and to be clear about the specific purpose(s) of life story work in your situation. This chapter will help you to better understand and be able to respond to these common apprehensions. It is important that you do not let your own concerns prevent the use of life story work with people who want to participate.

Consent and privacy

Before starting to use life story work with a person with dementia, it is important to work with the person and their family to assess whether they want to take part and whether there is anything that needs to be considered. Some helpful questions to guide this conversation are:

- Has the person with dementia been happy to talk about their life in the past?

- Are they someone who enjoys sharing their memories with others now?

- Are there any aspects of their life story that they might prefer to avoid discussing or that may cause distress?

If the person is from a black or minority ethnic group, it can help to consult with someone from their community to highlight any specific cultural issues to consider. If interpretation is required, consider whether the person would be happy to talk about their life in front of someone from the same community, or whether a same language speaker from another community might be more acceptable. Life story work does not necessarily involve discussion of sensitive or private topics, but some people may want to speak freely about things that go against cultural norms.

The questions suggested above are only a guide and people can change their preferences. Someone who has in the past not enjoyed reminiscing may enjoy doing so now, and similarly a person who was happy in the past to share their story and memories may now be reluctant to do so. It is important to move with the person's wishes and preferences and not rely on what their choices would have been in the past.

Consent to taking part in life story work is complex and not a one-off decision. However, it can equally be made over-complicated and people can be excluded from what can be a very enjoyable and worthwhile activity by care staff who may consider consent very rigidly (Gibson 1991).

For a person to give consent, they need to understand what will be involved, but also informed that what they discuss as part of life story work is their choice. With their permission, their memories and recollections will be recorded in some way, so that they can be reminded of what they said and so that, again with their permission, others, such as care staff, can see the record to help them understand and know them better as a person.

The person needs to know that nothing will be recorded without their agreement and that they can change their mind at any point in the process. There is no guidance on whether a consent form needs to be completed – the authors feel that such a rigid process may exclude people who cannot demonstrate informed consent. Moreover, being asked to sign forms can be unsettling for people with memory problems, who may remember signing something but may not be able to recall later what it was they agreed to. Good practice is to document conversations around the consent process in care records and to take a 'process approach' to consent by continually assessing whether a person wants to remain involved and is happy for their information to be shared (Dewing 2007; McKeown, Clarke, Ingleton and Repper 2010). Verbal and non-verbal cues should be noticed – for example: Is the person engaged in the activity? Do they seem relaxed or show enjoyment? Do they seem disinterested? Are they restless or upset? A certain amount of judgement is required to assess whether the person wants to participate or not. However, one especially good or difficult day should not determine whether or not future attempts are made at life story work. Continual assessment on different occasions is needed.

Privacy is another important factor. Find out from the person if there is anyone they would prefer not to view their life story record – some may only want to share this with their close friends or family. Others may have some things they are happy to share widely, but other things that they would like to record just for themselves, to help preserve precious memories.

Upsetting memories

Should a person become upset by their recollections, it is important that care staff acknowledge the feelings and support the person until they feel better. We can all identify with becoming upset now and again about sad memories, but this does not necessarily indicate that we do not wish to talk about them. One participant with dementia in the University of York research (see Chapter 5) sums this up:

> People may cry, or become distressed as they remember but to steer people away because that might make you feel uncomfortable is wrong…it is important that those engaged in this work are able to make themselves emotionally available, to be alongside people with dementia who might be accessing sources of distress or discomfort.

Staff need the necessary skills and training to support a person who is sharing their feelings. Whether or not you continue with life story work depends on whether the person indicates that they would like to proceed.

The time to consider seeking more specialised assessment and support is if a person becomes 'stuck' in upsetting memories – for example, wartime experiences, traumatic bereavements or abusive relationships. In these situations, it may be necessary to seek the more specialist assessment from a clinical psychologist or specialist mental health team member. The person's GP would be a good person to discuss this with initially.

Personal disclosures

Care staff sometimes have concerns about life story work as they worry they will uncover upsetting memories or family secrets. Although this is not an outcome from life story work per se, this could occur during the process of gathering information. The likelihood can be minimised by considering the preparatory questions referred to above, but even with the best preparation these issues can sometimes emerge.

It is important to recognise life story work as a 'therapeutic activity' – that is, an activity that may improve wellbeing and enjoyment for the person with dementia; however, it is certainly not 'therapy', which aims to help a person review and resolve aspects of their life. A useful analogy, which builds on the Skilled Helper Model of Counselling (Egan 2013), is provided by Dawn Brooker. It depicts a chest of three drawers, in order to understand the sort of personal information that may be shared during life story work (see Table 16.1).

Table 16.1 Life story work information: chest of drawers analogy

Drawer	Type of personal information
Top	Information freely available about a person that is often kept on case notes and may be collected on admission. May include: demographics, what the person did for a living, family members, basic preferences.
Middle	Information a person may choose to disclose in the context of a friendship or caring relationship and that might be disclosed when using life story work. May include: thoughts, feelings, beliefs, significant relationships, more personal memories.
Bottom	Information that may be private to a person or perhaps a few close others and not for the public domain. May include: Family secrets, private or traumatic memories.

Adapted from Brooker (2010)

However sometimes people can divulge personal information even when not invited to do so. They may value the individual time offered to them by a friendly and trusted staff member and share private feelings and memories.

It is important that staff listen and don't stop the person mid-conversation. They could divert the conversation at a relevant point if the information is especially sensitive and the staff member is not confident in responding. If sensitive information relevant to a person's care, or perhaps indicating the root cause of upset or anxiety, is disclosed, it may be prudent to discuss this with your manager or a clinician. It is important that sensitive information shared is not recorded in the life story work record without the person's full agreement and understanding of any potential consequences. Gibson (2011) recommends that private disclosures are not excluded from conversations but do not get recorded in a public life story work record. It is important that staff receive the necessary support and supervision to ensure that decisions are made in the best interests of the person with dementia in order that their dignity and that of others are retained.

Whose story is it?

Being clear at the start that the story belongs to the person with dementia is an important guiding principle. Any life story will involve other people and this should be considered, but for the purpose of this work the person with dementia needs to remain central to the process. Family members may suggest photographs or stories to include, but where possible the person whose story it is should be supported to decide what to include and what to leave out. Similarly, it is possible that care staff may become so enthusiastic in developing the life story work record that they may forget to prioritise the views of the person whose story it is.

Sometimes a person may describe an event in a different way from how a relative saw it, but it is important to represent the person's story as they tell it. Staff may need to negotiate differences with relatives and explain that valuing the person with dementia's subjective reality is more important than having all the facts correct; it is a life story, not a historical record. It can sometimes be helpful to encourage a family member to develop their own life story record so that they feel they are able to record their own version of events.

Also it needs to be established where the record is kept. Ideally this should be with the person, perhaps in their room. Care and respect should be given to original photographs and documents and it is advised that copies are taken and used in the life story record and that originals are returned to the person or their family. Photographs can be reproduced through scanning, photocopying or photographing with a digital camera. Copies of photographs that are scanned can be saved onto a memory stick or disc and given to the person, ensuring that copies are erased from organisational computers.

Care staff who have participated in life story work have sometimes found it helpful to develop their own life story record. This helps them to better understand the process and to consider some of the challenges discussed in this chapter.

Quality of the life story record

The life story work record should not diminish the person or their story. The daughter of a person with dementia noted her mother's reaction to spelling errors in her life story book (McKeown *et al.* 2015): 'Mother and I look at it quite often and every time she comments that things are not spelt correctly etc; she and I have always been very fussy about the correct use of English' (p.248). An editorial meeting with care staff, the person and family carers can ensure there are no spelling mistakes, grammatical errors or inaccuracies, with the caveat that the story belongs to the person with dementia and as such should reflect their recollection and understanding of life events, including the use of any local idiom or dialect.

As explored in Chapter 1, it is important to consider the purpose of the record and how it is to be used, before planning its format. For example, a beautifully embellished and delicate life story book may be a fantastic testimony to a person's life but may not be robust enough for care staff to use on a daily basis with the person. An online web page may engage the grandchildren and computer literate members of the family but may be difficult for the person to view on their own or if in hospital.

It should also be remembered that written forms of the life story record are not relevant to everyone. Life story work undertaken with a group of older men from the Yemen living in Sheffield resulted in a film, which helped to overcome literacy issues and an absence of photographs and artefacts. As discussed in the Introduction to this book, there are many different ways of recording a person's life story.

Issues in the use of the life story work record
Under use

The life story process (the time spent gathering the information) and the life story record are both equally important. The process is the place where the person with dementia can feel valued and important and where they can have their voice heard and express the things in their life that are important to them. The record is the opportunity to ensure this information is documented so that it can then continue to be used with the person.

The life story record needs to be a living document, enabling care staff, for example, to get to know the person and plan care and activities. Visiting family members can use the record as a prompt for memories and conversation. Murphy (2000) reports that in some cases, staff did not know that residents had life story books and consequently they were not used. The record is the means to remind and connect with the person about their life; and yet so often it remains locked in a cupboard for safety, or not known about by the majority of care staff or is taken home by relatives.

Locating the person in the past

It is also important that the life story record does not locate the person in the past (Adams, Bornatt and Prickett 1998) or freeze them in time). An adviser to the research on life story work conducted by the University of York, who himself had dementia, said:

> What you like and dislike changes over time...The danger is, especially if life story work is done at a very early stage, which it should be of course – is that the person becomes set in stone and defined by that life story for the rest of their lives.

People's preferences and choices may change and it is important that staff adjust to these changes. All of our life stories are continually changing and developing and that is no different for people with dementia. Similarly, as new things happen in the person's life these can be added to the life story product, keeping it current. It is also worth including things that people are looking forward to – this could be an event (Christmas, a birthday) or an ambition (to stroke a donkey or to visit a monument, for example). If the person can be supported to achieve these ambitions, this too can be recorded in the life story.

Overuse

Sometimes the record can be overused. Care staff and relatives need to be vigilant if their interest is overtaking that of the person with dementia, who may be feeling tired or overwhelmed. This was reflected by McKeown *et al.* (2015), who noted that a nurse manager observed that volunteers especially could sometimes overuse the book with a particular woman with dementia:

> I think you also have to be aware that she tires very easily and I think what we've had to watch out for is that she's not actively engaged for the full day…so I think it's our job to look for signs that she's wanting a bit of a rest. (p.248)

Life story work is not for everyone

Life story work should be explored on an individual basis. As Polly Kaiser discussed in Chapter 1, relatives and care staff can feel compelled to persevere with life story work because they have been advised that this is 'a good thing to do'. As one participant in the York life stories research explained:

> With [husband], a couple of times, people have tried to do life story work with him…but it wasn't very successful…he didn't want to go back. And very, very early on, he really didn't like looking at photographs, and particularly photographs of people who were dead.

Not everyone wants to revisit the past, and this person clearly did not respond well to photographs. Take your cues from the person and be sensitive to how they respond. If they don't want to be reminded of the past, try building a life story around their current interests or listening to familiar music with them.

Just because life story work is not right at a particular time, it does not mean that it is never right for a person. Through her clinical work one of the authors (JM) approached a relative to see whether she would let her husband, who had dementia, take part in life story work.

She refused at the time. A few years later JM met the relative in a different care setting. She explained that previously she was coming to terms with her husband going into care, she was not well herself and it just felt too much; but now that she was feeling better and her husband was settled in a nursing home, she had developed a book with him and they both found it enjoyable.

It is important to remind staff and family carers that it is never too late to undertake life story work with a person with dementia. It is ideal to start life story work when the person with dementia can fully contribute themselves and make decisions on what to include and exclude. However, if every effort is made to involve a person with more advanced dementia in the process, there are still gains for the person by being reminded about their lives and their achievements and for activities and interactions to be planned around things that were known to interest the person.

Conclusion

For the most part, life story work is an enjoyable and valuable experience for many people. Our aim in this chapter has been to reassure care staff, often the 'gatekeepers' to life story work for people with dementia, that with some thoughtful and sensitive preparation life story work can be a successful activity. However, challenges can present; sometimes these can be overcome and with negotiation and ongoing assessment life story work may continue to be used. It does need to be acknowledged, however, that life story work is not for everyone. In such situations other approaches to engage a person with their identity and stimulate interaction may be considered – for example, music, non-recorded reminiscence or interaction with dolls or animals.

It is important that staff receive the necessary training and supervision to undertake life story work to ensure it remains an activity that can improve wellbeing and quality of life for people with dementia and their carers.

·𝒬· **TOP TIPS**

- Make sure that everyone involved understands what life story work involves and what will happen.

- Decide near the start what the purpose of the life story work is, as that will guide the best way to record it.

- Remember life story work is not for everyone; a person may begin and decide it is not for them.

- Be prepared that people may sometimes become upset – offer them time to express their emotions.

- Remember that the person with dementia 'owns' their story, even if it is not seen as accurate by family members.

- Make sure the final life story work record is checked for spelling mistakes and is agreed with the person.

- Ensure staff have training and supervision so that they can undertake life story work in a safe and sensitive way.

17

Arts, Dementia and Life Story Work

Every Picture Tells a Story

Maria Pasiecznik Parsons

Introduction

The creative arts and arts appreciation are proving to be of particular value for people with dementia for whom they offer a constellation of different ways to communicate their experiences, thoughts and feelings to others that are not reliant on speech or cognitive ability. Poetry, painting, song, drama and dance amongst other arts are used in a conscious and purposeful way to enable people with dementia to reminisce and share their life stories. Observable positive outcomes for arts and dementia have encouraged arts practitioners, organisations and venues to develop projects and programmes, often in partnership with statutory and voluntary organisations. This chapter will describe a range of initiatives that illustrate the breadth and depth of what is a fast-growing dementia specialism that is helping people with dementia remain connected with their own lives and with the activities that they enjoy.

Lola's story

In July 2015, I took Lola, my 89-year-old neighbour, to a dementia-friendly screening of the Wizard of Oz at the Ultimate Picture Palace, the second of a year-long, once-monthly *Meet Me at the Movies* programme.[1] Lola could not remember what we were going to do or how we got to the cinema, yet was word perfect when she sang along about going 'off to see the Wizard'. In contrast to her usual restless pattern of walking resolutely to the local shops several times a day, Lola remained seated throughout the one-hour and 52-minute-long film. Other members of the audience, including care home residents, became visibly less stressed and more relaxed as they settled down in the velvet seats that clearly evoked memories of the traditional cinema of their youth. Contented stillness coupled with smiles, laughter, humming and singing suggested a high level of engagement with dear Dorothy and her journey to Oz. Choosing an ice cream was clearly a nostalgic and joyful activity that most of the audience had not participated in for a very long time.

Driving home after the outing, Lola laughed as she told me about a pair of shoes she had painted red (to be like Dorothy's), her fiendish lacrosse tactics when she played at boarding school and her student days in post-war Oxford – an astonishing amount of detail, that even her family carer had never heard before. Lola's experience clearly shows the power of the arts to unlock confusion, bring back memories and reveal the story of a life!

Arts and dementia: what are we talking about?

In the last decade the purposeful use of the creative arts to promote the health and wellbeing of people with dementia has increased exponentially. These encompass visual arts such as drawing, painting, craft, ceramics and sculpting; performing arts that comprise music, song, dance movement and drama; literature including creative writing, novels and poetry; and multimedia arts from photography and film to digital productions. Specially curated museum tours or attending a dementia-friendly performance of a play are also activities that make up what is often referred to as 'arts and dementia'.

This specialist field is multidisciplinary, cross-sectoral and diverse. Commissioners of arts for dementia include arts venues, NHS trusts, Public Health, voluntary organisations and not-for-profit and commercial care providers. Most commissioned projects involve partnerships between arts venues, statutory authorities or voluntary organisations, arts groups and arts practitioners with diverse sources of funding involved – much of it is short-term, which is why the majority of those engaging people with dementia through arts tend to be freelance or work part time and often on time-limited projects. Those employed in the field range from professionals, including registered therapists in dance, drama, art and music and arts graduates who have developed expertise in working with people with dementia, to non-professionals such as self-taught artists, care home activities organisers with skills and enthusiasm, or volunteers (some with teaching, health or care backgrounds) who want to work with people with dementia.

Arts, dementia and wellbeing

Many of the drivers for the development of arts and dementia are to do with changes in how dementia is understood and how people with dementia are now valued in society. As Polly Kaiser and others in this book have described, the negative social construction of dementia was challenged by Kitwood (1997), who fostered a new culture of care that led to a surge of powerful personal narratives (Bryden 2005) that attested to the uniqueness of the person with dementia and a desire to be, as far as possible, active and involved in their lives and the world around them. These publications, public appearances and later blogs by people with dementia played a part in shattering therapeutic nihilism associated with the old culture of dementia care.

Moreover, developments in neuroscience and brain imaging show that despite damage to the brain, many people remain creative sentient beings, at least in the early part of the dementia journey. Whilst the regions of the brain involved in planning, attention, complex task performance and factual (learned) memory are fairly soon compromised by dementia, making or appreciating the arts involves a range of sensory, perceptual and cognitive functions involving widely distributed brain systems. As the brain does not harbour a single arts centre, creative expression can and should be encouraged, especially as arts activities such as painting, clay modelling, felting and collage can help individuals discharge anxiety and lift mood. Studies conducted in the fast-growing field of cognitive neuroscience of how music affects the brain (Williamson 2014) show that rhythmic responses are reliant on procedural memory and since they require little or no cognitive or mental processing remain intact well into dementia (Sacks 2008).

Similarly, people with dementia can recall words of songs, popular poems and stories, pen or brush strokes, object use, sewing, knitting, folding and working with tools or other well-rehearsed activities. Indeed, despite forgetting what they had for breakfast or the name of the place where they were born, many people with dementia retain sense memories, emotional memories, body memories, collective memories, autobiographical memories and memories that are hard wired, such as the sun or smiles, through repetition and practice (Zeisel 2009).

Some caution is needed in accessing memories, for not all are pleasant (as explored in greater detail in Chapters 1 and 16) and not all are available. Those using arts to trigger reminiscence should note that reported memories are not evenly spaced through the life span: a consistent pattern emerges whereby a period of childhood amnesia until the age of four is followed by increased reported memories that peak between 16 and 25 with a pronounced 'reminiscence bump'. The spike in reported memories of mid-to-late adolescence is probably due to the effects of puberty, the intensity of 'first times' when the experiences and events were encoded and the number of times when these were subsequently recalled (Glück and Bluck 2007). A recency effect and a reminiscence bump in reported memories of adults aged 60 and over may be due to their relative freshness.

Art forms and life stories

Given the growth of arts and dementia, it is useful to think about its application in life story work. Kaiser and Eley's definition in the Introduction to this book may help:

> Life story work is, above all, a process that involves having helpful conversations to elicit, capture and use stories about a person in order to promote their personhood and their wellbeing and keep them connected with family.

A strength of the arts forms discussed here is in helping to elicit individuals' life stories – as with Lola. In many instances these life stories are then used individually or collectively, shared in community settings, which not only promote wellbeing and connection, but also the opportunity to elicit more individual life stories. They are also examples of challenging the narrative of stigma and shaping new stories about dementia in our wider society.

Reminiscence

A study of the work of over 200 professional art organisations and companies that engaged older people in the arts showed that reminiscence was a core theme in their writing, producing and performing plays and shows and developing materials about their lives (Cutler 2009). A number of well-established community arts organisations such as Equal Arts, Age Exchange and Entelechy Arts also began to champion participatory arts with people with dementia, and were soon joined by hundreds more. This rapid growth in practice was fostered by reports of positive outcomes for art in dementia, including improved quality of life (Young, Camic and Tischler 2015) – in particular psychological wellbeing, preservation of self-identity, self-esteem, communication and self-expression, and motivation for participation in spontaneous activity (Zeilig, Killick and Fox 2014). Physical health improvements, including breathing, mobility, posture and falls reduction, were reported from a study of care home residents' participation in singing, dance and movement (Guzman-Garcia *et al.* 2013). Importantly, the arts have been shown to reduce loneliness amongst older people, by promoting socialisation through participation in cultural and creative activities, and are therefore strongly recommended as an intervention for dementia as those affected experience high levels of loneliness (Cutler 2012).

More recently, arts venues have discovered that not only can they enrich the lives of people with dementia but they also stand to gain from cross-disciplinary and cross-sectoral links with health, social care and academia. In addition to the moral case for enabling people with dementia to remain active and engaged in their communities or in institutional care, there is also a business case for improving access and programming for audiences or visitors with dementia, which is imperative if arts venues intend to be relevant to contemporary Britain and in particular, an ageing society.

Museums in particular have had to respond to fiscal pressures and social change by changing the way they engage with individuals, communities and society (Museums Association 2012). Most museums house unique collections of local and national heritage with which visitors are encouraged to interact and reminisce about past times. The Museum of Liverpool's House of Memories[2] provides an exemplar of how one museum successfully made its local collection more accessible to people with dementia and their carers. Along with more traditional memory boxes and a memory tour, a pioneering Memory app was developed, which enables its users to explore objects and artefacts. Similar holistic experiential programmes have been developed by other museums. Hence, the sights and smells of the monarchs of the Georgian era feature in Sensory Palaces, the Historic Royal Palaces programme for people with dementia whilst, at the other end of the social scale, the lives of working miners are being evoked in a dementia-friendly project at Beamish Museum that will see a row of miners' cottages restored and authentically furnished.

A number of art galleries have developed innovative ways of enabling visitors with dementia to explore the collections and exhibitions by using artists to lead engagement programmes. In Manchester's Whitworth Gallery artists are involved in the well-established 'Coffee and Cake' programme for people with dementia; in the Ashmolean Museum in Oxford, two artists are working with members of Young Dementia UK and their carers on self-portraiture as part of 'Me, Myself and Manet', and in the Dulwich Picture Gallery a range of arts-related activities include art workshops for older people and people with dementia.[3] Perhaps one of the largest and most complex programmes has been the 'Journeys of Appreciation' programme (JOAP), a three-year project focusing on the life stories of in-patients with a range of mental health problems including dementia at the Maudsley in south London. Ward staff, patients and carers from the hospital worked with Cinema Museums, Dulwich Picture Gallery, Horniman Museum and Gardens, Tate Modern and Tate Britain (Shearn 2013).

Theatres and cinemas are also taking steps to make their venues more inclusive of audiences with dementia by training staff and volunteers in supporting individuals and carers. West Yorkshire Playhouse, Liverpool Everyman Theatre and Shakespeare's Globe have also developed dementia-friendly performances that share some features of successful autistic-friendly performances. Cueing into memories of 'going to the pictures' in the 1940s and 1950s, Tyneside Cinema and The Macrobert Arts Centre at Stirling University offer dementia-friendly film showings.

A critical component of all of these programmes is partnership between arts venues, health and social care and voluntary organisations, in particular local Alzheimer's Societies or Age UK. Their role in providing information about arts activities and organising transport and support in getting into, around and out of arts venues is crucial.

In order to inspire arts venues, a guide was developed by a group representing arts venues and arts organisations convened as part of the Prime Minister's Dementia Challenge Working Group on the Arts

(Alzheimer's Society 2015). More case studies collected by the group have been uploaded to the Culture Hive.[4]

Memory boxes

Memory boxes are often made by staff and residents (and family members) as part of the process of getting to know the individual life history of people with dementia who are admitted to care. Many care homes display the boxes near the resident's bedroom door to prompt memory and to facilitate conversation between care staff, residents and families. The process of collecting personal objects that are meaningful for the individual is perhaps of more importance than the outcome. As Victoria Metcalfe suggests in Chapter 13, this process should go at a pace that is comfortable for the person with dementia and prompts should be used to identify artefacts and other items of personal significance.

Besides objects, those using the arts to engage people with dementia in activities often use personal ephemera, photographs and pictures to trigger memories. Thus art has a life beyond its original function or aesthetic purpose and provides an authentic link to the past. It can be a medium for representing objects in ways in which they can be re-experienced in the sense that the emotions, feelings and thoughts that they trigger can stimulate memories. For example, in clearing my mother's house I found a box she had stored away for many years, and in it was something that had belonged to me as a child. Along with elation, there was momentary sadness as I connected with her again.

Entelechy Arts 'Little Boxes' project in Lewisham[5] drew on a model from Brazil that used a memory box as part of a performance to an audience. Older performers from Casa das Fases theatre group created miniature theatres from recycled cardboard boxes. These boxes, worn around the neck like usherette's trays, contained personal objects that performers paraded and shared in public squares, school playgrounds and many other community settings. An evaluation of the work in Lewisham highlighted the effectiveness of arts practitioners using crochet, song, dance, music, sketches and poetry to collect life histories of community-dwelling elders, care home residents and older patients recovering from stroke in hospital. This material was used to design two composite memory boxes – a steel shopping trolley lined with chequered plastic that held Dora's memories, including a plastic hollyhock, which her fiancée had plucked out of a front garden when he proposed to her, and step-cleaning brushes. Solomon's memories were in two leather suitcases filled (amongst other personal mementoes) with crinkly blue flying fish and a London Transport conductor's ticket machine. Actors and older volunteers *performed* these Little Boxes by encouraging audiences of children with special needs and older people to interact with artefacts and objects that were taken out and handled, facilitating a range of sensory experiences and promoting communication.

Visual art including arts appreciation

When the effects of dementia were studied through the paintings of artists who had frontotemporal dementia (FTD) and Alzheimer's disease, they showed differences in composition, style and other features that were attributed to damage to very specific parts of the brain (Gretton and ffytche (2014). Painter William de Uttermohlen provides one of the most poignant case studies of the effects of Alzheimer's disease. Diagnosed with early onset dementia, he continued to produce self-portraits and although his drawings become flatter and devoid of character over the trajectory of his illness, it is striking that he continued to communicate his life story through art. Clinicians who treated him were moved to celebrate his work as an 'example of continued artistic endeavour at a stage when Alzheimer's has blunted the craftsman's most precious tools [and] offers a testament to the resilience of human creativity' (Crutch, Isaacs and Rossor 2001, p.2133).

That we should not underestimate the capacity of people with dementia to enjoy art is clear from the results of a study of art preferences that found people with dementia were as able as people who did not have dementia to express a preference for particular pictures, and that these preferences remained consistent over time (Halpern *et al.* (2008). Such findings may have influenced the decision of the Museum of Modern Arts in New York to pilot curated gallery visits for people with dementia. These were very successful, showing that visitors with dementia had the ability to actively interpret paintings, often using insights drawn from their own lives (Rosenberg *et al.* 2009). In the UK, the Wallace Collection, the Royal Albert Memorial Museum and

Art Gallery and the Scottish National Gallery of Modern Art have all run similarly curated arts tours whilst the Camden Carers group organise gallery visits for people with dementia and their carers.

Craft work

Engaging people with dementia with impaired language in craft work can be an effective strategy since they can use sensory means of engaging with different materials and objects. Stroking or rubbing different types of textile has been found to reduce anxiety and promote relaxation in later stages of dementia. Often the textiles have been fashioned in some way to enhance their appeal – from small stitched pieces such as lavender bags and 'twiddle' blankets to state of the art sensory aprons that include sound, lighting and music. Like most arts activities used to promote reminiscence and facilitate life history work, crafts such as textile work are generally more successful in engaging women with dementia. To address this gender issue, the sensory aprons range includes an Aston Villa apron, which was designed to appeal to men. The 1970s *Match of the Day* theme tune can be heard when a small piece of leather football stitched into the apron is gently pressed (Treadaway and Kenning 2016). Addressing the higher prevalence of social isolation experienced by men with dementia and depression is recognised as a growing need, which various projects have tackled. A number of these use the actuality and imagery of 'Men in Sheds' as the basis for memory work (Milligan *et al.* 2013). Arthur+Martha have produced a creative 'recipe book' called *Making Memories* (Blackburn and Davenport 2015), which is a creative resource. In the course of these collective activities, people often share their individual stories.

Music

Triggering memory of the past through music and singing is one of the most widely used participatory art forms for people with dementia and is fundamental to life story work. The relationship between music and memory in dementia has developed due to: the accessibility of music for people at all stages of dementia; close links between music, personal identity and life events; and the importance of relationship-building through music making (McDermott, Orrell and Ridder 2014). Music performances have been found to increase communication, social contact and participation in people with mild dementia (Van der Vleuten, Visser and Meeuwesen 2012).

'The Tracks of My Life' is a project conceived by musician John Osborne who worked with Nottingham Social Services Home Care Department to develop individualised sound tracks for people with dementia. Stored on USBs or iPods, the soundtrack could be played by home care assistants coming into the client's home to provide care. An evaluation showed that the home care assistants frequently selected a gentle but upbeat 'morning call' track, which in time, clients associated with their visit. The portability of the USB meant that individualised sound tracks could be taken with the person with dementia into hospitals or into other services that they used.

The Alzheimer's Society's 'Singing for the Brain' is perhaps one of the best known programmes of song, which is run weekly in over 30 care homes nationwide and in many community settings. Leaders take time to get to know the residents, talk about music from their past and invite residents to choose songs they would like to sing. A study of an Australian Singing for the Brain group (Bannan and Montgomery-Smith 2008) found that their singing became more confident, louder and more resonant over the three weeks of the sessions, and this is attributable at least in part to the vocal contribution of the participants with Alzheimer's.

Moving Music concerts in Oxford, which combine community singing and performance, have been running quarterly for five years. Led by Sir John Lubbock or the soprano Christine Cairns, people with dementia living in care homes and in the community and their carers sing songs from the First World War, from popular musicals and the Beatles, after which Christine performs solo or, often, Derek Paravicini will play piano to the delight of all. Here it is possible to see that relationships between family or paid caregivers and people with dementia are enhanced when they participate in a pleasurable arts activity that has a link to a shared past. For people with dementia this may be a direct result of listening to live music, which studies conclude is significantly more effective in increasing levels of engagement and wellbeing, regardless of levels of cognitive impairment, than listening to recorded music (Sherratt, Thornton and Hatton 2004). Turtle Key Arts 'Turtle Song' projects bring together people with dementia, family carers, professional musicians and singers in order to encourage participants to compose a musical over a 10-week period. Turtle Song evaluations suggest that live music is a key element in the quality of the final pieces created and contributes to the levels of attention, concentration, involvement and motivation of participants.[6]

Music here is a good example of how listening might elicit individual memories, and that one's own musical life story can be developed through work like Osborne's 'Soundtrack'. It also demonstrates the power of listening to music in helping people to remain connected and helping to connect them with the wider community.

Drama

Drama work with people with dementia provides further therapeutic opportunities to act out present emotions, frustrations and sadness whilst glimpsing the past. Ladder to the Moon's performance of *The Grand Hotel* was enacted in a North London care home over several weeks. Residents, staff and families were immersed in live drama, led by actors, who engaged them in the dilemmas of a boy meets girl love triangle. As the action rolled through engagement to marriage, memories of love and marriage were shared by all those participating; and a video recording of these events, complete with musical interludes, continued to trigger positive memories when shown to the residents some months later (Parsons 2009).

Anne Davis Basting (2009) approached her care home improvisation work by encouraging care home residents to make up stories as the basis for plays. Faced with an impasse in one session, she tore a picture of Marlboro Man out of a magazine and asked the residents questions until they created a story – a method that became the basis of Time Slips. Intergenerational conversations about the myth of Penelope from Homer's *Odyssey* were used by a Wisconsin care home, including residents, families and staff, to stage *Finding Penelope* (2011). Story Box, a Manchester project, uses props and involves day centre users and care home residents in creating stories and staging improvisations.[7]

Digital technology

Digital storytelling has already been discussed in Chapters 1 and 6. Digital technology is increasingly being used to engage people with dementia in creativity. The 'Lost in Time and Space' project at Modern

Art Oxford[8] brought together young people, many of whom were disaffected and from mainstream school, and people with dementia and their carers. The project began with a guided tour of 'Lost in Time and Space', an exhibition by the artist Kerry Tribe, who addressed the themes of memory and identity through her installations, films and other multimedia pieces. The process of scripting and making a short video about dementia built relationships between the two marginalised groups, who worked together providing mutual support and learning new skills as they filmed short life histories of some of the participants with dementia. They then edited the subsequent short film, which toured Oxfordshire in a mobile cinema and was later shown across the world.

Evidence

Notwithstanding the proliferation of arts and dementia, much of the work in the field tends to be small scale and short term. Statutory funding has been substantially reduced and the majority of funding tends to be from grants (which are time limited) or income from commissions. As a result, programme or project evaluation is often limited to description. Most studies are qualitative and although a number are well designed and structured with clear results (MacPherson *et al.* 2009), there is a lack of systemic research into the effects of arts on measures related to dementia (Beard 2012). All the conclusions of a literature review of the evidence base for participatory arts for older people (Mental Health Foundation 2011) can be applied to arts for people with dementia: there is a need for better-designed, controlled research studies with larger samples as well as longitudinal studies, to improve the reliability and validity of claims that are made for the benefits of arts for people with dementia and to compare the effects of specific art forms.

More evidence for what works in the arts and dementia, and why, has been generated by research in the arts and health carried out by Canterbury Christchurch University, and will be forthcoming from 'Dementia and the Imagination', a national research study being led by Bangor University.[9] Students at TAnDem, a doctoral training centre in arts and dementia, founded as a collaboration between the Alzheimer's Society and the universities of Nottingham and Worcester in 2015,[10] will also, in future, contribute to the evidence base for arts and dementia.

Conclusions

The creative arts have a unique role to play in helping to elicit life stories of individuals. The 'reminiscence bump' of young adulthood provides a repository of memories that people with dementia can access, even at stages when language may be impaired, by utilising the senses and emotions. Not only are the arts effective as a medium for retrieving memories and reconnecting to past times, they are also beneficial in terms of connecting people and their stories in the present with the wider community. They maintain personhood through enabling those affected by dementia to participate in the arts.

Reported outcomes for health and wellbeing include psychological improvements and social benefits that help people to live well with dementia. This has encouraged the growth in the number of arts practitioners, organisations and venues now engaging people with dementia in the arts. The lack of controlled studies and longitudinal studies makes for a weak evidence base in arts and dementia, but this has not impeded what is fast becoming a specialist field of practice. Whilst the arts may not help a person with dementia get up in the morning, they do offer something to get up for, be inspired by and a way of staying active and involved with others.

Notes

1. Creative Dementia Arts Network: www.creativedementia.org
2. Liverpool Museums Memory App: www.liverpoolmuseums.org.uk/learning/projects/house-of-memories/my-house-of-memories-app.aspx
3. For further information, see Harper and Hamblin (2010).
4. For further information, go to Culture Hive: http://culturehive.co.uk
5. For an evaluation of Little Boxes of Memory go to www.creativedementia.org/resources
6. For further information, go to www.turtlekeyarts.org.uk/turtle-song
7. Story Box: www.manchesterculturalpartnership.org/case-studies/community-inspired/story-box
8. Dementia Lost in Time and Space, Modern Art Oxford on Vimeo https://goo.gl/XcQpWT
9. For further information, go to www.dementiaandimagination.org.uk
10. For further information, go to www.worcester.ac.uk/discover/tandem-phd-studentship.html

Part 5

Where Next?

18

A European Perspective

New Opportunities

Marie-Jo Guisset Martinez

Dementia is one of the most frequently occurring diseases affecting old age, and remains one of the most important challenges in European society. To live well with dementia, communities must accept and support people with dementia, and facilitate the expression of their remaining abilities. This raises enormous challenges for our ageing societies.

(Network of European Foundations NEF)

Introduction

The challenge of how to promote and respect an individual with dementia, to help them maintain their identity, dignity, relationships and connections, is not unique to the UK. This chapter will cover a range of innovative practices implemented in some European countries and aimed at promoting social inclusion and individualised care within various socio-cultural backgrounds. Whilst they are not examples of using life story work per se, they illustrate the principles of life story work and person-centred care, specifically focusing on people's abilities.

In recent years, care providers across Europe have increasingly recognised and prioritised the importance of individualised, person-centred approaches. In France, for example, important efforts have been made to move away from huge nursing homes, completely cut off from the community, where people's everyday lives were based on collective rules arising from a group approach. Such a collective way of living affects a person's interaction and autonomy; for human beings, social relationships are just as essential for the fulfilment of their individual needs. The two are inextricably linked.

Feelings of belonging to family, friends, village and community must be preserved even more for people with dementia, who are at risk of social exclusion (Van Gorp and Vercruysse 2011). Therefore, it is fundamental to service design that we combine promotion of, and respect for, the uniqueness of each person with interventions that give opportunities for connections and social links. Matching these two approaches will help promote on the one hand the person's individuality and on the other the community dimension. Chapter 10 illustrated how knowing a person's individual life story can help to keep people connected in their community and the importance of community stories and memories.

First, projects based on the societal and community perspective will be presented, followed by examples of individualised approaches. Finally, the chapter will address the key learning in terms of social inclusion and person-centred care drawn from the various examples.

Raising awareness and promoting social inclusion

When growing older in a city, everyday life is not always easy. A number of municipalities in Europe have decided to create opportunities for older people to make their voice heard. One example is in Barcelona (Spain) where an Old Age Citizens' Council – Consell Assessor de la Gent Gran de Barcelona (CAGG) – was established by the municipality more than 16 years ago.

This body is dedicated to issues concerning the life of older people in the community: wellbeing, care, transport, urban policy, safety, isolation and social life. Each district of Barcelona has its own *Gent gran* council, which acts as a forum for participation and consultation and from which delegates report to the general council. Every four years, before the municipal elections, a Convention ('The Wishes of the Elderly') brings together hundreds of older people: the 2015 theme was 'Actors in the Community'. This event was the outcome of several working groups in the districts, in which the inhabitants could express their dissatisfactions, ideas and wishes. The media attended and broadcast the content of the event. Such initiatives are essential to preserve the role of older people as citizens. It is also a way to communicate to local people that being old is not the end of the social commitment.[1]

However, people with dementia have to contend with the worries of others. The negative perception attached to dementia has a damaging impact on the image that people with dementia have of themselves and their quality of life, as we saw in Chapter 1. Anxiety, shame and feelings of rejection can make their lives difficult. Helping them is not only the concern of family and support staff; society as a whole is responsible for challenging the negative images of people with dementia so that they are better accepted and included. Different kinds of actions are needed to prevent exclusion. Promoting more positive images and stories could represent a first step in improving the quality of life for those with dementia.

Living with dementia in the community

Fortunately, some initiatives aim to raise awareness among the public that people with dementia are still part of the human community, that they can take part in many activities with others and express their feelings to the extent to which they are listened to.

Flash mob in Treviso (Italy)

On 21 September 2014, an Italian public care provider in Treviso (Istituto Servizi Ricovero e Assistenza Anziani – ISRAA) organised a flash mob in the city's Piazza Duomo.[2] This innovative campaign aimed to raise awareness of what people with dementia feel. The question 'What are you afraid of forgetting?' was asked to passers-by on the street, who were then invited to write their answers on sticky notes which were attached to boards in front of the city's cathedral. Answers included: my name, my mother, my first kiss, our wedding ceremony, the day my child was born... The flash mob 'animators' – ISRAA staff – were dressed in white and wore white masks on their faces to symbolise the invisibility of a person with dementia. The event was reported widely in the media, including regional TV and radio. The slogan of the flash mob was 'So we don't forget – let's build a collective memory'.

Life story work can be seen as a tool to contribute to this collective memory, especially in how it can be implemented in these community settings.

Konfetti im Kopf (Germany)

Since 2009, 'Konfetti im Kopf' (confetti in the head) has launched many campaigns based on photo-exhibitions in public places in Berlin and Stuttgart, such as railway stations and public buildings, in order to change the image of dementia and fight the stigmatisation that people suffer. Created by Michael Hagedorn, Konfetti im Kopf has worked closely with many local groups and various stakeholders to build an effective partnership.

More recently, Konfetti im Kopf was awarded a grant by the European Foundations' Initiative on Dementia (EFID 2014) to implement an action programme for a whole year in Hamburg, using artistic and cultural events (music, theatre, visual arts, humour and a Konfetti Parade). Here, too, the purpose is to raise citizens' awareness through creative actions bringing together people with and without dementia in their local community.[3]

Dementia-friendly communities all over Europe

In 2002 the Robert Bosch Foundation in Germany launched the programme 'Living with Dementia'. As part of this strategy, in 2006 the city of Arnberg was the first 'Projekt Demenz' to receive funding. Since 2007, 'Aktion Demenz' has been responsible for the Foundation's programme – 'People with Dementia in the Community', through which hundreds of municipalities have developed dementia-friendly communities. These local initiatives involve the inhabitants, key figures and organisations in the social life of their communities, including shopkeepers, banks, schools, sports and cultural groups, and sometimes specific groups such as police officers or staff at railway stations. This programme inspired cities across Belgium, with the support of the King Baudouin Foundation, to develop dementia-friendly communities. Various countries including the UK then followed. Some of these initiatives were described in Chapter 2.

Real improvements to the situation of people with dementia can only happen when forms of common ownership are developed and become part of life in cities and communities. Communities are places where citizens, policy-makers and civil society can create an environment where people with dementia and their families can live well and be active participants.

A day care centre with farming activities in Haarlem (Netherlands)

De Blinkert is a Dutch nursing home located in Haarlem, in an area that still has a village atmosphere with houses and gardens surrounded by fields. In 2012, the nursing home manager, a neighbour with a large piece of farmland and a farmer together decided to create a farm next door to the home. This was realised with the support of the municipality and a large partnership of organisations and individual people.

The farm is managed by two staff: a gardener and a social worker. When the farm opened, an advertising campaign was organised in public places such as the local market. Now, more than 150 people from the neighbourhood have taken out a subscription to buy a basket of fresh vegetables each week. They come on Friday afternoon, either to pick the crops themselves or to choose produce from the shop.

More than 40 volunteers participate in the project. The residents of the nursing home have access to the farm so they benefit from this attractive and lively environment, which is a pleasant place to visit with their families. Accessible paths make it easy to take a walk through plants, trees and flowers. In this astonishing place, children, young adults and older people can enjoy the animals, such as chickens, foals and rabbits, together.

In addition, a day care centre focused on the farming activities is open five days a week for up to 30 people. When registering for day care, older people can choose the 'traditional' indoor service or the farming one. If they choose the latter, they participate in a wide range of farming tasks, either doing what they are familiar with or learning new skills with the support of the care professional in charge of the project. During the winter there is a lot to do inside the barn: preparing the seeds, and fixing or repainting tools and equipment. Having coffee breaks with the staff and volunteers is an enjoyable event surrounded by nature. The day care users take advantage of the opportunities for intergenerational activities that the farm provides.

This last example has a double characteristic: combining social inclusion in the community through the farm with a person-centred care approach, thanks to the various day care activities offering choice to everyone.

Promoting the person's individuality

The following initiatives illustrate individualised care at home as well as in care homes. Living at home is the first choice for most people; nevertheless, those living alone can experience long periods of isolation and boredom, apart from when they are visited for a few hours a day by the domiciliary care staff. Some professionals, with the encouragement of their managers, take initiatives beyond their designated care tasks to bring more interest to the daily life of the people they care for.

Bringing life to everyday existence at home: Moissac (France)

In Moissac, a home carer noticed that an old woman who no longer speaks hummed along with her as she sang while cleaning her house. So the carer recorded some old songs in her MP3 player so that when she comes to this woman's home they can sing together, making the old lady very happy. Another professional explained that one of the people she cares for at home often complained that she was no longer able to visit her husband's grave at the cemetery because she got lost. Additional care time has been allocated once a month for the carer to go with her to the cemetery. The lady puts flowers on the grave, they clean it together and after a while, she feels at ease.

These actions show the importance of listening to people to find out what matters to them and to help them in an appropriate way. Listening and being aware of the person's preferences increases respect for their uniqueness and provides the opportunity to share pleasant moments in meaningful activities. Life story work can be a key tool to support this.

Living as a couple in an institution in Louvain (Belgium)

All too often, couples are separated when one of them needs constant attention or extensive care because of illness or disability that the other cannot provide. To solve this difficult problem, the De Wingerd home has devised an original solution. By providing apartments for couples when one partner has dementia and needs constant care and attention, their lives together are preserved. This facility takes in 128 people in different sectors: day care, a respite care unit, small residences for 8–15 people and nine apartments for couples. The latter comprise a bedroom with two beds, a bathroom and a living room, as well as a small kitchen and a private terrace. Breakfast is taken in the apartment; lunch and dinner are served in the common dining room unless the couple prefers to stay in their home. A staff member is present from 2–10 pm and two auxiliary nurses come in the morning to provide personal care. Activities are available during the day, as well as respite time for the caregiver partner. In this case, the needs of both partners are met by finding the balance between professional care, the feeling of safety and the respect of privacy.

The slightest things make sense (France)

Since 1994, Agevie, a non-profit organisation, has implemented a range of care and housing solutions for older people in a rural region. It includes a small housing unit of 23 apartments, two respite homes of 20 rooms each for short stays (three days to three months) and a mobile day care service that covers 15 villages. Twice a week, every village benefits from the day care team in a local public building. The Agevie philosophy of care is to give to each resident or day care participant the opportunity to live according to their own preferences and to address the older people's needs even when they are more complex. For example, every Friday evening one of the homes welcomes an old woman who lives in a remote farm with her brother, when he goes to play cards in the local café. His sister can enjoy having dinner in the home with the residents, then chatting or watching TV before he collects her to go home to their farm. She enjoys this outing, which also gives her brother a break and enables him to maintain his social life.

Another woman was no longer able to live alone after a severe health problem. The staff at the home noticed that she was very elegant and solicitous about her clothing and appearance. She also had pretty hands with very well-polished nails, so the staff had to learn how to manicure! At social events and celebrations, the woman was proud to be complimented by her neighbours. This attention to her frivolous nature meant that her priorities and particular needs were met, preserving her identity and sense of her own dignity.

Key learning points

In this chapter I have attempted to give a flavour of some awareness-raising campaigns, social inclusion initiatives and individualised care examples in different European countries. They result from care providers and staff being willing to promote wellbeing and social life for people with dementia. Projects that seem quite ordinary have aspects that are really pioneering. These examples are like little sparkles in the routines of everyday life for older and frail people and they hinge on getting to know and understand them as individuals.

The risk of exclusion requires creativity to make society aware. Inviting local residents to take part in a social event such as a flash mob or public events like those initiated by Konfetti im Kopf gives people a chance to discover or better understand what dementia means for those living with it. Such events involving a whole city in a dementia-friendly approach require a long and careful process of information sharing and dialogue to ensure that key figures and representatives of local organisations are convinced of the essence of the project. The same issues applied when creating the farm in Haarlem.

The initiatives that focus on the person's individuality raise an important issue: how do we hear the person's voice when they have communication difficulties? It is necessary to try to understand what is essential for an elderly person (being chic, continuing living with his spouse, having social relationships), so that the activities proposed will make sense; some older people may hate having their nails painted. The initiatives presented result from listening, observation and dialogue. They are also based on working as a team to put together pieces of a puzzle in which life story work is particularly relevant. The person's empowerment is a significant dimension of these projects.

Empowerment and positive person-centred examples, however, still raise ethical dilemmas that need to be considered or cannot be ignored. The promotion of interventions, be they individual or collective, can raise questions about the balance between risks, safety, freedom and choice. In our desire to keep people safe or in terms of our duty of care there may be many different views about empowerment. How these are resolved can raise ethical dilemmas for family and staff alike around a person's rights and their safety. This shows that even with practice that is innovative, staff can face ethical issues. Some of these challenges were explored in greater detail in Chapter 16.

? Reflection points

- Can you think of a time when you worked with someone who wanted to do something but there was conflict with family or staff as to how safe it was? What did you do to assess and manage the risks?

- What does empowerment mean for you?

- What do some of these examples help you to think about?

- Are there any ideas about including and empowering people with dementia that you could explore?

Conclusion

This all takes time, energy and courage. Life story work and narrative approaches are helpful tools in building relationships of trust and respect. They certainly require people to be creative.

The overview of creative practice described illustrates the importance of respecting the uniqueness of individual people combined with community initiatives. The diversity of countries where the projects take place opens windows of opportunity for us to learn from each other.

TOP TIPS

The examples presented suggest the following necessary conditions for implementing good practice:

- Ensure coherence between values, principles and actions.

- Build a relationship of trust with the person who has dementia.
- Adopt an attitude of respect for the person and implement it on a daily basis.
- Encourage and dare staff to be creative.
- Take advantage of new opportunities.
- Be willing to build effective partnerships.

Notes

1. Further information about CAGG is available at http://w110.bcn.cat/portal/site/ConsellAssessorGentGran
2. See the ISRAA (Istituto Servizi Ricovero e Assistenza Anziani) video at www.youtube.com/watch?v=XHdQDp1napk
3. More information about Konfetti im Kopf is available at www.11enhaus.de

19

Conclusions and Looking Ahead

Polly Kaiser and Ruth Eley

This chapter draws together the themes from the book and looks ahead to what the future might hold for life story work and narrative practices.

This book has given us an insight into how life story work can help us connect with people with a diagnosis of dementia in ways that are creative, enjoyable and relevant, wherever they live and however severe their dementia. Our fellow contributors have shown how taking the trouble to get to know people, to understand their histories and to validate their future hopes and aspirations can improve their sense of self, transform their lives and help to make person-centred care a reality.

As we have seen in earlier chapters, listening for the story – as opposed to interrogating for a chronology – is crucial and the process of life story work is as important as a finished product. Building rapport and establishing respectful relationships enable us to elicit the stories about people's extraordinary lives to help to have shared meanings.

Technological change is so rapid that it is hard to predict how life story work will evolve over the next generation. As boundaries between what is private and what is for public consumption become increasingly blurred, how will paid carers of the future approach the task of getting to know individuals with dementia? Will they go to their Facebook page or check them out on LinkedIn or whatever social networking sites are popular at the time? Will family carers be by-passed in the process? In a digital age, documents and photographs may not exist or may be difficult to retrieve. It has been said that this generation in the future will be the most undocumented age because the technology to retrieve photographs and memories might not be available. Yet the case example in Chapter 6, illustrating the use of a digital story with an elderly woman, highlights the potential of using different media.

Here is a reminder of our definition of life story work:

> Life story work is, above all, a process that involves having helpful conversations to elicit, capture and use stories about a person in order to promote their personhood and their wellbeing and keep them connected with family, friends and communities.

This book will have given you ideas of how to *elicit* and have helpful conversations with people. Chapters 4, 14 and 15 particularly focused on areas such as spirituality, sexuality, culture and end of life that can be challenging. Chapters 9, 12, 13 and 17 discussed various ways to *capture* and record life stories. Rachel Thompson provided useful information in Chapter 12 about some of the products available. Most of the book should help you to *use* life stories across a range of settings to promote wellbeing and personhood. In particular, you should now see how it helps people to remain *connected* in the present and into the future. We are delighted that the views of people with dementia are part of this book and in this chapter we will echo some of their views.

Our contributors have presented different ideas and applications of life story work. How can all of these practices be life story work? Terms and definitions will continue to be defined, refined and redefined as research and practice progress. In order to summarise and bring these practices and ideas together, we want to leave you with an overall framework for locating and describing life story work in your particular context that might be useful now and for the future – whatever the technologies that emerge.

To help us understand what we mean by life story work in practice across so many varied settings, we suggest that there are Five 'Ps' that are helpful to consider in undertaking life story work (see Figure 19.1):

- person
- principles
- purpose
- product
- process.

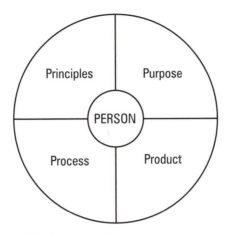

Figure 19.1 Framework for life story work

Person

Not surprisingly, the person and their needs are at the centre. Does the person want a life story? Do they want to be involved? As Jane McKeown and colleagues discussed in Chapter 16, has the person given consent? If they don't want to do it themselves, might it be undertaken as part of good care, as Ken Holt did when he told the care home about Alice and her wartime fears? A carer recently told me how her father had not wanted to do a life story, so when he went into a care home she was told she could not do it without him. They did not know him as well as she would have liked. Had they known a few snippets from Day One – for example, the importance of his Catholic faith and seeing a priest, being addressed as Mr Smith and not 'love' or 'pet' and his beloved Manchester United – his care, like that of Alice Holt's, could have been so much better. As life story work has become more established good practice, it seems to have acquired rigid rules of 'musts, shoulds and can'ts' and we are in danger of forgetting that it is about promoting personhood. It is no good having a beautifully produced life story book if the person cannot see or it does not become translated into good care plans. Life story books might be 'easy to make but difficult to do well' (Kindell *et al.* 2014). In Chapter 7, people with dementia expressed their concerns that their 'books' should not necessarily be seen as the 'true' representation of who they are and that their views expressed then should not outweigh those of the people that they have become.

This framework aims to help you to explore why you might be doing it, for whom and for what purpose and to guide you through some of those conversations and decisions.

Principles

These were outlined in Chapter 1 and can be summarised as those that promote personhood using the key tenets of narrative practice, namely:

- The stories of people's lives are socially constructed.

- Stories have real effects in shaping our futures.

- People's lives are multi-storied.

- Stories of ability are enabling.

The stories might not be chronological or linear. The best life story I ever saw was done by an eight-year-old. She photocopied photos on lined school paper, such as a drawing of a bonsai and birds – things she knew her grandad loved. She did a mind map of the things that were important to him. It was neither linear nor chronological but delightfully captured what was important to her grandad.

The Purpose

As we have seen, the purpose of life story work will vary according to individual needs and circumstances and the setting in which it is taking place. Jane McKeown and colleagues include a helpful table about the different purposes in Chapter 16. Much of it has been from a clinical perspective.

The Purpose for people with a dementia

If I'm on my own and feeling sad, I look at it and it makes me smile when I remember some of the things I've done...if I had to go into hospital and I couldn't remember things it would help people to understand me a bit more. I think it would help them to connect with what you are feeling and what you are going through. (Ray, Oldham Memory Service)

The purpose of life story work for Ray is not just to recall and remember; it also lifts his mood in the present and he hopes it will help others to connect with him and understand him now and in the future. As the people in Steve Milton's chapter (Chapter 7) said, it has a number of purposes:

It gives me something to talk about.

It gives me a chance to think about who I am and what I am about.

It might help me to remember me. (Advisory Group member)

Last but not least... It can be really enjoyable!

This was echoed by another group Polly has worked with recently, who said that they would like to do it:

• as something to do

• to trigger memories

• to spark conversation

• to share stories.

The purpose for a carer might be to keep hold of precious connections and relationships and to pass on stories to the next generation, whereas for staff it is to inform the care they give.

One product may serve all these purposes, but it is important to clarify and define these from the outset. Jean's father, George, (see Chapter 8) had a life story book that he did with a psychologist, but I think it served all those functions. Particular purposes may vary according to who you are and the setting you are in. So if your purpose is to aid life review and improve self-esteem after a diagnosis of dementia, structured life review resulting in a book might be what is required – a process that may take some time. If you are a carer collecting and cataloguing important moments in your life together, you may decide to use an online photo album. The process will be very different: you might do it as an activity together or put it together for the person. If, like Ken, you want staff in a care home to know important snippets that will inform good care practices, you might do a short life story or make up a one-page profile. The purpose will guide and indicate which product is needed.

Some of these purposes have been well summarised by Kindell and colleagues (2014, p.159):

- **Emotional connections**: as a psychological process with couples/families to help them positively connect as a couple or family unit...to help the person with dementia connect with their own identity in a positive way and to feel valued and feel that they matter. In this area the focus and outcome is emotions and coping at a psychological level

- **Interactional connections**: to produce a resource (book, board, box) that in an on-going way can support memories and conversation

- **Building new connections**: as a process to help build supportive relationships and partnerships in care between staff

- **Practical care connections**: in order to provide an appropriate care plan and activities for a person with dementia built around their particular needs

From our experience we would add the promotion of community connections to this list.

The words of someone from Steve Milton's chapter (Chapter 7) sum it up eloquently and are worth echoing again:

> I've had a real chance to think about what is most important to me – and that's my relationships...it's love. (Forget Me Not member)

The Product

Life story work does not necessarily result in a book. However, as Bob Woods and Ponnusamy Subramaniam point out in Chapter 6, there is some evidence that the production of a book is not only greatly valued but that this is also associated with improvements in cognition and quality of life when done in the context of the process of life review (Subramaniam *et al.* 2014).

The product can be a sheet of A4, a collage, a timeline or a collection of photographs in a scrap book. It might be a DVD or a set of significant songs as in in 'Soundtrack of my Life'.[1] We have been privileged to see many examples of different formats: a mosaic, a set of cartoons, a semi-fictional tale, a granddaughter's drawings on a sheet of paper, a tapestry, a digital story, a specially composed song and a DVD. Maria Parsons described many creative approaches to eliciting and presenting life stories in Chapter 17.

Bomber's Moon quilt, made in collaboration with older people in Derbyshire by arts organisation arthur+martha

Digital storytelling was pioneered by Joe Lambert in the 1980s. As technologies have developed, so has the technology of digital stories. They are short narrated films using non-linear narrative.

Typically, they are produced in intensive workshop situations with skilled facilitators and strong ethical principles (Lambert 2012). Digital storytelling combines the art of storytelling with multimedia features such as photography, animation, text, audio and voiceover. It has had wide usage in education, media, health, social care and community development (e.g. Silence Speaks). It is gaining ground and is being used in this arena. One of the first people we trained as part of 'Your Story Matters' is a member of the largest digital story project in the UK, taking place in the North East of England – Culture Shock.[2] This uses museum and gallery collections to inspire people to create their own digital stories, which are also being added to the relevant museum collections. A full review of available products was carried out by Kindell *et al.* (2014).

The Process

As we have said from the outset, a key tenet of life story work is that it is a *process* that involves having helpful conversations. Many of the chapters, such as those that consider spirituality and end of care, include pointers and tips for how to begin to have these conversations. How we listen to and for the stories is important (Shotter 2009), as is how we think about issues of risk and consent and ensure good management and supervision are in place. As Jane McKeown (Chapter 16) and Kindell *et al.* (2014) have pointed out, life story work can be a complex process. In Chapter 7, people with dementia on the advisory panel for the York research recognised that 'the person needs to be really skilled and sensitive'. They also explained that life story work involves not just looking back on the past but looking forward to future hopes: 'So talk to me, my life isn't over yet.'

What does the future of life story work hold?

As people are increasingly diagnosed early in their illness, more are likely to choose to do their own life stories as part of 'taking stock' of their lives and planning for their futures. As our understanding of what constitutes compassionate and person-centred care grows, we are hopeful that paid staff will be able to use the principles of life story work to provide individual care and use people's own life stories in care and support plans. As the evidence base for the methodologies of life story work grows, we anticipate less rigid views about what it is and how it should be undertaken, perhaps using narratives that do not rely on linear or more chronological approaches – for example, creative arts, music and digital story work.

What are timeless are the underlying principles that we have described, based on social constructionism and the work of Tom Kitwood around personhood. As we read in Part 1, these principles are not only enshrined in policy but also legislation, such as the Human Rights Act (1998) and the Equality Act (2010).

Alongside people with a dementia being active in their own movement for change and taking control of their own stories, there will always remain a need for skilled support to help and elicit these narratives. This includes family carers, friends and volunteers being supported to undertake the task, as well as paid staff.

Principles will remain, the purpose of good support or care will remain, the types of conversations may or may not vary much. The principles and skills of our human interaction, empathy and rapport with each other need still to be evident. What we don't know are what future products will emerge, some of which might change the processes. What is different now seems to be that more people are willing to hear the voice of people themselves with a dementia.

We have been telling each other stories since the dawn of time. We all have stories to tell. We put our prized memories in albums (or, increasingly, on CDs, DVDs, Instagram or Facebook). Stories need to be heard as well as told and sometimes it may feel hard to 'bear witness' to more difficult stories. So it may seem strange that we have to institutionalise these activities and write a book about what many of us do and have done for so long. But 'we sometimes need a little help doing what we'd naturally do'.[3] This book has aimed to do just that.

We think Ken Holt would be surprised.

Notes

1. See http://musicworksnet.co.uk
2. See www.cultureshock.org.uk/about.html
3. Dan Harmon, www.goodreads.com/quotes/770671-storytelling-comes-naturally-to-humans-but-since-we-live-in

Useful Resources

Alzheimer's Society

www.alzheimers.org.uk

Provides advice, information and resources about all kinds of dementia.

Association for Dementia Studies, University of Worcester

www.worcester.ac.uk/discover/association-for-dementia-studies.html

Established in 2009 at the University of Worcester, the aim of the Association of Dementia Studies is to make a substantial contribution to building evidence-based practical ways of working with people living with dementia and their families that enables them to live well. They do this primarily through research, education and scholarship.

Bradford Dementia Group

http://dementiapartnerships.com/project/bradford-dementia-group

Bradford Dementia Group, based at Bradford University, is a multidisciplinary, multi-professional group committed to making a difference to policy and practice in dementia care, through excellence in research, education and training.

Carers UK

www.carersuk.org

This organization provides information, advice and resources to support carers.

Christian Council on Ageing

www.ccoa.org.uk

The Christian Council on Ageing (CCOA) acts as a Christian voice and action on issues that matter to older people in church and society. It encourages churches to make provision for appropriate pastoral care, affirming fellowship, meaningful worship and relevant ministry for their older members. The CCOA also publishes a range of helpful books and resources on spiritual care and older people.

Dementia Action Alliance

www.dementiaaction.org.uk

The aim of the Alliance is to bring about a society-wide response to dementia. Organisations can join at a national or a local level by producing an action plan setting out what they intend to do to become more dementia-friendly. There are over 200 local alliances.

Dementia UK

www.dementiauk.org

Supports carers of people with dementia through Admiral Nurses.

Leveson Centre

www.leveson.org.uk

The Leveson Centre was formed in 2001. It brings together for study, reflection and exchange of ideas those of every faith and none.

Innovations in Dementia

www.innovationsindementia.org.uk/who.htm

A community interest company that works directly with people living with dementia to help them get their voices heard and influence policy and practice.

Life Story Network

www.lifestorynetwork.org.uk

Information, resources and courses, including *Family Carers Matter*.

On Our Radar – Dementia Diaries

www.dementiadiaries.org

This is a web-based resource that enables people with dementia to tell their stories on special handsets that are linked to a dedicated voicemail and are automatically sent to the editorial team at On Our Radar. The team listen to, transcribe and curate it for publication.

Mental Health Foundation

www.mentalhealth.org.uk

The Mental Health Foundation is a charity that provides support and research for good mental health. It has a range of useful publications, including resources about spirituality and mental health at www.mentalhealth.org.uk/a-to-z/s/spirituality

National Council for Palliative Care: Difficult Conversations for Dementia

http://shop.ncpc.org.uk/public/shop/default.aspx?Search=Difficult+Conversations+for+Dementia

This guidance aims to help anyone, paid or unpaid, caring for someone with dementia to open up conversations about end of life wishes and preferences, in order to enhance quality of life. It is based on conversations with around 50 people affected by dementia: people with dementia, carers and former carers.

Pilgrim's Friend Society

www.pilgrimsfriend.org.uk

The Pilgrim's Friend Society has developed resources about dementia-friendly churches.

Staffordshire University, Centre for Spirituality

www.staffs.ac.uk

Tide

www.lifestorynetwork.org.uk/tide

Tide – together in dementia everyday: National Family Carers Involvement Network for carers of people with dementia.

Endnote

My mother did not want me to do her life story... 'You only want to do it because I am dying', she insisted. My creative, talented singer songwriter sister, Sarah Gillespie, has, however, written a song and made a video – illustrating the best non-linear life story I could ever wish for.[1]

For my mum - who taught me life is not linear and so so much more.

---

1   *Glory Days* by Sarah Gillespie available on iTunes and Amazon.

References

Adams, T. (2009) 'The applicability of a recovery approach to nursing people with dementia.' *International Journal of Nursing Studies 47*, 626–634.

Adams, J., Bornatt, J. and Prickett, M. (1998) 'Discovering the Present in Stories about the Past.' In A. Brechin, J. Walmsley, J. Katz and S. Peace (eds) *Care Matters*. London: Sage.

Algar, K., Woods, R.T. and Windle, G. (2014) 'Measuring the quality of life and wellbeing of people with dementia: A review of observational measures.' *Dementia*, published online 24.6.14, DOI: 10.1177/1471301214540163.

All Party Parliamentary Group on Dementia (2011) *The £20 Billion Question: An Inquiry into Improving Lives through Cost-effective Dementia Services*. London: HMSO.

All Party Parliamentary Group on Dementia (2014) *Building on the National Dementia Strategy in England*. London: HMSO.

Alzheimer's Society (2009) *Counting the Cost: Caring for People with Dementia on Hospital Wards*. London: England.

Alzheimer's Society (2010) *My Name Is Not Dementia*. London: Alzheimer's Society.

Alzheimer's Society (2011) *Home from Home: Quality of Care for People with Dementia Living in Care Homes*. London: Alzheimer's Society.

Alzheimer's Society (2013) *This is me*. Available at www.alzheimers.org.uk/site/scripts/documents_info.php?documentID=1290, accessed on 8 July 2016.

Alzheimer's Society (2014a) *Dementia UK: 2014 Edition*. London: Alzheimer's Society.

Alzheimer's Society (2014b) *Fact Sheet: End of Life Care*. Available at www.alzheimers.org.uk/site/scripts/download_info.php?downloadID=1460, accessed on 2 March 2016.

Alzheimer's Society (2015) *Becoming a Dementia-Friendly Arts Venue: A Practical Guide*. London: Alzheimer's Society. Available at www.alzheimers.org.uk/arts, accessed on 3 March 2016.

Anderson, H. (2012) 'Collaborative relationships and dialogic conversations: Ideas for a relationally responsive practice.' *Family Process 51*, 1, 8–24.

Archibald, C. (2006) 'Meeting the nutritional needs of patients with dementia in hospital.' *Nursing Standard 20*, 45, 41–45.

Aries, P. (1982) *The Hour of Our Death: The Classic History of Western Attitudes Toward Death Over the Last One Thousand Years*. Harmondsworth: Penguin.

Bai, X., Ho, D.W., Fung, K., Tang, L. *et al.* (2014) 'Effectiveness of a life story work program on older adults with intellectual disabilities.' *Clinical Interventions in Aging 9*, 1865–1872.

Banerjee, S., Samsi, K., Petrie, C.D., Alvir, J., *et al.* (2009) 'What do we know about quality of life in dementia? A review of the emerging evidence on the predictive and explanatory value of disease specific measures of health related quality of life in people with dementia.' *International Journal of Geriatric Psychiatry 24,* 1, 15–24.

Bannan, N. and Montgomery-Smith, C. (2008) 'Singing for the brain: Reflections on the human capacity for music arising from a pilot study of group singing with Alzheimer's patients.' *The Journal of the Royal Society for the Promotion of Health 128,* 2, 73–78.

Barrett, R. (2010) *Fundamentals of Cultural Transformation: Implementing Whole System Change.* Available at www.valuescentre.com/sites/default/files/uploads/2010-07-20/Fundamentals.pdf, accessed on 21 April 2016.

Barrett, R. and Clothier, P. (2013) *The United Kingdom Values Survey* [online]. Available at www.valuescentre.com/uploads/2013-01-23/UK%20National%20Values%20Values%20Assessment%20Report%20-%20Jan%2024th%202013.pdf, accessed on 21 April 2016.

Basting, A.D. (2009) *Forget Memory: Creating Better Lives for People with Dementia.* Baltimore, MD: John Hopkins University Press.

Beard R.L. (2012) 'Art therapies and dementia care: A systematic review.' *Dementia: The International Journal of Social Research and Practice 11,* 5, 633–656.

Bélanger, E. (2011) *A Historical Essay about Notions of a 'Good Death': Toward Shared Decision-Making at the End of Life.* Presented as a plenary talk at the 1er Congrès Francophone d'Accompagnement et de Soins Palliatifs in Lyon, France, June.

Béphage, G. (2008) 'Meeting the sexuality needs of older adults in care settings.' *Nursing and Residential Care 10,* 9, 448–452.

Berger, P. and Luckman, T. (1966) *The Social Construction of Reality: A Treatise in the Sociology of Knowledge.* New York: Random House.

Bernstein, D. (1996) 'Involuntary autobiographical memories.' *Applied Cognitive Psychology 10,* 435–454.

Bewley, T. (undated) *Madness to Mental Illness: A History of the Royal College of Psychiatrists.* Available at www.rcpsych.ac.uk/pdf/Online%20archive%2025%20(b)%20(vi)%20Old%20age%20psychiatry.pdf, accessed on 3 October 2015.

Bird, M. and Moniz-Cook, E. (2008) 'Challenging Behaviour in Dementia: A Psychosocial Approach to Intervention.' In B. Woods and L. Clare (eds) *Handbook of Clinical Psychology of Ageing,* 2nd edn. Chichester: Wiley.

Blackburn, L. and Davenport, P. (2015) *Making Memories.* Available at http://robinblackburn1.blogspot.co.uk/2015/05/making-memories.html, accessed on 21 April 2016.

Bohlmeijer, E., Roemer, M., Cuijpers, P. and Smit, F. (2007) 'The effects of reminiscence on psychological well-being in older adults: A meta-analysis.' *Aging & Mental Health 11,* 3, 291–300.

Bohlmeijer, E., Smit, F. and Cuijpers, P. (2003) 'Effects of reminiscence and life review on late-life depression: A meta-analysis.' *International Journal of Geriatric Psychiatry 18,* 1088–1094.

Botsford, J. and Harrison Denning, K. (2015) *Dementia, Culture and Ethnicity: Issues for All.* London: Jessica Kingsley Publishers.

Bower, G. (1981) 'Mood and memory.' *American Psychologist 36,* 2, 129–148.

Bradbury, M. (2000) 'The "Good Death?"' In D. Dickenson, M. Johnson and J.S. Katz (eds) *Death, Dying and Bereavement*. London: Open University/Sage.

Bradley, R.J., Moulin, C.J.A. and Kvavilashvili, L. (2013) 'Involuntary autobiographical memories.' *Psychologist 26*, 3190–3193.

Bridges, J. and Wilkinson, C. (2011) 'Achieving dignity for older people with dementia in hospital.' *Nursing Standard 25*, 9, 42–47.

Brodrick, D., Lewis. D., Worth, A. and Marland, A. (2011) 'One page patient passport for people with learning disabilities'. *Nursing Standard, 25*, 47, 35–40.

Brooker, D. (2007) *Person Centered Dementia Care: Making Services Better*. London: Jessica Kingsley Publishers.

Brooker, D. (2010) 'The VIPS Model and the Importance of Life Story Work'. Presentation to The First National Life Story Work Conference. Leeds. 12 February 2003.

Brooker, D. and Latham, I. (2015) *Person-Centred Dementia Care: Making Services Better with the VIPS Framework*. London: Jessica Kingsley Publishers.

Bruce, E. and Schweitzer, P. (2010). 'Working with Life History'. In M. Downs and B. Bowers (eds) *Excellence in Dementia Care: Research into Practice*. Maidenhead: Open University Press.

Bruner, J. (1991) 'The narrative construction of reality.' *Critical Inquiry 18*, 1–21.

Bryden, C. (2005) *Dancing with Dementia: My Story of Living Positively with Dementia*. London: Jessica Kingsley Publishers.

Burnham, J. (2013) 'Developments in Social GRRAACCES: Visible-invisible, Voiced-unvoiced.' In I. Krause (ed.) *Cultural Reflexivity*. London: Karnac.

Butler, R.N. (1963) 'The life review: An interpretation of reminiscence in the aged.' *Psychiatry 26*, 65–76.

Butler, R.N. (1987) 'Ageism.' In G. Maddox (ed.) *The Encyclopaedia of Ageing: A Comprehensive Resource in Gerontology and Geriatrics*. New York, NY: Springer.

Care Quality Commission (2014) *Cracks in the Pathway*. Available at www.cqc.org.uk/sites/default/files/20141009_cracks_in_the_pathway_final_0.pdf, accessed on 21 April 2016.

Cheston, R. (1998) 'Psychotherapeutic work with people with dementia: A review of the literature.' *British Journal of Medical Psychology 71*, 3, 211–231.

Ciulla, J.B. (1999) 'The importance of leadership in shaping business values.' *Long Range Planning 32*, 2: 166–172.

Claire, D. (2009) 'Snakes and ladders: the ups and downs of a self-harming life style.' *The International Journal of Narrative Therapy and Community Work 1*, 1–12.

Clarke, A., Hanson, E.J. and Ross, H. (2003) 'Seeing the person behind the patient: Enhancing the care of older people using a biographical approach.' *Journal of Clinical Nursing 12*, 697–706.

Clayton, M., Fredman, G., Martin, E., Anderson, E. *et al.* (2012) 'Systemic practices with older people.' *PSIGE Newsletter, 121*, October.

Clissett, P., Porock, D., Harwood, R.H. and Gladman, J. (2013) 'Experience of family carers of older people with mental health problems in the acute general hospital: A qualitative study.' *Journal of Advanced Nursing 69*, 12, 2707–2716.

Cohen, K., Johnson, D., Kaiser, P. and Dolan, A. (2008) 'The roles and meanings of life story work among older people and their carers: A qualitative evaluation of Oldham's Age Concern Life Story Project.' Lancaster University, D. Clin. Psych small scale research project. Lancaster University.

Comfort, A. (1972) *The Joy of Sex*. London: Crown Publishing.

Comfort, A. (1974) 'Sexuality in Old Age.' *Journal of the American Geriatrics Society 22*, 10, 440–442.

Commission for Health Improvement Investigations (2003) *Investigation into Matters Arising from Care on Rowan Ward, Manchester Mental Health & Social Care Trust.* London: The Stationery Office.

Convention on the Rights of Persons with Disabilities (2006) Available at www.un.org/disabilities/convention/conventionfull.shtml, accessed on 21 April 2016.

Cook, A. (2008) *Dementia and Well-Being: Possibilities and Challenges.* Edinburgh: Dunedin Academic Press.

Cornwell, J. (2015) 'Keeping compassion and respect for patients a top priority'. An open letter to the Secretary of State for Health from Jocelyn Cornwell, Chief Executive of The Point of Care Foundation (dated May 2015).

Cotelli, M., Manenti, R. and Zanetti, O. (2012) 'Reminiscence therapy in dementia: A review.' *Maturitas 72*, 3, 203–205.

Cowdell, F. (2010) 'Care of older people with dementia in an acute hospital setting.' *International Journal of Older People Nursing 5*, 5, 83–92.

Craig, P., Dieppe, P., Macintyre, S., Michie, S. *et al.* (2008) *Developing and Evaluating Complex Interventions: New Guidance.* London: Medical Research Council.

Crampton, J., Dean, J. and Eley, R. (2012) *Creating a Dementia-Friendly York.* Available at www.jrf.org.uk/report/creating-dementia-friendly-york, accessed on 21 April 2016.

Crutch, S.J., Isaacs, R. and Rossor, M.N. (2001) 'Some workmen can blame their tools: artistic change in an individual with Alzheimer's disease.' *The Lancet 357*, 9274, 2129–2133.

Cumella, S. and Martin, D. (2004) 'Secondary healthcare for people with a learning disability: Results of consensus development conferences.' *Journal of Learning Disabilities 8*, 1, 30–40.

Cutler, D. (2009) *Ageing Artfully: Older People and Professional Participatory Arts in the UK.* London: Baring Foundation.

Cutler, D. (2012) *Tackling Loneliness in Older Age: The Role of the Arts.* London: Baring Foundation.

Deal, T.E. and Kennedy, A.A. (1982) *Corporate Cultures: The Rites and Rituals of Corporate Life.* Harmondsworth: Penguin Books.

De Beauvoir, S. (1970) *Old Age.* London: Penguin.

De Jong, J.D. and Clarke, L.E. (2009) 'What is a good death? Stories from palliative care.' *Journal of Palliative Care 25*, 1: 61–67.

DH (Department of Health) (1999) *National Service Framework for Mental Health.* London: HMSO.

DH (Department of Health) (2001) *National Service Framework for Older People.* London: HMSO.

DH (2009a) *Living Well with Dementia: A National Dementia Strategy.* London: HMSO.

DH (2009b) *Halfway Home: Updated Guidance on Intermediate Care.* London: HMSO.

DH (2010) *Nothing Ventured, Nothing Gained: Risk Guidance for People with Dementia.* London: HMSO.

DH (2012a) *Compassion in Practice: Nursing, Midwifery and Care Staff – Our Vision and Strategy.* Available at www.england.nhs.uk/wp-content/uploads/2012/12/compassion-in-practice.pdf, accessed on 21 April 2016.

DH (2012b) *Prime Minister's Challenge: Delivering Major Improvements in Dementia Care and Research by 2012.* Available at www.gov.uk/government/publications/prime-ministers-challenge-on-dementia, accessed on 8 July 2016.

DH (2013a) *Making a Difference in Dementia: Nursing Vision and Strategy.* Health Education England and NHS Commissioning Board. Available at www.gov.uk/government/publications/making-a-difference-in-dementia-nursing-vision-and-strategy, accessed on 8 July 2016.

DH (2013b) *Dementia: A state of the nation report on dementia care and support in England.* Available at www.gov.uk/government/publications/dementia-care-and-support, accessed on 8 July 2016.

DH (2013c) *Six Lives: Progress Report on Healthcare for People with Learning Disabilities.* Available at www.gov.uk/government/uploads/system/uploads/attachment_data/file/212292/Six_lives_2nd_Progress_Report_on_Healthcare_for_People_with_Learning_Disabilities_-_full_report.pdf, accessed on 21 April 2016.

DH (2015a) *Department of Health Guidance: Response to the Supreme Court Judgment/Deprivation of Liberty Safeguards.* Available at www.gov.uk/government/uploads/system/uploads/attachment_data/file/485122/DH_Consolidated_Guidance.pdf, accessed on 8 July 2016.

DH (2015b) *Prime Minister's Challenge on Dementia 2020.* London: DH. Available at www.gov.uk/government/uploads/system/uploads/attachment_data/file/414344/pm-dementia2020.pdf, accessed on 21 April 2016.

DH (2015) *The NHS Constitution for England.* Available at www.gov.uk/government/publications/the-nhs-constitution-for-england/the-nhs-constitution-for-england, accessed 8 July 2015.

DH (2016) *Prime Minister's Challenge on Dementia 2020: Dementia Implementation Plan.* Available at www.gov.uk/government/uploads/system/uploads/attachment_data/file/505568/dementia-implementation-plan.pdf, accessed on 21 April 2016.

Dewar, B. and Christley, Y. (2013) 'A critical analysis of compassion in practice.' *Nursing Standard 28,* 10, 46–50.

Dewar, B. and Nolan, M. (2013) 'Caring about caring: Developing a model to implement compassionate relationship centred care in an older people care setting.' *International Journal of Nursing Studies 50,* 9, 1247–1258.

Dewing, J. (2007) 'Participatory research: A method for process consent with persons who have dementia.' *Dementia: The International Journal of Social Research and Practice 6,* 1, 11–25.

Dewing, J. and Dijk, S. (2014) 'What is the current state of care for older people with dementia in general hospitals? A literature review.' *Dementia 0,* 0, 1–19.

Downs, M. (1997) 'The emergence of the person in dementia research.' *Ageing and Society 17,* 597–607.

Drumm, M. (2013) The role of personal story telling in practice.' *Insights 23*, Evidence summaries to support social services in Scotland.

Dying Matters Coalition (2009) 'Survey reveals reluctance to discuss own death'. Available at www.dyingmatters.org/page/survey-reveals-our-reluctance-discuss-own-death, accessed on 21 April 2016.

Edelman, P., Fulton, B.R., Kuhn, D. and Chang C-H. (2005) 'A comparison of three methods of measuring dementia-specific quality of life: Perspectives of residents, staff and observers.' *The Gerontologist 45* (Special Issue), 27–36.

EFID (European Foundations' Initiative on Dementia) (2014) *Living Well with Dementia in the Community – European Foundations' Initiative on Dementia – Awards 2014.* Available at www.nef-europe.org/wp-content/uploads/2014/03/Infopack_Awards_2014.pdf, accessed on 21 April 2016.

Egan, G. (2013) *The Skilled Helper: A Problem Management and Opportunity-Development Approach to Helping*, 10th edn. Belmont, CA: Brooks/Cole.

Ekdawi, I. and Hanson, E. (2010) 'Working with Older People in the Context of Difference and Discrimination.' In E. Anderson, G. Fredman and J. Stott (eds) *Being With Older People: A Systemic Approach.* London: Karnac Books.

Eliot, T.S. (2009) *Four Quartets.* London: Faber and Faber.

Elwick, H., Joseph, S., Becker, S. and Becker, F. (2010) *Manual for the Adult Carer Quality of Life Questionnaire (AC-QoL).* Essex: Princess Royal Trust for Carers. Available at http://static.carers.org/files/adult-carer-qol-published-version-5571.pdf, accessed on 21 April 2016.

Employment Research/RCN (2011a) *Dignity in Dementia; Transforming General Hospital Care: Summary of Findings from Survey of Practitioners.* Available at www.rcn.org.uk/clinical-topics/dementia/understanding-dementia, accessed on 8 July 2016.

Employment Research/RCN (2011b) *Dignity in Dementia; Transforming General Hospital Care. Summary of Findings from Family Carers and People Living with Dementia.* Available at www.rcn.org.uk/clinical-topics/dementia/understanding-dementia, accessed on 8 July 2016.

Equality Act (2010) Available at www.gov.uk/guidance/equalityact, accessed on 28 June 2016.

EHRC (Equality and Human Rights Commission) (2011) *Care Close to Home: An Enquiry into Older People and Human Rights in Home Care.* Available at www.equalityhumanrights.com/en/publication-download/close-home-inquiry-older-people-and-human-rights-home-care, accessed on 8 July 2016.

EHRC (Equality and Human Rights Commission) (2012) *Human Rights Review 2012: How Fair is Britain? An Assessment of How Well Public Authorities Protect Human Rights.* Executive Summary. Available at www.equalityhumanrights.com/publication/human-rights-review-2012, accessed on 21 April 2016.

Erikson, E. and Erickson, J. (1997) *The Life Cycle Completed.* New York, NY: W.W. Norton & Co.

Evans, S., Brooker, D. and Thompson R. *et al.* (2015) 'Introduction to the transforming dementia care in hospital series.' *Nursing Older People 27*, 6, 18–24.

Evans, S. and Vallelly, S. (2007) *Promoting Social Well-being in Extra Care Housing.* Available at www.jrf.org.uk/report/promoting-social-well-being-extra-care-housing, accessed on 21 April 2016.

Falicov, C.J. (1995) 'Training to think culturally: A multidimensional comparative framework.' *Family Process 34*, 4, 373–388.

Fernando, S. (1991) *Mental Health, Race and Culture.* Basingstoke: Macmillan Press.

Flynn, M. (2015) *In Search of Accountability: A Review of the Neglect of Older People Living in Care Homes Investigated as Operation Jasmine.* Available at http://gov.wales/topics/health/publications/socialcare/reports/accountability   /?lang=en, accessed on 22 April 2016.

Flynn, M. and Citarella, V. (2012) *Winterbourne View Hospital: A Serious Case Review.* South Gloucestershire Safeguarding Adults Board. Available at www.hosted. southglos.gov.uk/wv/report.pdf, accessed on 8 July 2016.

Fox, H., Tench, C. and Tench, H. (2002) 'Outsider-witness practices and group supervision.' *International Journal of Narrative Therapy & Community Work 4*, 25.

Francis, R. (2013) *Report of the Mid-Staffordshire NHS Foundation Trust Public Inquiry.* London: HMSO.

Frank, A.W. (2000) 'The standpoint of storyteller.' *Qualitative Health Research 10*, 3, 354–365.

Furey, R. (1993) *The Joy of Kindness.* Davers MA: Crossroad Publishing Company.

Froggatt, M. and Mofffit, L. (1997) 'Spiritual Needs and Religious Practice in Dementia Care.' In M. Marshall (ed.) *State of the Art in Dementia Care.* London: Centre for Policy on Ageing.

Gergen, K.J. (1973) 'Social psychology as history.' *Journal of Personality and Social Psychology 26*, 309–320.

Gibson, F. (1991) *The Lost Ones: Recovering the Past to Help their Present.* Stirling: Dementia Services Development Centre.

Gibson, F. (1994) 'What can Reminiscence Contribute to People with Dementia?' In J. Bornat (ed.) *Reminiscence Reviewed: Perspective, Evaluations, Achievements.* Milton Keynes: Open University Press.

Gibson, F. (2011) *Reminiscence and Life Story Work: A Practice Guide.* London: Jessica Kingsley Publishers.

Gilbert, P. (2003) *Guidelines on Spirituality for Staff in Acute Care Settings.* Staffordshire University: National Institute for Mental Health Excellence. Available at http://coventry.gov.uk/sclf/download/downloads/id/244/spirituality_booklet/pdf

Gilbert, P. (ed.) (2011) *Spirituality and Mental Health: A Handbook for Service Users, Carers and Staff Wishing to Bring a Spiritual Dimension to Mental Health Services.* Brighton: Pavilion Publishing.

Gillon, R. (2013) 'Restoring humanity in health and social care.' *Clinical Ethics 8*, 4, 105–110.

Gladman, J., Porock, D., Griffiths, A., Clisset, P. *et al.* (2012) *Better Mental Health: Care of Older People with Cognitive Impairment in General Hospitals. Final Report.* NIHR Service Delivery and Organisation Programme. Available at www.nets.nihr. ac.uk/__data/assets/pdf_file/0004/85072/FR-08-1809-227.pdf, accessed on 8 July 2016.

Glück, J. and Bluck, S. (2007) 'Looking back across the life span: A life story account of the reminiscence bump.' *Memory and Cognition 35*, 8, 1928–1939.

Goldsmith, M. (2004) *In a Strange Land: People with Dementia and the Local Church.* Southwell: 4MPublications.

Gretton, C. and ffytche, D.H. (2014) 'Art and the brain: A view from dementia.' *International Journal of Geriatric Psychiatry 29*, 111–126.

Guardian (2013) 'Levels of life.' *Interview by Blake Morrison with Julian Barnes on 10 April.* Available at www.theguardian.com/books/2013/apr/10/levels-life-julian-barnes-review, accessed on 8 July 2016.

Guss, R., Middleton, J., Beanland, T., Moniz Cooke, E. Watts, S. and Bone, A. (2014) *A Guide to Psychosocial Interventions in Early Stages of Dementia.* British Psychology Society.

Guzmán-Garcia, A. Hughes, J. C. James, I. A. and Rochester, L. (2013) 'Dancing as a psychosocial intervention in care homes: A systematic review of the literature'. *International Journal of Geriatric Psychiatry, 28*, 914–924

Haight, B.K. (1992) 'The structured life-review process: A community approach to the ageing client'. In G.M.M. Jones and B.M.L. Miesen (eds) *Care-giving in Dementia.* London: Routledge UK.

Haight, B.K., Bachman, D.L., Hendrix, S., Wagner, M.T., Meeks, A. and Johnson, J. (2003) 'Life review: Treating the dyadic family unit with dementia.' *Clinical Psychology & Psychotherapy 10*, 165–174.

Hallford, D. and Mellor, D. (2013a) 'Reminiscence-based therapies for depression: Should they be used only with older adults?' *Clinical Psychology: Science and Practice 20*, 4, 452–468.

Hallford, D.J. and Mellor, D. (2013b) 'Cognitive-reminiscence therapy and usual care for depression in young adults: Study protocol for a randomized controlled trial.' *Trials 14*, 1, 1–16.

Halpern, A.J., Ly, J., Elkin-Frankston, S. and Connor, M.G. (2008) 'I Know What I Like': Stability of aesthetic preference in Alzheimer's patients.' *Brain and Cognition 66*, 1, 65–72.

Hansebo, G. and Kihlgren, M. (2000) 'Patient life stories and current situation as told by carers in nursing home wards.' *Clinical Nursing Research 9*, 3, 260–279.

Harper, S. and Hamblin, K. (2010) *This is Living. Good Times: Art for Older People at Dulwich Picture Gallery.* Oxford: Oxford Institute of Population Studies.

Haywood, K. L. (2006) 'Patient-reported outcome I: Measuring what matters in musculoskeletal care.' *Musculoskeletal Care 4*, 4, 187–203.

Health Care Commission (2007) *Caring for Dignity: A National Report in Care for Older People while in Hospital.* Available at http://i.telegraph.co.uk/telegraph/multimedia/archive/00669/nwards127_pdf_669224a.pdf, accessed on 8 July 2016.

Heathcote, E. (2014) *The Meaning of Home.* London: Frances Lincoln.

Hedtke, L. (2003) 'The origami of re-membering.' *International Journal of Narrative Therapy and Community Work 4*, 51–59

Heliker, D. (1997) 'A narrative approach to quality care in long term care facilities.' *Journal of Holistic Nursing 15*, 1,1 68–81.

Hennell, J. (2015) 'A Double Diagnosis.' In L.Whitman (ed.) *People with Dementia Speak Out: Creative Ways to Achieve Focus and Attention by Building on AD/HD Traits.* London: Jessica Kingsley Publishers.

Hewlett, S.A. (2003) 'Patients and clinicians have different perspectives on outcomes in arthritis.' *Journal of Rheumatology 30*, 4, 877–9.

Holme, A. (1981) *Housing and Young Families in London.* London: Routledge and Kegan Paul.

Human Rights Act (1998). London: HMSO.

Hunter, P., Hadjistavropoulos, T., Smythe, W., Malloy, D., Kaasalainen, S. and Williams, J. (2013) 'The Personhood in Dementia Questionnaire (PDQ): Establishing an association between beliefs about personhood and health providers' approaches to person-centred care.' *Journal of Aging Studies 27*, 276–287.

Hussain, F. and Raczka, R. (1997) 'Life story work for people with learning disabilities.' *British Journal of Learning Disabilities 25*, 2, 73–76.

James, I., McClintock, K., Reichelf, F.K. and Ellingford, J. (2007) 'Are staff reliable informants? Identifying the triggers to challenging behaviour in dementia.' *International Journal of Geriatric Psychiatry 22*, 6, 598–600.

Jewell, A. (2011) *Spirituality, Personhood and Amnesia.* London: Jessica Kingsley Publishers.

Johnson, G., Scholes, K. and Whittington, R. (1992) *Fundamentals of Strategy.* Prentice Hall: Financial Times. Available at www.mindtools.com/pages/article/newSTR_90.htm, accessed on 16 January 2016.

Johnson, M. (1976) 'That Was Your Life: A Biographical Approach to Later Life.' In J.M.A. Munnichs and W.J.A. Van Den Heuval (eds) *Dependency & Interdependency in Old Age.* Netherlands: Springer.

Jolley, D. (2005) 'Why Do People with Dementia Become Disabled?' In M. Marshall (ed.) *Perspectives on Rehabilitation and Dementia.* London: Jessica Kingsley Publishers.

Jones, L. (2010) 'Good Practice.' Internal workshop at Woodlands Hospital, Salford in April 2010.

Jorm, J.F., Kortn, A. and Hendersen, A.S. (1987) 'The prevalence of dementia: a quantitative integration of the literature.' *Acta Psychiatrica Scandinavica 76*, 465–478.

Joseph Rowntree Foundation (2014) *Delivering a Better Life for Older People in Scotland.* Available at www.iriss.org.uk/resources/delivering-better-life-older-people-high-support-needs-scotland, accessed on 8 July 2016.

Jutla, K. (2015) 'Dementia and Caregiving in South Asian Communities.' In J. Botsford and K. Harrison Denning (eds) *Dementia, Culture and Ethnicity: Issues for All.* London: Jessica Kingsley Publishers.

Jurgens, F.J., Clisset, P., Gladman, J.R. and Harwood, R.H. (2012) 'Why are family carers of people with dementia dissatisfied with general hospital care? A qualitative study.' *BMC Geriatrics 12*, 57.

Kaiser, F.E. (1996) 'Sexuality in the elderly.' *Urologic Clinics of North America 23*, 1, 99–109.

Kaiser, P., Holt, K., Green, L., Newton, C. et al. (2008) 'Life story work in Oldham – embedding into practice.' *PSIGE Newsletter 104*, 6–11.

Kasl-Godfrey, J. and Gatz, M. (2000) 'Psychosocial interventions for individuals with dementia: An integration of theory, therapy and a clinical understanding of dementia.' *Clinical Psychology Review 20*, 6, 755–782.

Katsuno, T. (2003) 'Personal spirituality of persons with early-stage dementia: Is it related to perceived quality of life?' *Dementia 2*, 315–35.

Katz, J., Holland, C., Peace, S. and Taylor, E. (2011) *A Better Life: What Older People with High Support Needs Value.* York: Joseph Rowntree Foundation.

Keady, J. and Jones L. (2010) 'Investigating the causes of behaviours that challenge in people with dementia.' *Nursing Older People 22*, 9, 25–29.

Keady, J. and Nolan, M.R. (1994) 'Younger onset dementia: Developing a longitudinal model as the basis for a research agenda and as a guide to interventions with sufferers and carers.' *Journal of Advanced Nursing 19*, 659–669.

Keady, J., Williams, S. and Hughes-Roberts, J. (2005) 'Emancipatory practice development through life story work: Changing care in a memory clinic in North Wales.' *Practice Development in Health Care 4*, 4, 203–212, DOI:1002/pdh/18.

Keady, J., Williams, S. and Hughes-Roberts, J. (2007) 'Making mistakes: Using Co-Constructed Inquiry to illuminate meaning and relationships in the early adjustment to Alzheimer's disease: A single case study approach.' *Dementia 6*, 343.

Kellett, U., Moyle, W., McAllister, M., King, C. and Gallagher, F. (2010) 'Life stories and biography: A means of connecting family and staff to people with dementia.' *Journal of Clinical Nursing 19*, 11–12, 1707–1715.

Kelly, B. (2003) *Worth Repeating: More Than 5,000 Classic and Contemporary Quotes.* Grand Rapids, MI: Kregel.

Kennedy, J. (2014) *John Kennedy's Care Home Inquiry.* Available at www.jrf.org.uk/sites/files/jrf/Care_home_inquiry_FULL_0.pdf, accessed on 21 April 2016.

Kevern, P. (2011) '"I pray that I will not fall over the edge": What is left of faith after dementia?' *Practical Theology 4*, 283–294.

Killlick, J. (1997) *You are the Words.* London: Hawker Publications.

Killick, J. and Allen, K. (2001) *Communication and the Care of People with Dementia.* Buckingham: Open University Press.

Kindell, J., Burrow, S. ,Wilkinson, R. and Keady, J.D. (2014) 'Life story resources in dementia care: A review.' *Quality in Ageing and Older Adults 15*, 3, 151–161.

Kings Fund (2013) *Patient-Centred Leadership.* Available at www.kingsfund.org.uk/search/site/patient-centred%20leadersh, accessed on 21 April 2016.

Kitwood, T. (1993) 'Towards a theory of dementia care: The interpersonal process.' *Ageing and Society 13*, 51–67.

Kitwood, T. (1997) *Dementia Reconsidered: The Person Comes First.* Buckingham: Open University Press.

Kitwood, T.M. and Bredin, K. (1992) *Person to Person: A Guide to the Care of Those with Failing Mental Powers.* Laughton Gale Centre Publications.

Koenig, H.G., McCullough, M.E. and Larson, D.B. (2001) *Handbook of Religion and Health.* Oxford: Oxford University Press.

Kotter, J.P. (1996) *Leading Change.* Boston, MA: Harvard Business School Press.

Kotter, J.P. (2014) *Accelerate: Building Strategic Agility for a Faster-Moving World.* Available at www.kotterinternational.com/the-8-step-process-for-leading-change, accessed on 21 April 2016.

Lake, C. (2015) *New Year, Renewed Commitment.* Available at www.leadershipacademy.nhs.uk/blog/new-year-renewed-commitment, accessed on 21 April 2016.

Lambert, J. (2012) *Digital Storytelling: Capturing Lives, Creating Community.* London: Routledge.

Leung, P.P.Y. (2010) 'Autobiographical timeline: A narrative and life story approach in understanding meaning-making in cancer patients.' *Illness, Crisis & Loss 18,* 2, 111–127.

Levin, J. (2001) *God, Faith, and Health: Exploring the Spirituality-Healing Connection.* New York, NY: John Wiley and Sons.

Life Story Network (2012a) *Life Story Network Celebrates Successful Conclusion of Your Story Matters Project.* Available at http://www.lifestorynetwork.org.uk/life-story-network-celebrates-successful-conclusion-of-your-story-matters-project, accessed on 21 April 2016.

Life Story Network (2012b) *Your Story Matters.* Internal document (unpublished).

Life Story Network (2013) *Your Community Matters.* Available at www.lifestorynetwork. org.uk, accessed on 21 April 2016.

Life Story Network (2014) *Family Carers Matter in Hartlepool: Adult Carer Quality of Life questionnaire (Ac-QoL) Assessment Report.* Available at www.lifestorynetwork.org. uk/wp-content/uploads/downloads/2015/01/Hartlepool-Carers-AC-QoL-Assessment-Nov-2014.pdf, accessed on 21 April 2016.

Lintern, T. (2001) *Quality in dementia care: Evaluating staff attitudes and behaviour.* (Unpublished doctoral dissertation.) University of Bangor, Bangor, Wales. Available at http://e.bangor.ac.uk/4310/1/DX216907.pdf, accessed on 8 July 2016.

Linton, M. (1982) 'Transformations of Memory in Everyday Life.' In U. Neisser (ed.) *Memory Observed: Remembering in Natural Contexts.* San Francisco, CA: Freeman.

Lishman, A.W. (1978) *Organic Psychiatry:The Psychological Consequences of Cerebral Disorder.* Oxford: Blackwell Scientific Publications.

Litherland, R. and Robertson, G. (2014) 'Mindfulness meditation: Can it make a difference?' *Journal of Dementia Care 22,* 3.

Local Government Association (2012) *Developing Dementia-Friendly Communities – Learning and Guidance for Local Authorities.* Available at www.local.gov. uk/c/document_library/get_file?uuid=b6401bb0-31a8-4d57-823b-1fde6a09290e&groupId=10180, accessed on 21 April 2016.

Logsdon, R.G., Gibbons, L.E., McCurry, S.M. and Teri, L. (2002) 'Assessing quality of life in older adults with cognitive impairment.' *Psychosomatic Medicine 64,* 3, 510–519.

Mace, J. (2007) *Involuntary Memory.* Oxford: Blackwell.

MacKinlay, E. (2010) *Ageing and Spirituality across Faiths and Cultures.* London: Jessica Kingsley Publishers.

MacPherson, S., Bird, M., Anderson, K., Davis, T. and Blair, A. (2009) 'An art gallery access programme for people with dementia: "You do it for the moment".' *Aging & Mental Health 13,* 5, 744–752.

Marie Curie (2014) *What are palliative care and end of life care?* Available at www. mariecurie.org.uk/help/terminal-illness/diagnosed/palliative-care-end-of-life-care, accessed on 8 July 2016.

Marmot, M. (2010) *Fair Society, Healthy Lives: The Marmot Review.* Available at www. instituteofhealthequity.org/projects/fair-society-healthy-lives-the-marmot-review, accessed on 21 April 2016.

Marshall, M. (ed.) (2005) *Perspectives on Rehabilitation and Dementia.* London: Jessica Kingsley Publishers.

Mattera, D. (1987) Untitled poem on the home page of the District Six Museum website. Available at www.districtsix.co.za, accessed on 21 April 2016.

McAdams, D. (2001) 'The Psychology of Life Stories.' *Review of General Psychology 5*, 2, 100–122.

McAdams, D.P. (1993) *The Stories We Live by: Personal Myths and the Making of the Self.* New York: William Morrow.

McDermott, O.. Orrell, M. and Ridder, H. (2014) 'The importance of music for people with dementia: The perspectives of people with dementia, family carers, staff and music therapists.'*Aging & Mental Health 18*, 6, 706–716.

McKee, K., Wilson, F., Elford, H., Goudie, G. and Chung M.C. (2003) 'Reminiscence: is living in the past good for wellbeing?' *Nursing and Residential Care 5*, 489–491.

McKeown, J., Clarke, A., Ingleton, C. and Repper, J. (2010) 'Actively involving people with dementia in qualitative research.' *Journal of Clinical Nursing 19*, 1935–1943.

McKeown, J., Clarke, A., Ingleton, C., Ryan, T. and Repper, J. (2010) 'The use of life story work with people with dementia to enhance person-centred care.' *International Journal of Older People Nursing 5*, 2, 148–158.

McKeown, J., Clarke, A. and Repper, J. (2006) 'Life-story work in health and social care: Systematic literature review.' *Journal of Advanced Nursing 55*, 237–247.

McKeown, J., Ryan, T., Clarke, A. and Ingleton, C. (2015) '"You have to be mindful of whose story it is": The challenges of undertaking life story work with people with dementia and their family carers.' *Dementia: The International Journal of Social Research and Practice 14*, 238–256.

McNamara, B. (2003) 'Good enough death: Autonomy and choice in Australian palliative care.' *Social Science and Medicine 58*, 929– 938.

Mecocci, P., Von Strauss, E., Chenubini, A. *et al.* (2005) 'Cognitive impairment is still the major risk for development of geriatric syndromes during hospitalization: results from the GIFA study.' *Dementia & Geriatric Cognitive Disorders 20*, 262–269.

Mencap (2007) *Death by Indifference: Following up the 'Treat me Right' Report.* London: Mencap.

Mental Capacity Act (2005). London: HMSO.

Mental Health Foundation (2011) *An Evidence Review of the Impact of Participatory Arts on Older People.* Edinburgh: Mental Health Foundation.

Michael, J. (2008) *Healthcare for All: Report of the Independent Inquiry into Access to Healthcare for People with Learning Disabilities.* London: HMSO.

Middleton, D. and Hewitt, H.L. (1999) 'Remembering as social practice: Identity and life story work in transitions of care for people with profound learning disabilities.' *Narrative Inquiry,9*, 1, 97–121.

Milligan, C., Dowrick, C., Payne, S., Hanratty, B. *et al.* (2013) *Men's Sheds and Other Gendered Interventions for Older Men: Improving Health and Wellbeing through Social Activity. A Systematic Review and Scoping of the Evidence Base.* Lancaster University Centre for Ageing Research.

Milton, A. and Hansen, E. (2010) 'Moving from Problems to Possibilities with Older People.' In G. Fredman, E. Andresen and J. Stott (eds) *Being with Older People: A Systemic Approach.* London: Karnac.

Moniz-Cook, E., Agar, S., Gibson, G., Win, T. and Wang, M. (1998) 'A preliminary study of the effects of early interventions with people with dementia and families in a memory clinic.' *Ageing and Mental Health 2*, 3, 199–211.

Moos, I. and Bjorn, A. (2006) 'Use of life story in the institutional care of people with dementia: A review of intervention studies.' *Ageing & Society 26*, 431–454.

Morgan, A. (2000) *What is Narrative Therapy? An Easy-to-Read Introduction.* Adelaide: Dulwich Centre Publications.

Morgan, S. and Woods, R.T. (2010) 'Life review with people with dementia in care homes: A preliminary randomized controlled trial.' *Non-Pharmacological Therapies in Dementia 1*, 43–59.

Moyle, W., Lorenshaw, R,. Wallis, M. and Borbasi, S. (2008) 'Best practice for the management of older people with dementia in the acute care setting: A review of the literature.' *International Journal of Older People Nursing 3*, 121–130.

Murphy, C. (1994) *It Started with a Seashell: Life Story Work and People with Dementia.* Stirling: Dementia Services Development Centre.

Murphy, C. (2000) 'Crackin' Lives: An Evaluation of a Life Story-Book Project to Assist Patients from a Long Stay Psychiatric Hospital in their Move to Community Care Situations.' Unpublished work, reported in McKeown *et al.* (2006).

Murphy, C. and Moyes, M. (1997) 'Life Story Work.' In M. Marshall (ed.) *State of the Art in Dementia Care.* London: Centre for Policy on Ageing.

Museums Association (2012) *Museums 2020: A Discussion Paper.* Available at www.museumsassociation.org/campaigns/museums2020/about-museums2020, accessed on 8 July 2016.

Myerhoff, B. (1980) *Number Our Days: A Triumph of Continuity and Culture Among Jewish Old People in a Jewish Ghetto.* New York: Simon & Schuster.

Myerhoff, B. (1982) 'Life History Among the Elderly: Performance, Visibility and Re-membering.' In J. Ruby (ed.) *A Crack in the Mirror: Reflexive Perspectives in Anthropology.* Philadelphia, PA: University of Pennsylvania Press.

National Audit Office (2007) *Improving Services and Support for People with Dementia.* London: HMSO.

National End of Life Care Programme (2010) *Care Towards the End of Life for People with Dementia: An On-Line Resource.* Available at http://webarchive. nationalarchives.gov.uk/20130718121128/http://www.endoflifecare.nhs.uk/ search-resources/resources-search/publications/imported-publications/care-towards-the-end-of-life-for-people-with-dementia.aspx, accessed on 22 April 2016.

Newbronner, L., Chamberlain, R., Borthwick, R., Baxter, M. and Glendenning, C. (2013) *A Road Less Rocky: Supporting Carers of People with Dementia.* London: Carers Trust. Available at www.carers.org/sites/default/files/dementia_report_road_less_rocky_final_low.pdf, accessed on 22 April 2016.

NHS Confederation (2010) *Acute Awareness: Improving Hospital Care for People with Dementia.* London: The NHS Confederation. Available at www.nhsconfed. org/~/media/Confederation/Files/Publications/Documents/Dementia_report_Acute_awareness.pdf, accessed on 22 April 2016.

NHS Wales (2014) *1000 Lives Plus: Improving General Hospital Care of Patients Who Have a Learning Disability*. Available at www.1000livesplus.wales.nhs.uk/ sitesplus/documents/1011/How%20to%20%2822%29%20Learning%20 Disabilites%20Care%20Bundle%20web.pdf, accessed on 22 April 2016.

NICE (National Institute for Health and Clinical Excellence) and SCIE (Social Care Institute for Excellence) (2006) *Dementia: Supporting People with Dementia and Their Carers in Health and Social Care*. Clinical Guideline 42. Manchester: NICE.

NICE/SCIE (2010) *Dementia Quality Standard. QS1*. Available at http://publications. nice.org.uk/dementia-quality-standard-qs1, accessed on 22 April 2016.

NICE (2011) *Common Mental Health Problems: Identification and Pathways to Care, Guideline CG123*. Available at www.nice.org.uk/guidance/CG123, accessed on 22 April 2016.

NICE (2015) *Mid-life Approaches to Delay or Prevent the Onset of Dementia, Disability and Frailty in Later Life (NG16)*. Available at www.nice.org.uk/guidance/ng16, accessed on 8 July 2013.

Nolan, M., Brown, J., Davies, S., Nolan, J. and Keady, J. (2006) *The Senses Framework: Improving Care for Older People through a Relationship-Centred Care Approach*. Sheffield: University of Sheffield.

Norris, A. (1986) *Reminiscence*. London: Winslow Press.

Office of Public Guardian (2014) *Mental Capacity Act 2005 Code of Practice*. London: The Stationery Office. Available at www.gov.uk/government/publications/ mental-capacity-act-code-of-practice, accessed on 22 April 2016.

Older People's Commissioner for Wales (2011) *Dignified Care? The Experiences of Older People in Hospital in Wales*. Available at www.olderpeoplewales.com/en/ Reviews/dignity-and-respect/Hospital-review.aspx, accessed on 22 April 2016.

Parliamentary and Health Service Ombudsman (2011) *Care and Compassion? Report of the Health Service Ombudsman on Ten Investigations into NHS Care of Older People*. London: HMSO.

Parsons, M.S. (2009) *Over the Moon: Effectiveness of Using Interactive Drama in a Dementia Care Setting*, Evaluation Report. London: London Centre for Dementia Care.

Patel, K. (2005) 'Counting on change.' Interview by Hélène Mulholland in *The Guardian*, 7 December 2005. Available at www.theguardian.com/society/2005/ dec/07/mentalhealth.socialcare, accessed on 8 July 2016.

Patel, N., Bennett, E., Dennis, M., Dosanjh, N. *et al.* (eds) (2000) *Race and Culture: A Training Manual*. Chichester: Blackwell.

Penhollow, T.M., Young, M. and Denny, G. (2009) 'Predictors of quality of life, sexual intercourse and sexual satisfaction among active older adults.' *American Journal of Health Education 40*, 1, 14–22.

Pennine Care NHS Foundation Trust (2009) *Making Connections Not Assumptions Project*. Available at https://vimeo.com/11103492, accessed on 15 August 2016.

Phillipson, C. (2013) *Ageing*. Cambridge: Polity Press.

Phillipson, C. (2015) 'Placing ethnicity at the centre of studies of later life: Theoretical perspectives and empirical challenges. *Ageing and Society 35*, 917–934.

Pinquart, M., Duberstein, P.R. and Lyness, J.M. (2007) 'Effects of psychotherapy and other behavioral interventions on clinically depressed older adults: A meta-analysis.' *Aging & Mental Health 11*, 6, 645–657.

Pinquart, M. and Forstmeier, S. (2012) 'Effects of reminiscence interventions on psychosocial outcomes: A meta-analysis.' *Aging & Mental Health 16* ,5, 541–558.

Porter, M.E. and Lee, T.H. (2013) 'Providers must lead the way in making value the overarching goal.' *Harvard Business Review 3*. Available at https://hbr.org/2013/10/the-strategy-that-will-fix-health-care/, accessed on 22 April 2016.

Posner, B.Z. and Munson, J.M. (1979) 'The importance of values in understanding organisational behaviour.' *Human Resource Management 18*, 3, 9–14.

Pot, A.M., Bohlmeijer, E.T., Onrust, S., Melenhorst, A.S., Veerbeek, M. and De Vries, W. (2010) 'The impact of life review on depression in older adults: A randomized controlled trial.' *International Psychogeriatrics 22*, 4, 572–581.

Preschl, B., Maercker, A., Wagner, B., Forstmeier, S. *et al.* (2012) 'Life-review therapy with computer supplements for depression in the elderly: A randomized controlled trial.' *Aging & Mental Health 16*, 8, 964–974.

Robson, P., Sampson, A., Dime, N., Hernandez, L. and Litherland, R. (2008) *Seldom Heard: Developing Inclusive Participation in Social Care*. Social Care Institute for Excellence, Position paper 10. Available at www.scie.org.uk/publications/positionpapers/pp10.pdf, accessed on 8 July 2016.

Roper-Hall, A. (2008) 'Systemic Interventions and Older People.' In R. Woods and L. Clare (eds) *Handbook of the Clinical Psychology of Ageing*, 2nd edn. Chichester: John Wiley and Sons Ltd.

Rosenberg, F., Parsa, A., Humble, L. and McGee, C. (2009) *Meet Me: Making Art Accessible to People with Dementia*. New York: Museum of Modern Art.

Royal College of Psychiatrists (2009) *Good Psychiatric Practice Third Edition*. College Report CR154. London: Royal College of Psychiatrists.

Rubin, D. (1989) *Autobiographical Memory*. Cambridge: Cambridge University Press.

Russell, C. and Timmons, S. (2009) 'Life story work and nursing home residents with dementia.' *Nursing Older People 21*, 4, 28–32.

Russell, S. and Carey, M. (eds) (2004) *Narrative Therapy: Responding to your Questions*. Adelaide: Dulwich Centre Publications.

Sabat, S.R. (2001) *The Experience of Alzheimer's Disease: Life Through a Tangled Veil*. Oxford: Wiley Blackwell.

Sabat, S.R. and Harre, R. (1992) 'The construction and deconstruction of self in Alzheimer's disease.' *Ageing and Society 12*, 443–461.

Sacks, O. (2008) *Musicophilia-Alzheimer's/The Power of Music*. Available at https://goo.gl/bGejVk, accessed on 22 April 2016.

Sampson, E.L., Gould, V., Lee, D. and Blanchard, M.R. (2006) 'Differences in care received by patients with and without dementia who died during acute hospital admission: a retrospective case-note study.' *Age and Ageing 35*, 187–189.

Sampson, E.L., Blanchard, M.R., Jones, L., Tookman, A. and King, M. (2009) 'Dementia in the acute hospital: Prospective cohort study of prevalence and mortality.' *The British Journal of Psychiatry 195*, 61–66.

Sanderson, H. (2016) *One-Page Profiles*. Available at http://www.helensandersonassociates.co.uk/person-centred-practice/one-page-profiles, accessed on 22 April 2016.

Sartre, J.P. (1936/2000) *Nausea*. London: Penguin Modern Classics.

Schachter, D.C. (1996) *Searching for Memory: The Brain, the Mind and the Past.* New York, NY: Basic Books.

Scherrer, K.S., Ingersoll-Dayton, B. and Spencer, B. (2014) 'Constructing couples' stories: Narrative practice insights from a dyadic dementia intervention.' *Clinical Social Work Journal 42,* 90–100.

Seabrooke, V. and Milne, A. (2004) *Culture and Care in Dementia: A Study of Asian Community in Northwest Kent.* London: Mental Health Foundation.

Senior, P. and Bhopal, R. (1994) 'Ethnicity as a variable in epidemiological research.' *British Medical Journal 309,* 327–330.

Sewell, H. (2009) *Working with Ethnicity, Race and Culture in Mental Health: A Handbook for Practitioners.* London: Jessica Kingsley Publishers.

Seymour, J.E. (1999) 'Revisiting medicalisation and "natural" death.' *Social Science and Medicine 49,* 691–704.

Shearn, H. (2013) *Journeys of Appreciation (JOAP)* Museums and Gallery Partnerships with NHS Inpatient Services for Older People with Mental Health Services and Dementia. South London and Maudsley NHS Foundation Trust.

Sherratt, K., Thornton, A. and Hatton, C. (2004) 'Emotional and behavioural responses to music in people with dementia: An observational study.' *Aging and Mental Health 8,* 3, 231–241.

Shotter, J. (2009) 'Listening in a way that recognizes/realizes the world of "the Other".' *The International Journal of Listening 23,* 1–23.

Singer, J. (1995) 'Seeing one's self: Locating narrative memory in a framework of personality.' *Journal of Personality 63,* 429–457.

Singer, J. and Salovey, P. (1993) *The Remembered Self.* New York, NY: Free Press.

Skills for Care (2011) 'Common core principles for supporting people with dementia: A guide to training the social care and health workforce.' Available at www.skillsforcare.org.uk/Documents/Topics/Dementia/Common-core-principles-for-dementia.pdf, accessed on 8 July 2016.

Sloane, P.D., Brooker, D., Cohen, L., Douglass, C. *et al.* (2007) 'Dementia care mapping as a research tool.' *International Journal of Geriatric Psychiatry 22,* 580–589.

Smith, S.C. Lamping, D.L., Banerjee, S., Harwood, R.H. *et al.* (2007) 'The development of a new measure of health related quality of life for people with dementia: DEMQOL.' *Psychological Medicine 37,* 737–746.

Steeman, E., Dierckx de Casterlé, B., Godderis, J. and Grypdonck, M. (2006) 'Living with early-stage dementia: A review of qualitative studies.' *Journal of Advanced Nursing 54,* 6, 722– 38.

Steinhauser, K.E., Christakis, N.A., Clipp, E.C., McNeilly, M., McIntyre, L. and Tulsky, J.A. (2000) 'Factors considered important at the end of life by patients, family, physicians, and other care providers.' *Journal of the American Medical Association 284,* 19, 2476–2482.

Stokes, G. and Goudie, F. (1990) *Working with Dementia.* Bicester: Winslow Press.

Strauss, C., Cavanagh, K., Oliver, A. and Pettman, D. (2014) 'Mindfulness-based interventions for people diagnosed with a current episode of an anxiety or depressive disorder: A meta-analysis of randomised controlled trials.' *PLoS ONE 9,* 4, p.e96110.

Subramaniam, P. and Woods, B. (2010) 'Towards the therapeutic use of information and communication technology in reminiscence work for people with dementia: A systematic review.' *International Journal of Computers in Healthcare 1*, 2, 106–125.

Subramaniam, P. and Woods, B. (2012) 'The impact of individual reminiscence therapy for people with dementia: A systematic review.' *Expert Reviews in Neurotherapeutics 12*,5, 545–555.

Subramaniam, P., Woods, B. and Whitaker, C. (2014) 'Life review and life story books for people with mild to moderate dementia: A randomised controlled trial.' *Aging and Mental Health 18*,3, 363–375.

Tadd, W., Hillman, A., Calnan, S., Clanan, M., Bayer, T. and Read, S. (2011) 'Right place – wrong person: dignity in the acute care of older people.' *Quality in Ageing and Older Adults 12*, 1, 33–44.

Thompson, R. (2010) 'Realising the potential: Developing life story work in practice.' *Foundation of Nursing Studies Dissemination series 5*, 5, 1–4.

Thompson, R. (2011) 'Using life story work to enhance care.' *Nursing Older People 23*, 8, 16–21.

Thompson, R. and Heath, H. (2013) *Dementia: Commitment to the Care of People with Dementia in Hospital Settings.* London: Royal College of Nursing. Available at www.rcn.org.uk/professional-development/publications/pub-004176, accessed on 22 April 2016.

Thompson, R. (2015a) 'Transforming dementia care in acute hospitals.' *Nursing Standard 30*,3, 40–48.

Thompson, R. (2015b) 'The use of patient profiles in supporting the care of people with dementia in acute care settings: a feasibility study.' Unpublished MSc Dissertation. King's College, London.

Treadaway, C. and Kenning, G. (2016) 'Sensor e-textiles: Person centered co-design for people with late stage dementia.' *Working with Older People 20*, 1.

Trigg, R., Watts, S., Jones, R. and Tod, A. (2011) 'Predictors of quality of life ratings from persons with dementia: The role of insight.' *International Journal of Geriatric Psychiatry 26*, 1, 83–91.

Van der Vleuten, M., Visser, A. and Meeuwesen, L. (2012) 'The contribution of intimate live music performances to the quality of life for persons with dementia.' *Patient Education Counselling 89*, 3, 484–488.

Van Gorp, B. and Vercruysse, T. (2011) *Framing en reframing: Anders communiceren over dementie.* Koning Boudewijn Stichting.

Van Puyenbroeck, J. and Maes, B. (2008) 'A review of critical, person-centred and clinical approaches to reminiscence work for people with intellectual disabilities.' *International Journal of Disability, Development and Education 55*, 1, 43–60.

Walshe, K. and Higgins, J. (2002) 'The use and impact of inquiries in the NHS.' *British Medical Journal 325*, 7369, 895–900. Available at www.ncbi.nlm.nih.gov/pmc/articles/PMC1124388/#B2, accessed on 22 April 2016.

Warmington, J., Afridi, A. and Foreman, W. (2014) *Is Excessive Paperwork in Care Homes Undermining Care for Older People?* York: Joseph Rowntree Foundation.

West, M., Dawson, J., Admasachew, L. and Topakas, A. (2011) *NHS Staff Management and Health Service Quality: Results from the NHS Staff Survey and Related Data.* Available at www.gov.uk/government/uploads/system/uploads/attachment_data/file/215455/dh_129656.pdf, accessed on 22 April 2016.

White, M. (1988) 'Saying hullo: The incorporation of the lost relationship in the resolution of grief.' *Dulwich Centre Newsletter Spring*, 29–36.

White, M. (1997) *Narratives of Therapists' Lives.* Adelaide, Australia: Dulwich Centre Publications.

White, M. (2000) *Reflections on Narrative Practice: Essays and Interviews.* Adelaide: Dulwich Centre Publications.

White, M. and Epstein, D. (1990) *Narrative Means to Therapeutic Ends.* Adelaide: Dulwich Centre Publications.

Whittamore, K.H., Goldberg, S.E., Bradshaw, L.E. and Harwood, R.H. (2013) 'Factors associated with family caregiver dissatisfaction with acute hospital care of older cognitively impaired relatives.' *The American Geriatrics Society 62*, 2252–2260.

Williamson, V. (2014) *You Are the Music: How Music Reveals What it Means to be Human.* London: Icon Books Ltd.

Willis, R. and Holland, S. (2009) 'Life story work: Reflections on the experience by looked after young people.' *Adoption & Fostering, 33*, 4, 44–52.

Wilmott, M. and Young, P. (1957/1986) *Family and Kinship in East London.* London: Routledge and Kegan Paul.

Woods, B. and Russell, I. (2014) 'Randomisation and chance-based designs in social care research.' *NIHR School for Social Care Research Methods Review 17.* London: NIHR SSCR. Available at http://sscr.nihr.ac.uk/PDF/MR/MR17.pdf, accessed on 22 April 2016.

Woods, B., Specter, A., Jones, C., Orrell, M. and Davies, S.P. (2005) 'Reminiscence therapy for dementia.' *Cochrane Database of Systematic Reviews 2005*, Issue 2. Art. No.: CD001120. Available at http://onlinelibrary.wiley.com/doi/10.1002/14651858.CD001120.pub2/abstract, accessed on 22 April 2016.

Woods, R.T. (1996) 'Psychological "Therapies" in Dementia.' In R.T. Woods (ed.) *Handbook of the Clinical Psychology of Aging.* Chichester: Wiley.

Young, R., Camic, P.M. and Tischler, V. (2015) 'The impact of community-based arts and health interventions on cognition in people with dementia: A systematic literature review.' *Aging & Mental Health 20*, 4, 1–15.

Zeilig, H., Killick, J. and Fox, N. (2014) 'The participative arts for people living with a dementia: A critical review.' *International Journal of Ageing and Later Life 9*, 1, 7–34.

Zeisel, J. (2009) *I'm Still Here: A Breakthrough Approach to Understanding Someone Living with Alzheimer's.* New York, NY: Penguin Group.

Zhang, S.J., Hwu, Y.J., Wu, P.I. and Chang, C.W. (2015) 'The effects of reminiscence therapy on depression, self-esteem and life satisfaction on institutionalized older adults: A meta-analysis.' *Journal of Nursing & Healthcare Research 11*, 1, 33–42.

Subject Index

Author Index

Polly Kaiser has worked with people with dementia since 1984, first as a researcher in England and France and subsequently as a clinical psychologist. She was the National Lead for Mental Health in Later Life for the National Mental Health Development Unit (NMHDU - 2009-2011). She was a founding director of the National Life Story Network. She is a consultant clinical psychologist in Pennine Care NHS Foundation Trust and is an honorary lecturer at the University of Manchester doctoral training program for clinical psychologists.

Ruth Eley is a qualified social worker and former deputy Director of Social Services. As the former National Programme Lead for Older People and Dementia in the Department of Health she contributed to the development of the English National Dementia Strategy and led its implementation support. She is a trustee of a Housing Association in Wales.